The Rev. Fr. Saturnino Lohure

A Roman Catholic Priest Turned Rebel, the South Sudan Experience

By
Steve A. Paterno

PublishAmerica
Baltimore

ISBN: 1-4241-9483-0
PUBLISHED BY PUBLISHAMERICA, LLLP
www.publishamerica.com
Baltimore

Printed in the United States of America

Dedication

This book is dedicated to my father, Colonel P.S.C. Paterno who was an aide to Fr. Saturnino Lohure during the Anyanya liberation struggle and had felt that the struggle for freedom, equality, justice and peace was to continue in its second phase in 1980s, where he was reported to have convinced his colleagues that the *struggle we have started should continue*. Unfortunately, my father could not stay a little bit longer to witness this book being written as the harshness of struggle consumed even his very existence of life, the fact that shows the high price for those who offer to struggle for the people of Sudan.

Acknowledgment

A work of such great depth, breadth, and compelling information would not have been possible without others who, in one way or another chip in with their contributions and assistances. For that, I am so ever grateful for those who allow me to interview them to obtain the information compiled in this book. I am also grateful for the members and supporters of Otuho Speaking Community of North America (NACO) with the assistances and discussions leading into the compiling of this book. In that, I will not forget my gratefulness to the members of Sudanese Internet forums in which I am a member, for their discussions, interactions, and insights have pretty much contributed to the directions of this book.

My special thanks go to Jane R. Hogan, Assistant Keeper of Archives and Special Collections at Durham University Library for availing to me necessary research materials for this book. I also thank Marit Magelssen Vambheim who has just completed her master's thesis on the Roundtable Conference of 1965, for letting me have her research materials. For Tong Deng Anei of the United States Agency for International Development (USAID) in South Sudan, I say, thank you for providing to me development project materials being undertaken in South Sudan.

The efforts of Fr. Hilary Boma in providing significant information, assisting in translations of foreign languages materials, and traveling all the way to Uganda to not only pay homage to the tombs of Fr. Satrunino Lohure and Fr. Anywar Leopoldo, but to also conduct interviews for this book will forever be appreciated. The efforts and encouragements of Fr. Neno Contran in making sure this book is completed are also greatly appreciated. Equally appreciated are the efforts of Fr. Celestino Murras, the Rector of St. Paul's National Major Seminary at Khartoum for agreeing in collecting materials related to this book.

The contributions and critiques of some experts and leading authorities on issues discussed in this book are highly commendable. This includes, Uncle Oliver Albino who has not only intimately involved in the issues discussed in this book, but who is also a researcher and an accomplished author on these issues. Also among this group is a renowned Southern Sudanese historian, Dr. Robert O. Collins, Professor Emeritus, Department of History at the University of California in Santa Barbara. This also includes another accomplished author, Dr. Amir H. Idris who is an Assistant Professor of African Studies at the Department of African & African American Studies in Fordham University. And there is also Dr. Abannik O. Hino, an Associate Professor of History at Wingate University in North Carolina whom his contributions are equally valuable.

This cannot go by without acknowledging the great insights and intellectual contributions of Rogato Ohide, which very much shape the directions of this book. Equally requires acknowledgment is Benaiah Duku for his friendship, knowledge and support, which helps the shaping of this book. And finally, this book could not have been possible without the support and encouragement of my huge family members who are stretched far and beyond, from the periphery of Washington, D.C. to the hills of Pittsburg in Pennsylvania and all the way to the Great Lakes of Erie, Pennsylvania, for they have been the source of great encouragements.

With all these supports, contributions, and encouragements, I, and only I, take full responsibility for ideas and opinions expressed in this book and in the context in which they are expressed as well as I take full responsibility on the mistakes which may have inadvertently slipped through the crack into this book.

Table of Contents

The Rev. Fr. Saturnino Lohure

A Roman Catholic Priest Turned Rebel, the South Sudan Experience

Introduction

Sudan, the largest country in Africa in the land mass is also one of the most trouble countries not just in African but in the world. Like many countries, Sudan has been the subject of foreign invasions and colonialisms. Sudan has systematically been invaded and colonized for the same reasons that countries have been invaded and colonized. But before it could even declare its own independence, Sudan had found itself embroiled in the conflicts from within. Thus, Sudan has been the subject of intellectual excitements and curiosities, given its unique and tragic unfolding circumstances. And to contribute to these intellectual excitements and curiosities, the perspective and background of those who directly experienced the tragedy and intimately involved in the whole affairs of Sudan is highly relevant. It was Ralph Waldo Emerson who once wrote, "there is properly no history; only biography."[1] This in essence is true because in greater part, history revolves around people— the ideas they hold, the values they embody, and the choices they make, intricately shape events, set trends, and create forces that form history. It is through this concept of people influencing the course of history this book is written. This book takes into historical accounts to analyze in

13

more details how the personal experience and political life of Fr. Saturnino Lohure profoundly impacts the history of the South Sudan liberation struggle for justice, peace, freedom and equality. In a contextual sense of the history of South Sudan liberation struggle, this book definitively concludes that Fr. Saturnino Lohure as an individual is among those people—some of whom are profiled in this book—who are either for better or for worse, greatly influence the history of South Sudan liberation struggle through their ideas, values, and choices they make in life.

For some apparent reasons, the Southern Sudanese historians and intellectual adventurers in their excitements and curiosities completely ignore and neglect the great contributions of Fr. Saturnino Lohure in their discourse of South Sudan liberation struggle, relegating his significant role into the anecdotal footnotes of history. As a result, more often than not, the history and discourse of South Sudan liberation struggle is discussed, but yet with rather some serious constraints and limitations without accounting for the much instrumental role played by Fr. Saturnino Lohure. Therefore, this book though profoundly in general contributes to the intellectual discourse of the South Sudan liberation struggle like the other books written previously, it uniquely sets itself apart in attempting to explain and analyze how the life of Fr. Saturnino Lohure, which went undocumented, profoundly contributes to the history and discourse of the South Sudan liberation struggle. In short, the book brings into public view, the undocumented historical facts to add into the ongoing discussions of the South Sudan liberation struggle.

Chapters' Structures

The book is laid out into seven chapters. Chapter one explores different factors which possibly shape the life of Fr. Saturnino Lohure from childhood into adulthood and as well as into his political life. Among those factors are cultural influences, educational background, religious orientation, and inspirations from notable individuals. The book goes on to lay out the background of those factors and in details explains how profoundly they influenced the ideas, values and choices of Fr. Saturnino Lohure. Among the many lessons one will learn from this chapter is that individuals' ideas, values and choices are shaped through their background in culture, education, religion among many factors.

Chapter two traces the historical impact of the two monotheistic religions, mainly the Islamic and Christian religions, which fortunately or unfortunately always tend to divide Sudan into Southern and Northern parts. It examines how religious adventurers from the period of Mahdi revolution used Islamic fanaticism as a means in attaining political power and how that in turn set into motion a precedent in which one can only succeed in building large political movement in modern Sudan by appealing into Islamic fanaticism. Such precedent is very much responsible in modern Sudan failing as a nation state since the country is unable to build nationalistic consciousness.

In a more interesting twist, the chapter presents Christianity not just as a religion alternative to the deadly and encroaching Islamic fanaticism, but it also presents Christianity as a political counterbalance to the Islamic ideologies envisioned by the Islamic religious adventurers, starting from Muhammad Ahmad al-Mahdi to the successive Northern Sudanese governments including the present government, which took power with strong emphasis on Islamic fanaticism under no better designation than National Islamic Front (NIF). This chapter demonstrates that Fr. Saturnino Lohure, a Roman Catholic priest and a leading personality in Sudan's politics became more or less a symbol of threat to Islamic fanaticism and its religious adventurers. This is illustrated by the fact that in 1960s, the Northern Sudanese government in Khartoum did not hide the reasons for expelling Christian Missionaries from Sudan as they reasoned that the personality of Fr. Saturnino Lohure was one of the major reasons for expelling the Christian Missionaries. This fact is evidenced in the numerous citations of Fr. Saturnino Lohure's name in the Christian Missionary Act, an act that drove the Christian Missionaries out of the South Sudan. If there is any important lesson one can take from this chapter, it will be that the use of Islamic fanaticism as a substitute for nationalism by various Islamic religious adventurers did not only eliminate none Islamic believers from meaningful participatory role in building of Sudan as a nation state, but is also a major reason for the separation of the South and North of Sudan. It further proves that Sudan can never succeed to exist as a one nation given the bitter and bloody religious encounters and conflicts among Sudanese competing multi-religious society.

Chapter three traces the political history of the South and North of Sudan and concludes that the South and North of Sudan had maintained separate status from time immemorable to the present. Through historical analysis, it concludes that Sudan had never been a one country. The chapter went as far as dismissing many of the false historical myth being advanced by the Northern Sudanese Arabs such that the colonial rule was responsible for the division of the South and North of Sudan or that the Juba Conference of 1947, was a final affirmation by the Southern Sudanese of the unity of South and North of Sudan. If the colonial power was ever responsible for anything, it was that they maintained the already divided South and North of Sudan but tragically made a mistake in attempting to unite these two distinctive entities on their departure during the independence period. This chapter makes it very clear on why it cannot surprise anyone that the Northern Arab Sudanese could create a false myth surrounding the outcome of the Juba Conference of 1947. Given Sudan being a hybrid of African and Arab nationalities, the chapter further analyzes the over exaggerated emphasis of Arabism practiced by the Northern Sudanese Arabs. The chapter then points to the root causes of the inferiority complex faced by the Sudanese Arabs and its overriding psychological impacts, which tend to haunt the Northern Sudanese Arabs and in turn lead into the ongoing conflict in the Sudan. The chapter also highlights significant role the Southern Sudanese played in trying to resolve the Southern Problems in a more peaceful political process with Fr. Saturnino Lohure as a leading personality in that effort at the parliamentary government of 1958. This is the chapter that provides all the reasons on why the South of Sudan must be separated. By so reading this chapter, one will be able to make strong and informative argument for the case of separation for South Sudan.

Chapter four depicts the life of Fr. Saturnino Lohure and the Southern Sudanese politicians in exile. The chapter explains in a more detail account, how the Southern Sudanese politicians under the patronage of Fr. Saturnino Lohure mounted the first ever political and military resistance against the Khartoum government from exile. In short, the chapter illustrates the birth of South Sudan national liberation struggle movement. It is in this chapter that one will learn the political sophistication of Fr. Saturnino Lohure, which will make one to conclude that Fr. Saturnino Lohure was in fact born ahead of his time.

Chapter five is about the history of South Sudan military struggle. It highlights important points in the history of Sudan where military strikes were justified as the only means to achieve justice, peace, freedom, and equality for South Sudan. This is also the chapter where Fr. Saturnino Lohure is prominently featured not as just a soldier but a military thinker. If there is anything to make the people of South Sudan proud in this chapter, it will be the sheer bravery and honor that the people of South Sudanese demonstrated in their history of war of liberation.

Chapter six brought into public view, the ideologies and political thoughts of Fr. Saturnino Lohure. Those thoughts were valuable then, four decades ago, and are still valuable today in the context of national liberation of South Sudan. For their relevance, it even makes it more important and urgent for those views to be brought into public discourse. Those thoughts are drawn from Fr. Satutnino Lohure's master piece book, *The Problem of Southern Sudan*, in which he attributed its authorship to two of his prominent colleagues, Joseph Oduho and William Deng. Other thoughts in this chapter are drawn from documents, articles and speeches written by Fr. Saturnino Lohure. Those thought are laid out systematically in accordance to religion, political, economic, social, and education. Those were the most pressing issues that affected the stability of Sudan as a nation state and not surprisingly, those issues continue to be the challenges of today, which require to be addressed in the current situation. Here also, one will learn how the Southern Sudanese were negatively affected with respect to these issues and challenges.

Chapter seven covers the posthumous Fr. Saturnino Lohure. Given all the things known about Fr. Saturnino Lohure, the chapter makes an attempt to realistically fare Fr. Saturnino Lohure in his posthumous political life to the relative existing challenges. One of such challenges was the Addis Ababa Agreement of 1972, where an attempt is made to illustrate on how Fr. Saturnino Lohure would have handled the entire situation. The chapter also provides strong argument on how South Sudan should maintain its interest of separation amidst the external oppositions and challenges from other countries or organizations that may wish the South maintain a fragile united Sudan. This is also one of the chapters where one will learn ideas in order to make strong arguments for the separation of South Sudan, especially with respect to the external oppositions and pressure.

Many books have been written about the Southern Sudan struggle, and most of them make attempts to address the root causes of conflict of Sudan, however, none of them is clearly written from the Southern Sudanese perspective whereby majority of Southern Sudanese would identify with them like they would have with this book. Even though the book is a biography of Fr. Saturnino Lohure, it is written against the background of South Sudan liberation struggle, where every Southern Sudanese from all walks of life could plug themselves in the narrative as easily as they read along. As Emerson would say, "all history resolves itself very easily into the biography."[2] Therefore, this book does not only present the biography of Fr. Saturnino Lohure as an individual, but it also nicely and fittingly presents the history of South Sudanese people—their history of struggle in particular.

The book is an easy read. Though rich with historical facts and loaded with all the relevant concepts as well as addresses complex issues, it tries to avoid the convoluted phrases and sentences for easy understanding. Even though that is the case, certain points in the book need clarifications right from the beginning so as to avoid confusions. For example, the words "Sudan government" which is used in other quarters in describing the government in Khartoum is substituted with "Khartoum government" or in other cases it is substituted with the "Northern Sudanese government." This rule applies to anything that deals with the successive regimes in Khartoum where "Sudan" is substituted with either "Khartoum" or "North." The reason for this is simply because there has never been an existence of any Sudanese government, but that of Khartoum or Northern Sudanese government. There would only be Sudanese government if all the nationalities in the territorial Sudan are represented in some a sort of constitutional government arrangement, a strange phenomenon that never happened yet in Sudan, and probably will never happen as the present trend is indicating Sudan splitting up into pieces. Another thing that needs clarification is that the name "Fr. Saturnino Lohure" is in most cases written as the "Father." For one reason, this is his title as a Catholic priest, and for second reason, he was the National Patron for Southern Sudanese liberation movement, naturally earning him the title of the Father of national liberation for South Sudan. Other word which may cause confusion is the usage of the term Arab. The application of the term Arab in this book is taken from the Southern Sudanese perspective. In this perspective, it applies to the broader categories that include the Northern Sudanese Arabs, the successive regimes in Khartoum, and all those who collaborated with those regimes against the interest of South Sudan. A good example here is when a Southern Sudanese who was collaborating with the Khartoum government is quoted as he was lamenting on the fact, "I am now just considered as a Northerner, because I have been chosen by the North" to represent the interest of the Khartoum government as oppose to that of the Southerners in the Round Table Conference of 1965.[3] The fact that a Southern Sudanese collaborated with the Arab regime against the interest of the Southerners, he or she could be considered an Arab from the Southern point of view. To avoid falling trap into some foreign languages utilized in this book, a uniform approach is applied where terminologies and phrases used in this book which are none English are all translated into English language. And all the acronyms used in this book take their full written forms. Otherwise, the intent is not to mystify the readers in anyway or shape, and if there are those confounded terminologies, phrases, sentences, or concepts in the mix, they can easily be understood by the consistency of their usage and the context in which they are used.

This book is a result of extensive research and that can be evidenced by its numerous citations and bibliographies. Such does not only demonstrate the intellectual depth and horizon of the author, but this provides the readers, mainly the students and researchers with further sources for consultation on particular topics of interest. The sources are both primary and secondary, including oral. Most of the oral sources resulted from extensive discussions on a forum like settings. The sources are as much diverse to include information from those who intimately experience the subject matters first hand to the popular literatures ever written on the subject matters as well as to the grew literatures, which include the publications of government agencies, professional organizations, research centers, universities, public institutions, special interest groups, and associations or societies. These all add to the comprehensiveness of this book and for those with interest for the South Sudan liberation struggle, the book would further enrich their knowledge and hopefully stimulate their intellectual excitements and curiosities.

Chapter Endnotes

[1] Ralph Waldo Emerson, *A collection of 20 Essays by Emerson including Self-Reliance, The OverSoul, Experience, and Nature,* New York: Houghton Mifflin Company, 1883.

[2] Ibid

[3] Marit Magelssen Vambheim "Making Peace While Waging War:—A Peacemaking Effort in the Sudanese Civil War, 1965-1966" MA thesis in history, University of Bergen, Spring 2007.

Foreword

Steve Paterno's effort to highlight Fr. Saturnino Lohure's role in the liberation struggle for the liberation of Southern Sudan must be commended as one of the bold ways forward in portraying the true history of the leadership of that territory. Even what appears not to have dawned to the Southern Sudanese leadership, (headed by Dr. John Garand de Mabior) like the need for involvement of Northern Sudanese leadership from marginalized areas for the struggle of the people in the South had already been clearly articulated by Hon. Ezboni Mondiri Gwonza. It was, indeed, fear of his idea taking root that he was targeted for a very long imprisonment. After winning the same elections that Hon. Fr. Saturnino Lohure won, Hon. Ezboni Mondiri Gwonza was unable to take his seat as a result of such a persecution. What Dr. John Garang de Mabior did was to demonstrate the value of power. By building a formidable army, Dr. Garang managed to sway even some of the ordinary Northerners to join his movement; thus, strengthening it. Hon. Mondiri's being a mere political movement, died when he was imprisoned, and its disciples were frightened away.

I knew very little about Fr. Saturnino Lohure, prior to his offer to speak out for the Southern Sudanese cause. Most of the best Southern Sudanese Members of Parliament (MPs) were gifted, and very articulate in their own rights, given that the background of most of them ended in Intermediate (Middle) Schools only. Nevertheless, standards of learning were so high in those formative years that little could have been desired to brush up those gentlemen's parliamentary capabilities. They knew their minds, and were thorough over the North-South relations.

The British Administration was so thorough in what it did in the Sudan as a whole, that Honorable Buth Diu managed, not only to access the position of an administrator, but shone so brilliantly as the most respected spokesman in parliament for the South those days that a British Newspaper, 'The Daily Telegraph' could not help describing him as being "…from kitchen to parliament." Indeed, Hon. Buth Diu had only picked up his literacy while working as a cook for the wife of a British administrator. He must have been so good that the man and his wife decided to spend time teaching him for a better future than being just a cook. Furthermore, they must have equipped him with the ambition for self-improvement. While his English was not only virtually perfect; but, the man appeared to have been the best read Members of Parliament (MP) those days.

I was then a freshman; yet, a student leader in the University of Khartoum. The entry of Fr. Saturnino Lohure onto the political arena was very attractive to us in the student body for a number of reasons. Our Members of Parliament (MPs). came from very poor backgrounds, and that tended to subject them to temptations when offered bribes by Northern Sudanese Political Parties. The Father, as a priest, would live in a mission, where he would enjoy the same menu without the need to look outwardly for the wealth of this world. Needless to say, we in the student body held these views, regardless of the bad example that a Fr. Cosmos

Arbab (whom the Azande—from where he hailed, called Rababa; meaning a thumb harp) had already set. Something, which I do not know, must have told us that this individual (Fr. Saturnino Lohure) would be different. One most obvious thing must have been the differences in the lifestyles of the two.

Fr. Saturnino Lohure: A Revolutionary

When the parliament in which Fr. Saturnino Lohure was a member was inaugurated, the Southern Sudanese Members of Parliament (MPs) unanimously sided with the view of the student body that even though he was not a member of any of their parties, they should recognize him as the spokesman for the Southern Bloc. This was a solid body of twenty five, out of forty Southern Members of Parliament (MPs). It was in that capacity as the spokesman for the Southern Bloc, that he made his impressive speech, which left both the North and the South Sudanese, looking at their relations in terms of confirmation and denial of colonialism, if not slavery.

Unfortunately, this parliament did not do much business, because Northern Sudanese were nervous about its continuity. Several attempts were made by the then Prime Minister, Abdalla *Bey*[4] Khalil, to talk Southern Sudanese Members of Parliament into submission by threatening a hand over of his government to the army. It was Fr. Saturnino, the then spokesman, who firmly held the position that the South Sudan was never going to suffer alone from such a hand over. The North Sudan, which appeared to be already enjoying the fruits of independence, would suffer even more. It would also appear that when the government was already handed over to the army, it was Fr. Saturnino who came up in a secret meeting in Juba, with the signal of the already discussed disappearance into exile for serving the Southern Sudanese cause. Most of the Southern Sudanese Members of Parliament. from Greater Equatoria, left the country either for The Congo, or for Uganda. Little did I know until then, that I would one day find myself face to face with Fr. Saturnino; working together, hand-in-hand.

In the Town of Aru: Congo

When I took my round of exile, events in the country took me round the Congo to Aru, a little Congo township, just fifteen miles from Arua, in Uganda, and only seven miles from the Congo Uganda border. There were a number of refugees in Aru, and many of them came round to me with stories that Fr. Saturnino had been coveting the day he would set eyes on me, because it was his belief that I was the most sincere fighter for him to lay hands on. I did not even know that I was coming to a town where he lived. One of these people was a young man called Paterno. I had no reason to doubt him, since he was from the Father's Lotuko tribe. Indeed, the moment Fr. Saturnino learnt from Paterno that I was in town, he sent a driver with Paterno to fetch me. Having heard what I heard, we needed only to exchange a few words with the Father, and there was a complete meeting of the minds. What followed is a long story.

To cut a long story short, I found myself driving a German Opel Escort around virtually the whole of the Congo and sometimes venturing up to the Central African Republic (CAR), where the only language that opened doors for me was my Bangala language, taught to me in childhood by my father, for whom it was the language of the Christian Bible. My visiting Congolese cousins from my grandmother's side later polished that Bangala into Lingala. Amazingly, this language is spoken in most of the Congo and the adjacent parts of the CAR. Even in those parts where Lingala was rarely spoken, a broken Swahili, known as Kingwana, was spoken. That, too, helped fit me everywhere in that region.

My journeys around East Africa (Kenya, Tanganyika—as it then was—and Uganda, meeting people I would never have dreamt of seeing; all through contacts arranged by the Father. He must have assured them that they could trust me to explain the situation in the Sudan to them in very precise terms. I had always approached him with a desire to work, while others openly portrayed themselves as leaders—his equals—who had their extra edge of being unfettered by the restrictions of the Vatican. In short, Fr. Saturnino was seen as a politician, whose qualities for leadership were inhibited by his priesthood in the Catholic Church, and who had, therefore, to be used for upholding someone in a position of leadership.

It was then that rumors began to circulate that the Father was trying to build me up as a puppet, just to warm the seat of power for him. That I was guilty of infusing political ambition into the Father etc. The origins of such rumors were such politicians who were very close to him; even when he had appended the name of one of them as an author to a book he wrote single-handedly, to avoid being too political. The other, so-called author, while appearing not to care, was a believer in the predominance of the numbers of his tribe, as outlined and encouraged by Egyptian politicians. In both cases, the politics of the South had been turned into a theater for leadership ambition, especially when I tell you that the Father and I had nothing in mind at that stage, but only the salvation of the South Sudan. We even went to the extra extent of giving them the respect they appeared to demand.

Our partying of the ways with Fr. Saturnino was, if anything, an uncharted territory. Fr. Saturnino Lohure did not appear to know I valued my honor so much that I could read words, and even body language which did not respect that honor. A lucky event was the coming of the Congolese rebellion by the Simba. That appeared to have been the one that forced us apart. The fact was, however, different. I felt I was blamed for what to me was a matter that saved my life, along with the lives of my fellow travelers. For the first time, Fr. Saturnino Lohure had openly told me that he would have trusted the arms I had short-landed would have been put to better use had they gone to the Eastern Bank, *where there were Lotuko warriors*. Having known him all the time as an impartial worker for the Southern Sudan cause, I decided not to stay, and hear any more. While he might have thought that he was only rebuking me for what I had done, I saw the rebuke to have gone out of normal range as a result of the mention of his tribe. Our tribes are important to us. No amount of impartiality can erase that fact from our minds. While that fact is already reflected in the Comprehensive Peace Agreement (CPA), some of our leaders still behave as if they are there to live above certain natural facts. We need courage to face all the facts of our diversity, and to offer amicable solutions.

An Uncharted Parting of the Ways

Although I have deliberately chosen this heading as the title of this incident, I have a feeling; in my heart of hearts, that Fr. Saturnino will churn with rebuke to me in his grave. That may be because, while Fr. Saturnino Lohure was a priest, who had known the value of forgiveness of someone, I am a layman, who is unable even to understand my being forgiven. I had been under very close speed chase in the Congo. As the official gun-runner, I was carrying very dangerous weapons. What was even more dangerous was that I was being chased by the sellers of the weapons. That was obviously to say that we had stolen them. It was a situation where I felt even God would have allowed his only begotten son to let go, if that could let him be found without any evidence on him. However, God allowed me to out-speed my chasers into safety. That safety did not happen to coincide with my destination where the Father was. But, it did coincide with where one of the Father's trusted allies from the parliamentary days was. The Father had even at one time authorized that man to head one of my trips to the CAR. I handed him the weapons, and drove straight to my destination. On our being intercepted, nothing was found. After such a long service, gratis to the Fr., I, for the first time felt that my version of the story was not palatable to him. For me, that was the parting of the ways.

Shamefully for me, however, I was to strike on another of Fr. Saturnino's surprise recommendations for me, only after his death. He is said to have passed word through someone to Colonel Joseph Lagu that if he (Colonel Joseph Lagu) worked hand in hand with me, he (the Father) was confident that the South would one day be freed. This fact was confirmed by many different sources. It was then that I felt my emotions must have had the better part of me when I walked out on him in annoyance. Unfortunately, that is what we are as political animals—too quick to react to any sign of disrespect.

Fr. Saturnino Lohure's Revolutionary Activities and Ultimate Death

The Father died as a revolutionary. He had all his life shown himself— even to his superiors at the Vatican—to be a priest, with some obvious nationalistic zeal. However, I should like to humbly make a small correction regarding the contribution Joseph Lagu is said to have made to the Southern Sudan cause as a result of Fr. Saturnino's effort and prodding. If that is supposed to demonstrate Joseph Lagu's insolence to the Father, I should like to assure the author that Joseph Lagu had done that even with me. Nonetheless, we must give the devil his due.

Joseph Lagu was with me in school. He was among those whom I would count as Southern Sudanese national activists. We were the group that gave our Members of Parliament (MPs) support. The group that admired Fr. Saturnino, right from the start. Their connections to the Israelis came through their own separate ways. Those connections bore the hallmarks of the wit of the Israeli Intelligence Agency, the Mosad. For, contrary to the views expressed on the Leopoldville meeting, my views are that the Israelis might have used that brief small gathering as a diversionary tactic, through the Mosad; so that they could deliver assistance to the Southern struggle discretely. The facts were as bare to me as follows: while they were in Leopoldville, I was made to appear to be the only link with them from the South. My knowledge about Fr. Saturnino was thoroughly researched, and recorded. Within twenty-four hours, Fr. Saturnino Lohure's knowledge about me was thoroughly researched and recorded. That Father who was supposed to be in Leopoldville suddenly turned up in Nairobi. Let me add another simple fact: when an eager, inquisitive volunteer like Ibrahim Nyigilo was made to introduce Fr. Saturnino to a certain French source in Kampala, it might have been just a way of making Ibrahim lose sight of the pursuit. Ibrahim will, in the end, never manage to know where the man he had introduced the Father to have ended.

When it came to naming a person I thought could represent us militarily, I named Joseph Lagu; while it appeared Fr. Saturnino Lohure named former army Sergeant Major Lohioro. We were only aware of the presence of each other in the city through town gossips—not that we were necessarily enemies. We were simply made to go about the same thing without knowing each others activities, or even the other's whereabouts. All these activities took place within Nairobi. I was made to live in the same hotel with Aggrey Jaden, and we only discovered after three days that we checked in only an hour apart. The Israelis made each one of us act busily in isolation, without being given the chance of knowing about the presence of the other in the town. I cannot be surprised if Joseph Lagu was actually in Nairobi.

That may be why Lagu himself cannot, knowingly, and openly tamper with any facts regarding his final breakthrough with the Israelis. He knows that his passing the test before the Israeli side was the result of my sitting up all night to type out his elaborate list of military requirements. What was most important was that I had already prepared the ground for him, so that he did not have to answer questions that were political in nature. He was left to his comfort with military matters. In fact, it was the Nairobi contact that counted to his men on the days towards the end of the war. Should I catch Joseph Lagu uttering the words he is said to have uttered, he knows what kind of piece of mind he will get. However, he has to mind so many pieces of mind along his track too.

Oliver B. Albino
Portland, Maine.

Chapter Endnotes

[4] *Bey* is a Turkish Middle Ranking Officer like a colonel. It is also a title of respect.

Chapter One
In the Beginning

*In the beginning was the Word, and the Word was with God, and the
Word was God. He was in the beginning with God. All things were
made through him, and without him nothing was made that was made
(John Ch. 1: 1-3).*

The Beginning

Of course, in the beginning, there was God and perhaps there was the
Word as the Holy Scripture proclaims, but also in the beginning, before
Father Saturnino Lohure was born, there was the Lotuko community, the
whole ethnic group of people in which the Father was born in, and from
there everything else followed. The Father didn't emerge out into scenery
of political prominence in Sudan out of nowhere, but of a certain
community background, culture, and heritage profoundly established in
the history of Sudan and the history of humankind. A proverb attributed
to Africans because of Africans community nurturing behavior states, "it
takes a village to raise a child." It is through such background, culture and

heritage the Father came into existence, and to some extend it is through these attributes which shaped the Father's skills, attitudes, and experience in life. In other words, one's experience is shaped by one's environment or surrounding, especially the upbringing in the early age can shape one's life in most profound ways. Actually, they say, "culture permeates and influences every aspect of life."[5] That can apply for everyone who grow around certain culture and cultures.

The Lotuko People

In the case of the Father, his first life experience started among Lotuko people because he was born and raised among them. Later in his life, he lived and worked among the Lokuka people as well as among other communities, hence shaping his life experience even further. The Lotuko people are among many ethnic groups inhibiting the vast land of Sudan, more specifically inhibiting the mountain ranges and low plains in the Eastern Equatoria region of Southern Sudan. Legend had it that the Lotuko people have their origin in East, somewhere around the Ethiopia highlands and plateaus. They, the Lotuko people are said to have migrated to their present day territory in around 1600 A.D. in the migration wave that resulted many of their supposed counterparts such as the Masaai, and Kalenjin ended up in Kenya, the Iteso in Uganda as well as the Bari ending up along the River Nile in Equatoria region of South Sudan. The history of Lotuko people like many ethnic groups in South Sudan is short in a sense that it is not recorded in some form to provide and accurate picture. Their recorded history started recently with the arrival of the outsiders, mainly the colonial powers and the missionaries. The other part of the history is left for historians, archeologists, and anthropologists to try their best to piece out together part of the lost history and uncover some of the truth behind it. And the rest of history is shrouded in the mystery of legends pass onto generations after another through oral history.

On their first encounter with the outside world, the Lotuko people did not fail to impress, their new visitors. Francis R. Wingate, the British intelligent officer in Egyptian Army in his assessments of the Southern Sudanese ethnic groups, came to the conclusion that the Lotuko people were of a "pleasant and cheerful disposition."[6] For Samuel Baker, an English explorer, the Lotuko people stood out to be the "finest savage" he had ever seen. In his assessment, Baker remarked that the Lotuko people were "far from being the morose set of savages…they are excessively merry, and always ready for either a laugh or a fight."[7] Others such as Emin Pasha, the then governor of Equatoria, shared this same assessment and even went as far as supporting it with anthropometric data. In perspective, "a number of travelers and missionaries contrast the cheerful and gallant way by which they are received by the Bari and Lotuho with the uncomfortable, shy and clumsy approach of the Nuer and Dinka."[8]

Like most of the Southern Sudanese ethnic groups, the Lotuko people share some of their exhibited cultural characteristics with others, even though the Lotuko also retains some of their unique characteristics only to themselves. In South Sudan, the home of many ethnic groups, stereotyping is a first line of identity. It seems a Southern Sudanese would not be satisfied without identifying one of their own with something either related or stereotypical of their ethnic group or culture. Those stereotyping sometimes could be so negative to chill someone's nerves. They involve ethnic groups or cultures noted for killing, witch crafting, poisoning, sexual promiscuity, drunkenness, or even roaming around naked. This is so common that it becomes automatic to apply any of those stereotyping without having any thought about it, and this practice becomes widely acceptable.

In other societies, such as the Western societies, the notion of stereotyping is debated on whether they are healthy among societies. Stereotyping is scorned by others because they view it as prejudicial approach to reinforce certain discriminatory behavior toward certain individual or group of individuals, mostly the minority groups. However, stereotypes in and of themselves are not generally harmful. Their harmfulness can be determined on how they are used. Social scientists and psychologists have longed been researching the inevitability of stereotyping in major cases of human social interactions, and they came to the conclusion that stereotypes, "operate as a fundamental part of human social interaction. Their activation in the majority of cases is automatic and inevitable. In a minority of cases their activation may be thwarted."[9]

The Lotuko Cultural Influence

Given this scientific conclusions couple with the prevalent cultures of South Sudanese where stereotypes is considered more of a means of identity, one cannot help it but point some of the characteristics exhibited by Fr. Saturnino Lohure which can best be linked to the Lotuko culture or which can be stereotyped as a Lotuko culture. The first such distinctive characteristic is the name Lohure. The name Lohure, in its correct form Ohure, has significant cultural and historical meaning. Ohure is a noun deriving from an adjective *ahure*, which is hanger. Traditionally, the name Ohure is given to a male child born in time of famine. The Lotuko people, from time to time are hit by famine for a host of reasons. Even under normal circumstances, they still don't yield enough harvest to maintain food surplus that last beyond a year circle, hence facing famine in the beginning of every harvest season. Given this circumstances, the Father's first experience in the world was a harsh one, because he was met by a misery of famine, a lesson that later turned into crusade when he took it as his mission to fight the miseries and wickedness of the world that he found to be full of injustices and inequalities. Actually, the Father's "legend" as described in his eulogy, "is that he hated injustice, inequality and misery to the same degree as he loved justice, equality and prosperity."[10] It is said, the Father "has been delivered to God in untimely fashion through the wickedness of the world he talked of."[11]

Another characteristic reflected in the Father, which can be stereotypical of the Lotuko culture is the very manner in which he is identified whereby his Lotukoness is highly emphasized and stressed despite his status or accomplishments, which surpass beyond the confines of Lotuko culture, and despite all the glories that come with those accomplishments. In the volume of *Sudanese Catholic Clergy*, Fr. Vittorino Dellagiacoma wrote that Fr. Saturnino Lohure is "the first Lotuho priest."[12] Even if he was a priest, the Italian Comboni missionary, Fr. Dellagiacoma, felt that it is necessary to identify him as a Lotuko first and a priest second making him the first Lotuko who became a priest. The American, Robert Collins, a renowned South Sudanese historian, describes Fr. Saturnino Lohure, "an ambitious Latuka Catholic priest who remained an enigmatic figurehead of the southern movement."[13] Once again, even though he was "an ambitious leader," a "Catholic", and a "priest", his Lotukoness must be emphasized for the purpose of a complete identification. Otherwise people will wonder if such emphasis is not made clear. For all the good or bad reasons, in South Sudan, it is a norm to identify individuals based on their tribal affiliations. Given their diverse cultural affiliations and attitudes, the Southern Sudanese themselves started this phenomenon and began to fully practice it.

Unfortunately, the British took it a bit further to another level by instituting an entire policy of "Indirect Rule" in an attempt to identify some of the tribal attributes or these stereotypes, which can be suitable for colonial rules and exploitations. According to Lord Kitchener, the British intention was "to seek out the better class of native, through whom" the British would be able to influence the entire population of the South Sudan.[14] From the last time it was checked, the British failed miserably as they ended up fragmenting the societies "along ethnic, regional, and tribal lines, and also preventing a possibility of forging a national identity."[15]

Another Lotuko cultural attribute is that the Lotuko people have strong sense of duty through the generational system of *monyie-miji*. *Monyie-miji* is a Lotuko literal translation of the owners of a village but an implied reference to the generation who are in charge. This active generation or *monyie-miji* is a generation which attains power and responsibility to govern on matters related to the welfare of Lotuko people, and power to protect their villages and properties. The power is handed through a grand ceremony that take place every twenty two years called *efira*. In every one of these ceremonies, the power is handed down to a generation between the range of ages eighteen through forty years young. Even though the Lotuko people pays their allegiances to the king or queen, the decision to deal with matters related to the running of the village and welfare of the people lies to *monyie-miji*. The kings and queens duties are mostly to perform ceremonial rituals. It is through the appeal of *monyie-miji* that villages and their properties are protected. The Father took advantage of this social and cultural system to the fullest extent possible. During the struggled, he appealed directly to the *monyie-miji* sense of duty and responsibility to recruit them in the Anyanya movement. The concept of *monyie-miji* in a context of a modern state is patriotism.

After the death of the Father, the Sudan People Liberation Army (SPLA), which emerged in 1980s, was to gain immensely by appealing to the *monyie-miji* sense of duty for its recruitment. The Lotuko people were the first to join the SPLA struggle in Equatoria region in large numbers changing the face of SPLA from being viewed as a Dinka movement into a national liberation movement. When the first group of the recruits returned to the Lotukoland all they have to do to gain more recruits was to sing songs with appealing sense of *monyie-miji* or in other words, with appealing sense of patriotism. Songs were great morale boosters for SPLA recruitments and morale. They could go hungry, exhausted and sick but yet pumped up when they sing patriotic songs, which they simply refer to as morale. And for the Lotuko warriors, songs have special meanings, which they translate into national patriotism. In war time, songs are used as inspirations. One of the SPLA songs they brought in the Lotukoland to induce recruits was title, *Tihian Monyie-miji*. *Tihian* is a name of SPLA battalion. It is an Arabic word for valor. To paraphrase the meaning of this song and its sense of appeal: it asserts that there are no visible cowards among the Tihian Battalion, because they are all *monyie-miji*. It goes on to assert that the courage of Tihian Battalion once demonstrated, it explodes into flames, and that courage is only matched by none other than the courage of John Garang, the leader of SPLA and that of Commander Jada, the SPLA commanding officer in the Lotuko area at the time. Such song and others were so appealing that young boys had to abandon their dreams to join SPLA in droves. In his field research, Dr. Simon Simonse, an archeologist, discovered that the SPLA recruitments in Lotuko land were less violent than in other parts of Eastern Equatoria because the recruitment was voluntary. He wrote, "I did not come across men who said that they joined the SPLA just because they did not want to be victims of the new round of violence" of recruitment. He added that instead, the recruits joined willingly and the "SPLA attacks on the main road from Torit to Kapoeta were carried out in collaboration with the *monyie-miji*" who are by the way civilians.[16] Perhaps, it is only in Lotukoland where civilians actively participate in combat operations against the armed forces of Khartoum government. The Lotuko people have a culture in responding to emergencies in a more swift manner through the concept of *alulu*. *Alulu* simply means a cry, but in its conceptual application, it is an appeal to respond to crisis, emergencies, or to perform certain immediate task. When *alulu* is evoked, it means an announcement is made whereby people responded first and ask questions later. At a village level, *alulu* is used to alert people of tragedy such as funerals, attacks, raids or imminent danger of some sort. It is also used to get people to perform certain duties. Such a concept can also be translated into a national level, and in the South Sudan context, both the Anyanya and SPLA movements benefited from it.

Along this same Lotuko cultural ceremony performed during the initiation of a new generation to take control of the new leadership is that all the fires from all the Lotuko villages will be put off before the ceremony commenced. A new fire will be ignited in a ceremonious way at the sacred location where the initiation ceremony is taking place. This is done with style and a show of skills, by rubbing special sticks which have potential to produce the mother of all fires to light the households in the entire Lotuko villages. Capable and able individuals from each village would take a piece from this fire to start the new fires in their respective villages. Those individuals will diligently carry the torch and reach their respective villages as fast as they could no matter how far their villages may be. They must also make sure they reach their villages with the fire still lightening. In a symbolic way, the Father demonstrated this phenomenon at a national level. When the call for South Sudan liberation struggle came, the Father was the first Southern Sudanese individual to run with the torch of liberation struggle and set the flame for the liberation struggle to lighten throughout the South Sudan. Such effort would have earned him with ease the praise worthy title of *Ofeja* (being active and quick to respond) among the Lotuko people.

Other stereotypes or attributes the Lotuko people credited for themselves or they are noted for, stemmed from the competitive nature of Lotuko society. The Lotuko people are among the most competitive in the world perhaps on the par in their zealotry for competitions with ancient Roman gladiators or the ancient Greeks who started Olympic Games. Most of the Lotuko people are Olympians without gold metals. For example, before the arrival of guns, they used to javelin each other and their neighbors into death using spears. You can still see signs of that in their dance today where they shake the spears vigorously as if to throw it at someone. From childhold, males practice through several games the art of not only throwing the spear to the furthest distance, but also to throw it accurately on the target. By the time they grow up, they already master the art of handling the spear properly and they employ those skills to practically fight wars. As recently as mid 1980s, the spear was still the weapon of choice among the Lotuko people. In one report, it indicates that when the SPLA made its first incursion to "attack a police post in the village of Kiyala, many *monyie-miji* from Iloli and Lobira carrying their spears followed the troops. In the attack three villagers got killed by the spears of the enemy *monyie-miji*."[17]

With the arrival of powerful guns; they literally practice their sharp shooting skills on each other, their neighbors, and anyone or anything that happen to pass by including vehicles. Actually, it is written that the best marksmanship in the whole Sudan in 1950s was a Lotuko by the name, Emideo Tafeng. He never got a gold metal for his skills but instead prison time for the fear that he was a dangerous man.[18] With a specially designed beating stick known as *leluk*, they clobber each other breaking their skulls just like gladiators. Even more to the gladiatorial standard, they use a specially designed axe for chopping each other in challenging matches or in duels. Some of the reasons contributing to competitive nature of these seemingly sporting or athletic activities among Lotuko society are natural due to their environment. For example, running is natural due to the fact that members of the community are constantly active at all time to pursue the enemies or being pursued by the enemies on foot. Besides, there are no other means for mobility; therefore, they have to improvise with their feet for speed. But this is also not to undermine the pride invested into these activities, especially wrestling where those who are good wrestlers take great pride in wrestling just as fast runners also take great pride in running.

As for Fr. Saturnino Lohure, he certainly possesses some of the qualities desirable for competitiveness among the Lotuko society or qualities stereotypical of Lotuko people. Among those qualities the Father possessed, is valor and courage. Being timid among the Lotuko society is not an option as the environment requires one to stand up and face dangers and hardships with a resolute attitude and astute. The Father is an exemplary of this. Fr. Vittorino Dellagiacoma, the author of Sudanese Catholic Clergy noted the Father's courageous nature by describing him, as a "…courageous leader."[19] The Vigilant newspaper described the Father's "heroic stance in the Constitutional Draft Committee" as a man "brave enough to present the Southern viewpoint to the Constituent Assembly" of 1958.[20] Prior to his death, he was informed of Ugandan plan of sealing off the borders to intercept and contain possible *Anyanya* suspects and the flow of refugees into Uganda. The Ugandan army unit in Jinja barrack was transferred and deployed in the borders for this purpose. The Father rushed quickly from Nairobi to go to Sudan facing the danger of getting caught and killed on his way. While by the border, they could clearly sense the imminent danger. His companions cautioned him of the dangers crossing the border, and pleaded with him that they were willing to cross first leaving the Father behind in safety to inform the South Sudanese people of the Ugandan plan to seal the borders. He dismissed his companions' plea saying that it will be cowardice for him to stay behind in a safe place while the two risked their lives. So, they both courageously risked their lives in their attempt to cross the border, but it was only the Father who died as a result.[21]

One other characteristic the people of Lotuko are noted for is the ability to wrestle effectively and master the wrestling techniques to have a competitive advantage over opponents during the brawling. Wrestling among the Lotuko people is a big deal as it is used for punishing opponents, self defense, and for gaining respect among peers. For the Father, he even had an advantage given the size of his body, which gives him an edge against opponents. The Father's wrestling ability and techniques came handy in the last day of his life. With only bear hands, he physically wrestled down one of his Ugandan killers who were armed with automatic rifle. Such is only true in scenery of fictitious characters in the movies.

His athletic ability also came handy during his years of struggle as he used to paddle on bicycles and walk long distance on foot. For example, on the day of his death, he had already paddled over 80 kilometers on bicycle and walked additional 40 kilometers. He would be so hungry, tired and exhausted of long cycling and walking, but in the end he would say, "I go on", recalled Fr. Tarcisio Agostoni.[22] He has been remembered as the most restless person who moved "endlessly through ruined and unrecognizable land, encouraging the Christians and inviting resistance."[23] Another fellow priest remembered meeting the Father "on his return from one of his usual journeys inside his country. He looked tired, hungry and poorly dressed...incarnated in himself the sufferings of his oppressed people."[24] Had he not been athletically fit, and a person who can endure great amount of suffering, and very passionate about his work, he would not have done some of the things that he did.

Other Cultural Influences

It is not only the Lotuko culture, which significantly influenced Fr. Saturnino Lohure because he was also exposed to other different cultures, especially as he was growing older and began to encounter different cultures and moving to different places. Some of his attributes are also stereotypical of other cultures given their influence on him. The Father was born in Loronyo village one of the biggest Lotuko villages. Loronyo village is just situated few miles north of the major town of Torit at latitude and longitude of 4° 37' 60 N and 32° 37' 60 E respectively.[25] The village is right on a major road north bound from Torit town into Lopit villages along the mountain ridges as well as on the road that passes through to Lafon (Lokoro) villages.

Traditionally, Loronyo village enjoys some level of interactions with its neighboring villages of Lopit and Lafon. Those interactions are both peaceful and violent, depending on circumstances and occasions. Even though the people of Lopit speaks a language with slightly varying accent than the one the people of Loronyo speaks, people from both communities can be able to communicate with each other effectively. Not only that, both communities share many of their customary practices including the clan system where members of the same clan, who are supposedly related to each other through the clan system, can be found across those communities. Intermarriages between these two communities are not taboo as the intermarriages actually strengthen their relationships even more. Due to close cultural affinity and proximity to the Lopit people and their villages, the relationship between the people of Loronyo and Lopit people is far stronger than it is with the Lafon people who are of a different ethnic group, speaks different language, practice different culture, and situated at a much farther distance. The Father might have easily connected with the Lopit communities and gain some influence from them including their language.

One of the unique attributes of the Lotuko people is that they are willing to go out of their ways to forge a relationship wherever there is no blood, clan, or tribal relationship. This practice of forging a relationship or adopting a relative is commonly used among the Lotuko people when dealing with people from different ethnic groups or communities. The caveat though is that this relationship must be mutual in nature. Unlike the Lopit people who may have clan relationship with the Loronyo people, in the case of Lofan people, no such a relationship exist, therefore, the people of Loronyo would have to resort into forging or adopting those relationships due to their frequent interactions with the people of Lofan. Such a relationship is forged under friendship which goes beyond mere friendships to imply relationship of stronger type. The Lotuko uses the word *mote* in describing this forged and adopted relationship. *Mote* literally means friend, however, in a context of a forged or an adopted relationship, it implies a relative from a different ethnic group or a relative from different community. If relationships are ranked due to their imminence, *mote* or an adopted relative will be ranked next to a member of clan in that order of closeness in relationship. It is through this relationship people of both Loronyo village and Lafon can find comfort interacting with each other despite their cultural differences or occasional hostilities. And it would have been through such relationship that the Father would be intimately involved with the Lafon people at early age while in Loronyo.

Even though all these neighboring communities are trading with each other through a barter system, especially in times of drought and famine, Loronyo village is a significant attracting center as it is a destination stop for some people from Lopit and Lafon who travel to and from Torit town. Torit town is acting as a market destination for the exchange of goods and services to the surrounding communities. Therefore, the Lofan and Lopit people cannot avoid the temptation in trekking to Torit in order to take advantages of the exchange of goods and services just like the other surrounding communities. Among the commodities the people of Lafon offer on the market in Torit are smoked fish, smoked wild meat, *lulu* oil, honey and sorghum. While the people of Lopit offer peanuts and honey among other things. In exchange for these commodities, they will get back in return salt, medicines, clothing, beats, and money and trek back home.

It would have been in Loronyo village that Fr. Saturnino Lohure had a first encounter with large communities who are non-Lotuko community. This will later shape his experience as he moved on to Torit town and other places with more diverse communities. By the time he was posted as a priest in Lirya (Lokoya ethnic group area), in late 1940s, he already mastered the language of Pari (Lafon) people and visited Lafon several times. He also developed closed affinity with a prominent Pari leader of the time, Henry Bago. Fr. Hilary Boma, a young fellow priest who was a seminarian at the time, is greatly impressed by Fr. Saturnino Lohure linguistic competency and genius. He describes the Father, as "a walking library of tongues who switched from one language to another as occasion presents itself."[26] A good example of the Father switching from one language to another in the amazement of the young seminarians took place in Lirya in 1953. When the young seminarians were at a picnic, they observed the Father intervened to interpret among a Greek merchant, a Lulubo, and a Lokoya, literary juggling three different languages in resolving a situation that involved the three individuals. Of course, other examples are in his lively homilies when he would occasionally throw quotes in Latin and other languages in the mix to articulate his points. In fact, prior to Vatican II, the masses in Catholic Churches were conducted in Latin.[27]

"A library of tongues" that the Father was, he spoke many of the major world languages as well as the local languages making his interaction with other communities easier. For this reason alone, the Father distinguished himself from most of the Southern Sudanese leaders of his time as he could easily approach and interact with people of different backgrounds, ethnicities, nationalities, and languanges with a considerable amount of ease. Besides being fluent in the queen's language, he also spoke Arabic, French, German, Italian, Latin and Kiswahili fluently. In Yei, he is being heard preaching in Lingala, a language that is widely spoken in Congo and some of its neighboring countries. While traveling through Congo in the 1960s, it is reported that he would often asked the Bishops of those areas so that he would hear the confessions of the Christians whom he knew their languages and preach to them in those languages, which included French, Lingala, and Kiswahili.[28] The Father also knew Acholi language very well, and in this case, he had studied in Gulu for his philosophy and theology, mastering Acholi language in the process. He is also said to be fluent in Bari language, which has some similarities to Lotuko language. The little Madi language he knew might have come from his classmate, Fr. Avellino Wani who was ordained with him on the same day and served together with him in Lirya parish.[29] He also briefly served in Kopoeta and

47

Rumbek, however, there are no evidence that he spoke the Toposa and Dinka languages. In case of Toposa language, it is more similar to the Lotuko language in some ways, which leads to the possibilities that he might have picked up some of the Toposa in that short period of his service in the area. Nonetheless, in Rumbek, the Father and his fellow priest, Fr. Paulino Doggale are remembered or rather accused by the Arabs for inciting students to boycott Arabic teaching.

The Father also developed talent and passion in social and cultural activities such as music and dance. In Lirya, he is vividly remembered for participating in local activities like dancing, farming, and hunting. A parishioner at the time, Marina Lohide, claims that the Father was liked by the local people more than any priest who ever came to Lirya at that time, especially due to the fact that all the priests who were in Lirya prior to the Father's arrival there, were white Europeans.[30]

With respect to farming, the Father is remembered as the guy who tilted the land along with the locals. An interesting example of the Father being in a farm, showing his humility, occurred in Lirya. At that point, a messenger was delivering a personal parcel to the Father at the Lirya mission sent by Bishop Sisto Mazzoldi from Juba. Upon arrival at the mission in Lirya, the messenger found Fr. Avelino Wani who told the messenger that the Father was away at the mission's farm, but he was willing to keep the parcel and will hand it to the Father when he arrives. However, the messenger was strictly following the instructions when he then insisted that the parcel must be delivered directly to the Father, because it was urgent. As such, Fr. Wani provided direction to the messenger to go find the Father at the mission's farm, which was a bit distant, about three to five miles away. The messenger then rode of on his bicycle to the mission's farm. As he was by the gate, he found someone wearing a large and floppy hat, and at the same time carrying a bundle of firewood. That messenger never bothered a bit to asked the person. He just passed the person and went straight to the offices, and then peeking through the offices with the hope that he would find the Father sitting comfortably in one of those offices. But unfortunately there was no sign of the Father in the offices, because the person who was wearing the large and floppy hat while carrying the firewood by the gate was the Father, going about his business in the farm. In frustration, the messenger returned insisting that the Father was not at the farm. He was then sent for the second time to go and ask the workers at the farm, if at all the Father had left for some pastoral work. This time around, the messenger went to the farm and asked for the whereabouts of the Father. A small boy then escorted him to the Father who was at the time cooking food for the workers. When the messenger asked, the Father responded, 'yes, I am Fr. Saturnino.' The messenger was struck dump. He immediately fell into his knees and cried. Then moments later, from the top of his lungs, the messenger shouted, *'Hotwoho Yesu Kristo!'* (Praise Jesus Christ!).[31]

It is worth noting that the Catholic missionaries, the Verona Fathers in particular were keen on farming. They were not only farming so as to sustain their living, but most of those missionaries just like their founder, Saint Daniel Comboni, came from rural farming areas in Italy. This fact is support by the statistic, which indicates that all but only few of the Verona missionaries in Sudan came from the rural vicinity of Verona town in Italy.[32] But yet, the Father distinguishes himself from all the priests, locals and missionaries alike, by suppressing his privileges of a priest and actively participating with the workers as if he was not a priest.

It was also in Lirya that the Father is remembered for incorporating African traditions into Christianity, a radical transformation of Catholicism that would not have seated well with the Holy See at the period of pre Vatican II. And it was also in Lirya that he encountered the force of Islamization and Arabization where he vehemently opposed to it, and together with Fr. Avellino Wani, they instigated the students to boycott classes when the school that was run by Arabs was introduced. It was there and then that the Father understood the immediate threats posed by Arabs and Islam to the people of South Sudan.[33] And it was also in Lirya where he showed his compassion for the sanctity of human lives by protecting, in his own house the Arabs who were fleeing the 1955 Torit Mutiny, something that the Arabs who lust of eliminating him still appreciate to this day.[34] Perhaps demonstrating such act of compassion was not the influence of Lotuko culture nor was it stereotypical of Lotuko people. That must have been Christian faith. But had he instituted that Lotuko warrior instinct, the Arabs might have remembered the whole incident differently.

The Influence of Catholicism

Speaking of Christianity in general and the Catholic specifically, the faith has tremendous influences on the Father. If the name Lohure is stereotypical of Lotuko culture, then Saturnino is stereotypical of Catholic culture; that is to consider the context of South Sudan stereotyping standard. In English, they will say, Lohure is to Lotuko as Saturnino is to Catholic. Of course, as noted earlier, the Father was a Lotuko first and then he was converted into Christianity through baptism. For the people of South Sudan, to convert into Christianity or Catholicism in this case, one has to be competent as the process is not that easy. The most interesting thing about the Catholic is that no one is born as a Christian, not even the pope. All the Catholics must be baptized, in order, for them to become Catholics or be initiated in the Church. However, that makes it worse for the South Sudanese people, as there are no means to baptize people at a young age or at the moment they are born.

This is contrary to other countries, which baptize their babies the moment they are born. For example, the unfortunate Southern Sudanese would be surprise to learn that the current pope, Benedict XVI was among the blessed to be born and baptized in the same day. Moreover, it was on Holy Saturday, only a day before Easter Sudan. No wonder he is a pope. Reflecting on this blessed experience, the Pope wrote, "to be the first person baptized with the new water was seen as a significant act of Providence. I have always been filled with thanksgiving for having had my life immersed in this way in the Easter Mystery."[35] It is easier for some of those countries, which are able to baptize their children at a younger age partly because their babies are born in hospitals and in every hospital there is a chaplain or a priest who is readily available to baptize the new born. In South Sudan, most people are not born in hospitals, only few are born in hospitals, and they have to be sick to be born in the hospital anyway. After all, there are few hospitals and they are reserved for the sick, not the new born. Even then, the hospitals don't have chaplains or priests to carryout baptisms in the hospitals. The regular baptism has to be arranged with the church and is only performed on special day where a bunch of kids have to be baptized all together at once. And that takes place in Church.

In the case of the Father, he was baptized at age ten that means he had to endure ten years of being taunted as a pagan. By then, Catholicism was only eleven years old in the Lotuko land, meaning the majority of the people were pagans, at least as far as the Church was concerned. Before he was to be baptized, the Father was to first, successfully complete catechism course, which provides instructions about Christ, faith and the Church. During baptism, he has to choose a Christian name or he would be given one. In his case, the name Saturnino was the choice. Amazingly, it turns out that Saturnino is not just a Christian name but an Italian name as well. So, a Christian name can also be an Italian name this is because the Italian happened to embrace Christianity before the Lotuko people did, therefore, they monopolize Christian names, and perhaps Catholic faith, and that is why it is not surprising that Catholicism have its center in Italy even deriving part of its name from Rome such as Roman Catholic Church. This would mean, the Father was also influenced to same extend by the Italian culture, and that fact is manifested in his name and on the Italian language that he spoke.

Of a lively intelligence, the Father completed his primary school within only two years than the normal four years. He then went on to join seminary in Okaru. Becoming a priest was an idea that the Father manifested earlier on in his life. After rigorous years of studies in Okura, the Father passed on to Gulu in Uganda in 1938, where he studied philosophy and theology. On December 21, 1946, the Father and a fellow classmate, Fr. Avellino Wani were ordained priests in Gulu. The Father and Fr. Wani will later ended up serving in the same parish in Lirya. The Christmas of 1946, was not only the joyous for the people of Torit, but it was also historic in the sense that the people of Torit in disbelieve have to witness their own son, Fr. Saturnino Lohure officiating the mass at Christmas. In amazement, their son who left as a young boy is now back as a priest and they have to call him *Fadiri* (a corruption of Padre, an Italian for Father). It is interesting that the Lotuko culture, which had all along put so much emphasis in respecting the title of the Father to strictly be followed along the age lines, had dramatically drifted from such norm by having elders called the young Fr. Saturnino Lohure as Father. If there was a time of cultural revolutionary changes among the Lotuko social system, it was when the Father stepped in Torit and to be called as a Father even by the elders.

Martyrdom Inspirations

It was not only the cultures that had tremendous influence on Fr. Saturnino Lohure but also the inspirations of the blessed saints and Catholic martyrs, which had much impact on him. A devoted Catholic priest, he was greatly influenced by the martyrdom of Fr. Miguel Agustín Pro, a Mexican Roman Catholic Jesuit priest who was executed on behest of Mexican government for defying anti-Catholic laws in Mexico. Fr. Pro or Padre Pro, as he is popularly known, was a priest of extraordinary distinction. Padre Pro is described as, "an exquisite wit, never coarse, always sparkling."[36] Wrongfully accused of participating in assassination attempt, Padre Pro was executed on November of 1927. During his execution, he declined to be blindfolded. Instead, he armed himself with crucifix on one hand and a rosary on the other. Spreading his arms in imitation of Jesus Christ on the cross, he shouted out loud, "may God have mercy on you! May God bless you! Lord, Thou knowest that I am innocent! With all my heart I forgive my enemies!"[37] He concluded by shouting "*Viva Cristo Rey!*" (Spanish for "Long live Christ the King!"), and then he was executed in firing squad.

Inspired by this extraordinary courage and character, the Father would later write articles pleading for the persecuted people of South Sudan, proudly signing those articles under the name "Padre Pro."[38] It is interesting that the Father was inspired by an individual across the ocean in Americas, but after the death of the Father, an interesting phenomenon emerged in Americas known as the "liberation theology" something similar to what the Father was involved in throughout his lives. Now could it be that the Americas were inspired by the Father or it was the other way around?

Attributes

A leader of international scope and stature, the Father was viewed by others in the same caliber with those of Patrice Lumumba, a contemporary of his time who was the first legally elected Congolese Prime Minister who led Congo into independence. Patrice Lumumba who is declared a national hero and martyr continues to serve as inspirations to many in Congo, throughout Africa, the Black World, and all over the world.[39] Others see Lumumba's struggle for justice, freedom, equality, and controversial death, parallel to that of the Father. On the Father's death, a long report was carried on *The Vigilant* newspaper, which states, "once more, one more great African leader met violent death in very obscure circumstances."[40] Because the Father was arrested and dealt away with, without any due process of the law, the report goes on to parallel the two incidents that the Father "was in the custody of the Ugandan army, just as much as Lumumba six years earlier was supposed to be in safe hands of the Katangese Gendarmerie."[41] In their obscure death where no one is held responsible, the report says, "there was supposed to be a responsible government in Katanga, and one would suppose that there was a much more responsible government in Uganda than in Katanga. But yet, a man was arrested and done away with, without any due process of law." It then concludes, "as Lumumba lives and pervades the life and politics of the Congo; as so many great heroes lived after their physical death, so will Saturnino Lohure live in the South Sudan."[42]

Chapter Endnotes

[5] "Definition of Culture" [online] http://fog.ccsf.cc.ca.us/~aforsber/ ccsf/culture_defined.html

[6] Francis R. Wingate, *Mahdism and the Egyptian Sudan*, London: Macmillan & Co., 1891.

[7] Simon Simonse, *Kings of Disaster: Dualism, Centralism and the Scapegoat "King" in Southern Sudan*, Leiden: E.J. Brill, 1992. p. 81.

[8] Ibid

[9] Stereotype inevitability, From Wikipedia, the free encyclopedia [online] http://en.wikipedia.org/wiki/Stereotype_inevitability

[10] "Fr Saturnino is Dead but His Soul Liveth" *The Vigilant*, February 7th, 1967.

[11] Ibid

[12] Fr. Vittorino Dellagiacoma "Sudanese Catholic Clergy" Provincial Comboni House, Khartoum, Sudan. [online] http://www.dacb.org/ stories/sudan/ohure_saturnino.html

[13] Robert O. Collins, (forthcoming publication in 2007): "Chapter Five: Parliamentary and Military Experiments in Government, 1956-1969" *The History of the Modern Sudan*, Hollywood: Tsehai Publ.

[14] Amir Idris, *Conflict and Politics if Identity in Sudan*, New York: Palgrave Macmillan, 2005.

[15] Ibid. pp. 36—41.

[16] Simon Simonse, "Conflicts and Peace Initiatives in East Bank Equatoria, South Sudan: 1992-199" Report, Pax Christi, Netherlands, November 12th, 2000.

[17] Ibid

[18] Severino Ga'le, *Shaping a Free Southern Sudan: Memoirs of our Struggle*, Nairobi: Paulines Publications Africa, 2002.

[19] Fr. Vittorino Dellagiacoma "Sudanese Catholic Clergy" Provincial Comboni House, Khartoum, Sudan. [online] http://www.dacb.org/stories/sudan/ohure_saturnino.html

[20] "Fr Saturnino is Dead but His Soul Liveth" *The Vigilant*, February 7th, 1967.

[21] Fr. Neno Contran, *They Are A Target: 200 African Priests Killed*, Nairobi: Catholic Publishers in Africa, 1996.

[22] Ibid

[23] Ibid

[24] Adriano Bonfanti, "Padre Saturnino ha Compiuto la Sua Missione" *Nigrizia*, Aprile, 1967 Translate by Fr. Hilary Boma

[25] Eastern Equatoria-Sudan. Map Printed by CDE, University of Berne, Switzerland for the Federal Department of Foreign Affairs.

[26] Fr. Hilary Boma "Fr. Lohure questions" email, June 26, 2007.

[27] Ibid

[28] Fr. Neno Contran, *They Are A Target: 200 African Priests Killed*, Nairobi: Catholic Publishers in Africa, 1996.

[29] Fr. Hilary Boma "Fr. Lohure questions" email, June 26, 2007.

[30] Fr. Vitale Otililing Elia "Saturnino Ohure: Rev. Fr., Rebel and a Leader," May 23, 2006.

[31] Fr. Hilary Boma, "Humility of the Patron and Martyr of the South Freedom Movement," September 6, 2007.

[32] Karl-Johan Lundstrom, *The Lotuho and the Verona Fathers: A Case Study of Communication in Development*, Uppsala: EFS För̈laget, 1990.

[33] Fr. Vitale Otililing Elia "Saturnino Ohure: Rev. Fr., Rebel and a Leader," May 23, 2006.

[34] Fr. Neno Contran, They Are A Target: 200 African Priests Killed, Nairobi: Catholic Publishers in Africa, 1996.

[35] Joseph Cardinal Ratzinger, *Milestones; Memoirs 1927-1977*, San Francisco: Ignatius Press, 1998. p. 8.

[36] A friend of Fr. Pro, Pulido quoted by Mary E. Gentges, "Father Pro of Mexico" Angelus [online] angelusonline.org

[37] Catholic News Agency, "Blessed Miguel Pro Juarex, Priest and Martyr" [online]
   http://www.catholicnewsagency.com/saint.php?n=397

[38] Fr. Neno Contran, *They Are A Target: 200 African Priests Killed*, Nairobi: Catholic Publishers in Africa, 1996.

[39] Ludo De Witte, *The Assassination of Lumumba*, Trans. by Ann Wright and Renée Fenby, London: Verso, 2001. pp. 165

_____BBC News "Kabila party' formed in DR Congo" April 2, 2002. [online] http://news.bbc.co.uk/2/hi/africa/1907252.stm

_____BBC News "More killings in Algeria" February 6, 1998. [online] http://news.bbc.co.uk/1/hi/world/africa/54067.stm

_____BBC News "Naming children for a head start in Africa" December 15, 2003. [online] http://news.bbc.co.uk/1/hi/world/africa/3321575.stm

_____University of Belgrade "The Beograd Student Center" A Student Residence Hall named under Patrice Lumumba's name. [online] http://www.sc.org.yu or www.vodickrozbu.com/standard_en/st_centar_bg.htm -19k

[40] Fr. Neno Contran, *They Are A Target: 200 African Priests Killed*, Nairobi: Catholic Publishers in Africa, 1996.

[41] Ibid

[42] Ibid

Chapter Two
Path to Christianity

"I am dying but my work will not die" (Saint Daniel Comboni).

Early Christianity in Sudan

Exactly a hundred years after the birth of Saint Daniel Comboni and fifty years exactly after Saint Comboni's death, is when Fr. Saturnino Lohure, from deep inside South Sudan officially became a Christian and later on becoming an outstanding priest. In all, it fulfilled and reinforced, Saint Comboni's prophecy of willingness to give up his "life thousand times for the redemption" of Africa so as his "work" of "regenerating Africa through Africa itself...will not die."[43]

For centuries, most of the South Sudanese societies remained out of the influence of any of the world major monotheism religions, notably Christianity and Islam. The only religions most of these societies accustomed to were their traditional belief systems. Even so, to this day with advancement of Christianity and imposition of Islam, South Sudanese population is still largely considered animists, a derogatory term often used in describing African "primitive culture" of not comprehending real religion. Tragically, though, the arrival of the monotheism religions of Christianity and Islam in Sudan would later prove to be divisive as they facilitated to the division of the country between southern Christian and northern Muslim. And this further led into bloodshed and further conflicts.

As stated above, for centuries, the Southern Sudanese societies enjoyed a religious free environment that was not tainted by the religious atmosphere that visited them for the last two centuries. The first Christian sighting in the present Sudan in the sixth century A.D., if any, had little bearing to the majority of the current South Sudanese ethnic groups. For one reason, Christianity was particularly concentrated mainly in the deep north among the Nubian kingdoms. Secondly, during those periods, some of the current Southern Sudanese ethnic groups were not yet settled in their current territories for them to have opportunity to encounter the Nubian Christians. Third, there were no constant and active interactions between the South and North of Sudan to the level that would have facilitated massive exchange of cultures and in this case, the spread of Christianity. Dustan Wai summed it up well when he wrote, "prior to the Turkish-Egyptian adventures into the South, there had been no…political alliance or unity between North and South of the present Sudan."[44] These historical facts will continue to define the distinctive relationship between the South and North of Sudan to this day, and those distinctions contribute much to the conflict between these two regions as forceful and dubious attempts are being made by the Northerners to unify with the South.

The Arabic and Islamic Conquerors

The emergence of Islam with the zeal of conquest and with the rigor for Arab dominance in the seventh century had clearly posed greater threats to the Nubian Christian kingdoms in the Northern Sudan and that will centuries later have its negative effect to the South of Sudan. To his credit though, Prophet Mohammad managed to convert most of the Arab ethnic groups into Islam before his ultimate death in 632 A.D. However, Prophet Mohammad's death marked the spread of Islam through conquest where the Arabs became the perpetuators of those conquering force. After Prophet Mohammad's death, the Arab Islamic conquerors spread from the Arabian Peninsula in all directions like wildfires as they embarked on conquering territories and forcing people to submit into Islam. The Arab Muslim conquerors moved at such faster pace and successfully conquering large territories. Edward Gibbon, an eighteenth century British parliamentarian and historian succinctly depicts the Islamic conquest in his most important work, *The History of the Decline and Fall of the Roman Empire*, as he stated, "under the last of the Ommiades, the Arabian empire extended two hundred days' journey from east to west, from the confines of Tartary and India to the shores of the Atlantic Ocean."[45] To maintain their control, the Arab Muslim conquerors imposed political structures over the territories they conquered under the dictate of caliphs, the Prophet's successors who commands Islam on earth.

By 640 A.D., the Arab Islamic conquerors invaded and conquered Egypt. In 643 A.D., they won a conquest victory in Tripoli (present day Libya), sealing and guaranteeing their control in Northern Africa. This in turn, trapped the Nubian Christian kingdoms behind the enemy lines in the Southern edge, isolating them from the rest of the Christian World and weakening the powers of their kingdoms. In around the same time, several incursion attempts were made by the Arab invaders, to forcefully conquer the Nubian Christian kingdoms and have them submit to the new religion of Islam. Nonetheless, the Nubian Christian kingdoms fiercely fought back by putting stiffed resistance to the invading Arab forces. This forced the conquerors to abandon their invasion plans and renounce the use of force. Instead the Arab Islamic conquerors agreed on armistice and on signing a series of treaties with the Nubian Christian kingdoms, in order, to maintain a peaceful coexistence.

Although the treaties between the Arabs and Nubian Christian kingdoms led to these two distinctive communities to stay relatively peaceful, they later proved deadly for the survival of Nubian Christian kingdoms. For example, one of the provisions in these treaties allowed the Arabs to purchase lands in the Nubian territories and to stay in those territories. The Arab merchants took advantage of this offer and beginning to purchase and own chunk of lands in Nubian territories. Before they could know it, the Arabs were dominating the commerce activities, and Arabic became the dominant language in commerce, a serious sign for subsequent assimilation into Arabic culture. Islamization, then began to take an accelerated but gradual root through intermarriages, imposition of Islamic tax system, and intensification of slavery. It is worthy remembering that the Muslims justified the enslaving the non Muslims and slaves became the source for new converts. It was then that the Christian Nubian kingdoms began to witness a gradual and devastated declining of their powers, influence and the disappearance of their own identities—phenomenon that become too obvious of problems today. In 1315, a Muslim prince of a Nubian descent ascended to the throne of a king in the Nubian kingdom of Dongola. By fifteenth centaury, the Muslims constituted a majority in the Nubian areas and some of the inhabitants of those areas claimed direct descendents to the Arabian Peninsula and even direct lineage to Prophet Mohammad.

Even some of the modern Sudanese Arabs of today are still claiming direct ancestry to the Arabian Peninsula and deeply taking pride in their

Arabic roots. Abd al-Rahman al-Bashir is right in his observation when he says, "some of the Sudanese thinks of themselves as *Ashraf* (decedents of Prophets closet friends and associates). This might be forced, but it gives them satisfactory."[46] Ismail al-Azhari, the head of National Unionist Party (NUP) proudly declared, "I feel at this juncture obliged to declare that we are proud of our Arab origin, of our Arabism and of being Muslim. The Arabs came to this continent, as pioneers, to disseminate a genuine culture and promote sound principles which had shed enlightenment and civilization throughout Africa."[47] Sadiq al-Mahdi, who held a position of Prime Minister in Khartoum twice and is the head of Umma Party, contents that Arabization and Islamization are the "brightest and civilized" aspects of intercultural exchange that transformed Sudan. This is not to ignore the Muslim hypocrisy by calling the spread of Islamic religion and Arabic culture as "brightest and civilized" intercultural exchange while calling the spread of Western cultures and Christianity in the South Sudan as an evil European Imperialist imposing its language and cultures onto others.[48] The irony of all this hypocrisy is even more difficult to understand considering that Sadiq al-Mahdi is an educated product of missionary school system in Sudan and went on for advance studies in London, the capital of what those of al-Mahdi type consider evil imperialists.

To the insult of the African Sudanese, the Arab Sudanese Muslims even went as far as claiming to be the only authentic Sudanese of today. This very Sadiq al-Mahdi, who is by far considered a moderate Arab Muslim, wrote, "the dominant feature of our nation is an Islamic one and its overpowering expression is Arab, and this nation will not have its entity identified and its prestige and pride preserved except under an Islamic revival."[49] When Ali Abdallatif, a Muslim born to Dinka mother and a Nuba Father was promoting the idea of Sudanese nationalism during the British rule, his Sudanese authenticity immediately came into question by the Sudanese Arabs who considered him nothing but a black salve.[50] In trying to convince the Arabs in joining the Arab League Nations, the Khartoum government declared in its statement, "our relations with the Arab League will be based on our age-long blood ties and it will be our aim to strengthen relations between us and the governments and Nations of the Arab League and to work consistently toward friendship and sincere co-operation with them."[51] At the time this political declaration was made, those who identify themselves as Arabs were a minority, at about thirty-nine percent of the Sudanese entire population. Not surprisingly, a minority in control of the government was making a decision on behalf of all. This is a clear indication that if the Arabs North are talking of the unity of Sudan they actually mean an opportunity to dominate and oppress the non-Arabs Sudanese or otherwise.

Even though through the course of long history the Arab Muslim would eventually take a full control of the present northern Sudan by Arabizing and Islamizing the entire inhabitants of the northern areas, the attempt to do the same in the South was minimal. This was largely in part due to the following explanations by Francis Deng:

> Swamps, flies, tropical humidity, and the fierce resistance of the tribes kept the contact marginal, even though it was devastating violent. Furthermore, since the Arab Muslim was interested in the actual and potential value of the Negro as a slave, he did not desire to interact or integrate with him in the same manner as in the North.[52]

Colonialism

Even though most of the slaves were drawn from the South, the first most serious attempt and effort to conquer, Arabize, and Islamize the entire South came in the late nineteenth century during the Mahdi revolution. The Turko-Egyptian colonialists who came into the South in nineteenth century were more interested in economic benefit, slave trade in particular. The Mahdi movement was the most ambitious one in its grandiose plan of imposing its own vision of Islamization and Arabization. The Mahdi movement was led by a charismatic and an ambitious Islamist by the name Muhammad Ahmad ibn as Sayyid Abd Allah. From Danagala tribe, born at Dongola in 1848, to a family famous for building excellent boats, Muhammad Ahmad was recognized earlier on as an intelligent and promising child by his relatives. Physically tall and with a youthful built body, Muhammad Ahmad bore all the physical features for a well-bred gentleman. At twenty-two, he had already built great reputation for a Sheik and commanded wide admiration. His moving words drove men crazy that some wept, some beat their breast, and some even trembled uncontrollably. The women went nuts by praising his good looking and dedicating countless songs and poems for him.[53]

Soon then, Muhammad Ahmad proclaimed to be the Mahdi or the guided one, who had been prophesized to be the redeemer in Islamic religion. The concept of Mahdism varies considerably under different Islamic traditional sects. For the Sunnis sect, they expected the advent of Mahdi just as Messiah had been expected to be the redeemer in Judaism. As for the Shi'ites sect, the Mahdi will be their twelfth Imam, in accordance to the Caliphs, who succeeded Prophet Mohammed. According to this tradition, the Mahdi is hidden and will only appear in the advent of the judgment day, actually a day before judgment day. Not surprisingly, it was on the death of Prophet Mohammed that disagreement on who to succeed the Prophet arose among the Muslims, which led into division of two major Islamic sects. The Sunnis argued that the successor must be elected while the Shi'ites maintained that it should be hereditary. Thus, it resulted into division between Sunnis who were mainly Arabs and the Shi'ites, majority of whom were Persians.

Muhammad Ahmad of Sudan, a Dongolawi, took in the tradition of Shi'ite to model himself as the Mahdi. He then molded himself into mysticism and superstition, and even adopted Persian titles such as Dervish for his followers. Muhammad Ahmad began to preach anti-Turkish and anti-foreigners' sentiments which resonated very well with his followers. He claimed to be acting under divine instructions from Prophet Mohammad and Allah (the Muslim's God) to impose his vision of Islam on the world. He then went on declaring war against the Turko-Egyptian rule in Sudan. He started first with few religious followers, but he was soon joined by criminals, robbers, and slave-traders who were more motivated by lootings and booty. Rumors began to spread on how Muhammad Ahmad was the Mahdi and he was using miracles to win wars. Even though others do not believe in him, many more did believe him and joined him by thousands. His military victories, which came about as a result of his strategy or by mistake of his enemies or even sheer luck kept to reaffirm his position. By now even those who did not believe in him as the Mahdi had no choice but to join him for the fear of retribution. His recklessly brave Dervish soldiers who were driven with fanaticism couldn't manage to bring the poor but brave Nubas from the mountains under the control of Mahdi. After fighting fiercely, a treaty was signed between the Nubas and Mahdi, but unfortunately, Muhammad Ahmad had no incline whatsoever of honoring or respecting the treaty. The poor but brave Nubas were left with no choice. They took to mountains and were even more determined to die fighting rather than faced humiliation of the Mahdi.[54]

Equally a blow for the Mahdi quest was his failed attempts to conquer the entire South Sudan, the attempts which were forcefully repulsed with the help of Belgium colonialist from the neighboring present day Congo. Base on the published stories of those Dervishes who escaped from the onslaught in the South, the Mahdi expedition to South Sudan was dealt great blow. The warrior African ethnic groups of the South Sudan killed the Mahdi's Dervishes without any mercy, and those who were lucky to escape could barely survive the tropical diseases and the harsh Southern Sudan climate. As the Mahdists became aware that they could not establish a foothold in the South, they reluctantly sent only trouble makers on the expedition to the South as a means of exiling them. The last expedition of the Dervishes to be sent to the South refused to go, and they have to be dragged on board shackled with chains. Luckily though, for the Mahdists, they managed to get the King of Shilluk, one of the powerful ethnic groups of the South Sudan. The head of the Shilluk King was left dangling in Omdurman, which infuriated the Shilluks who would end up on fighting any foreign expedition to the South until well into the twentieth century.[55]

The Mahdi was also lucky to conquer Bahr el-Ghazel by winning the admiration of the Southern Dinka ethnic group who called him "Maadi" and viewed him as someone sent by God to free them from the oppression and slavery normally coming from the north. The Dinka received Mahdi's messianic message very well by easily interpreting it into their own traditional beliefs. According to Francis Deng, the Dinka "portrayed the Mahdi as a manifestation of the Spirit of Deng, their deity associated with rain and lightening as a manifestation of God's might."[56] The Dinka heaped a bunch of songs in praises of Mahdi, the Son of Deng.

Little did the Dinka know that Muhammad Ahmad was nothing than a cunning man who survived through lies and repressions of others. After the Mahdi's conquest, slavery in the South continued and he made an attempt of forced Islamization and Arabization, and that was when the Dinka turned and began to fight against him. It is worth remembering that slave traders joined Mahdi as they were promised that slavery will resume after Mahdi conquest, because by then, the British along with Christian missionaries were exerting much pressure in stopping slave traders, depriving the slave traders in process. In their effort in fighting the Mahdi, the Dinkas reversed the very songs they used to praise with Mahdi to fight against him.[57] The Mahdi plan for the South turned into failure.

With the Turko-Egyptians, the Mahdi forces managed to drive them out of the country. The bravery of the Mahdi's Dervish soldiers requires great commendation. With the beat of drums and loud shouts, the Dervish charged recklessly with only sticks in their hands to a well positioned army with intention of pulling away their guns from them, but to only be shot dead at closer range. Mahdi used all sort of lies to turn these Dervishes into fanatics who never fear death. It was their fanaticism, reckless bravery and sheer number which guaranteed them victory. Before the Mahdi revolution, there were estimate of 30,000 to 40,000 Turkey-Egyptian and European forces in Sudan, and by the time the revolution was over, barely a couple of thousands troops made it alive.[58] The Mahdi wiped almost all of them. The British Governor-General of Sudan, General Charles Gordon, nicknamed "Chinese" for his military victory in China, made some desperate failed attempts to pacify Muhammad Ahmad. In one of those desperate efforts, General Gordon addressed a letter to Muhammad Ahmad requesting him to give up rebellion in exchange for sultanate of Kordofan province. Along with the message, General Gordon included as a gift for Muhammad Ahmad, ceremonial red robes and a tarbush. This to Muhammad Ahmad was a joke, he laughed so hard over the message of General Gordon. Here was an ambitious man who controlled much of the country already and was poised to take control of Khartoum and beyond, but yet sarcastically being offered sultanate of Kordofan province. In his response to Gordon, he emphasized, "know that I am the Expected Mahdi, the Successor of the Apostle of God. Thus I have no need of the sultanate, nor of the kingdom of Kordofan or elsewhere nor of the wealth of this world and its vanity. I am but the slave of God, guiding unto God and to what is with Him."[59] Along with this message to Gordon, he sent back the gift Gordon offered him and instead offered Gordon a dress worn by his Dervish troops and an opportunity for Gordon to convert into Islam and join his forces. Gordon, a devoted Christian and a renowned British soldier, declined the offer.

As a result, the Mahdi forces marched into Omdurman in late 1884, there, they planned the siege of Khartoum. While in Omdurman, overlooking toward Khartoum through the While Nile, Muhammad Ahmed promised his forces that he could dry up the river like Moses did. This turned out to be lies because he never dried up the river and his forces had to really struggle to cross the river into Khartoum. Gordon with fewer troops could only do little in preventing the Mahdi fanatics from taking Khartoum. Gordon only hope was the British expedition, which never made it until when Khartoum fell, and on seeing the devastation from afar, the expedition had to hopelessly turn back. In his part, Gordon never survived the onslaught. On the final assault of Khartoum, Muhammad Ahmad unleashed his 50,000 wild Dervishes in Khartoum who began slaughtering people left and right. Gordon got out of his room walked down stairs and was met with angry Dervishes who were charging through into his house. He tried to talk to them, but they could not listen to him, instead one of them plunged his sharp spear through Gordon where he instantly fell forward. He was dragged through his stairs and repeatedly stabbed with the spears. Blood flow. His head was eventually chopped of for positive identification. When this news reached Muhammad Ahmad, he was furious not out of sympathy for Gordon but for the fact that Gordon refused to join him.

Killing Gordon was probably a mistake that would come and haunt the Mahdi forces later on since Gordon was popular in Great Britain to warrant revenge. After all, Gordon warned the Muhammad Ahmad through a massager by saying, "go, tell the Mahdi that I have only to stamp my feet on the ground, thousands of Englishmen will at once spring up."[60] In that effect, the Mahdi rule was short lifted, from 1884 through 1898. By 1881, the revolutionary leader, Muhammad Ahmed claimed that he was to live for forty more years so as to implement his agenda in the world, but he was only to live for short four years as he died abruptly in 1885, after his victory in Khartoum.[61] After conquering Khartoum, he hypocritically abandoned the notion of humble life; instead, he amassed himself with every luxury item he could loot. He had more concubines than he would have wished in his life. His fanatic followers were still intrigued by his mysticism and superstition. They would gather in front of his house in large numbers to just take a pick of him, but he disappointed them all the time as he spent most of his time rather sleeping. When he walked, to the mosque, which was about the only place he used to go to, the poor ignorant women rolled on the ground hysterically to come in contact with the footprint he left behind. The drop of water he washed with was said to be good for curing diseases and sins as people religiously drunk them. Worse yet, Muhammad Ahmad grew fatter than ever before as he accustomed to the live of idleness. He slept endlessly that his first wife, Aisha or better known by her fanatical admirers as *Om al-Mominin* (the Mother of the Faithful), had to always remind him by prayer times to wake up and pray. His fatness is actually said to have led to heart complications, which contributed to his sudden and ultimate death. It was only after his death that his fanatic followers were to learn that they were lied to all along. By then, it was too late, the damage was already done as thousands were robbed of so many things and many more died and the country was ruined.[62] The spirit of those thousands dead might have finally visited Mahdi, the guided one. Even though he was dead, he remind a legend and for others, they refuse to acknowledge that he was dead, but that he was rather removed.

The political and historical significance of Mahdism in Sudan's perspective is that it did not just diminish the notion of national consciousness, but rather set a precedent where political mobilization can only be built on Islamic fanaticism. One analyst who observed the raise and fall of Mahdi's revoution from close range for ten years concluded, "I do not think it is possible ever to start a movement on a large scale in a Muslim country unless it is based on some religious ground."[63] He went on to observe that the events surrounding the successes of Mahdi movement and the subsequent trends that followed demonstrated how easily "Muslims are imposed upon by religious adventurers."[64] Muhammad Ahmad managed to mobilize thousands of supporters who overran the foreign troops from Sudan and created a Mahdi state through his appealing sense on religion fanaticism. His successor, Khalifa Abdallah ibn Muhammad, though known quite well by good Muslims as someone who lacked religious piety, had to adhere into the rhetoric of religion fanaticism to consolidate and maintain his political power, concubines, and booty. Those who challenged Khalifa Abdallah unjust rule and mounted anti-Mahdi fights such as Abu Gemaizeh found no any other ground than religion to mobilize for their support. The Abu Gemaizeh example went to show that Islamic religion was taken for ride by those "religious adventurers" to the extent of achieving personal gain, ambition and glory, because according to one author, "those who had joined and left Mahdiism, thoroughly convinced of its fraud and deception, had unhesitatingly allied themselves to this new religious movement, which they inspired with almost greater enthusiasm than that they had just quitted," the Mahdi revolution.[65]

Unfortunately, this historical and political trend had established a permanent root and system in Sudan where successive governments must out-compete each other in religion fanaticism as a means of maintaining their grip of power. The first nationalism movement in Sudan during Anglo-Egyptian colonialism led by none Arabs such as Abdallatif was immediately shunned away because this nationalistic movement was not authentically Arabic in origin and Islamic in nature. It was only until when two Islamic sects of Ansar and Khatmiyya formed political parties that Sudan witnessed a real large scale mobilization toward self-governing. This was done on the exclusion of none Islamic sects such as the Southern Sudanese, the Communist party and other political forces, which were not religion fanatically oriented. This situation even did exacerbate because upon Khartoum's independence, the South of Sudan, which majority of whom are none Muslims and all of them are none Arabic either in origin, temperament, orientation or otherwise, becomes part of this complex equation where Islamic religion is the norm and Arabic authenticity is the overriding identity. Thus, for these Islamic religious zealots, the South becomes the ground for competition to be won through religious fanaticism. The military regime of Dictator General Ibrahim Abboud was brought in power so that it could force through military discipline the unity of Sudan by enforcing Arabic culture and

Islamic fanaticism in the South of Sudan. As Abboud's regime failed, he was overthrown, and the new government that came in of Muhammad Magoub was even more determined in its zealotry of Arabic culture and Islamic fanaticism to maintain popularity. From then onward, each government would have to prove on how fanatical they are so they could stay in power. The opportunistic and none religious Numayri had to sign a pact with Islamic fundamentalist movement as a means of staying longer in power. The current military government of dictator Omer Hassan al-Basher came to power under the banner of National Islamic Front (NIF), and the regime had to maintain power through its appeal of Jihad, waging a holy war against the none believers.

Back to the status of Mahdi and its conquest, it became apparent that the death of Muhammad Ahmad could never stop the British advancement to re-colonize Sudan and avenge the death of their General, Chinese Gordon. The British mobilized its troops with Egyptian troops and under a renowned General Lord Kitchener, they then converged into Sudan. The British moved forcefully with superior fire power. For one, they were coming to avenge the death of their popular General, Chinese Gordon and for another reason to swiftly secure their interest in the Suez Canal and along the Nile Valley as the French and Belgian, the other imperial powers were already eying those interests. They dislodged the Mahdi forces by winning a decisive victory at the battle of Omdurman in September of 1898. Khalifa Abdallah ibn Muhammad, the successor of Mahdi fled in disarray, but he was eventually caught and killed in Kordofan. As the British were advancing deeper south, they met with the French troops who were about to secure Fashoda, a village lying strategically along the White Nile, in Upper Nile region of Southern Sudan. Both the British and the French claimed legal ownership of Fashoda and that was when their fleets were lined up and guns drawn, the closest the British and French ever got on the verge of war over imperial territorial dispute in eastern part of Africa. In the end, the British won the dispute in diplomacy, and it was there that the phrase *fashoda syndrome* made its way into diplomatic vocabulary while *fashoda incident* became a significant historical reference.

The Rebirth of Christianity

After securing the entire country, British together with Egypt took control of the country for themselves. They established a joint condominium rule where the British was the one actually running the country. During the Turko-Egyptian rule, the British were ruling Sudan through Egypt but now they have a full control. Interestingly, the British brought along with them Christianity to be imposed by the missionaries to its newly conquered territories. During the Turko-Egyptian rule, Christian missionaries' activities were limited and Mahdi was to put them completely out of business, killing and imprisoning most of them during the revolt. But that all changed, thanks to the British Empire for reviving Christianity in one of the most hostile regions in the world where Christianity was completely dead.

The missionaries, which came to Sudan, were consisted of three main groups that included the United Presbyterian Church of North America from United States of America, the Anglican, more specifically, the Church Missionary Society (CMS) from Great Britain, and the Roman Catholic Church from Italy. Unfortunately, these missionaries neither could reclaim the lost Nubian Christian kingdoms nor could they Christianize the population of the north who are by now all Muslims and to high degree are all Arabized like that Sadiq al-Mahdi guy. As such, the missionaries have to scramble south to rather deal with the animists southern ethnic groups. Soon then, the Southern Sudanese were told that they were pagans who required conversion to Christianity for the redemption of their sins, the sins that were supposedly original and were inherent in human souls. To accomplish this effort of conversion, the main Christian groups, divided the South according to their sphere of influence. This was in away to stop rivalry among these Christian missionaries. The system, however, provided ethnic and regional monopoly to the missionaries. The British then facilitated their activities while discouraged those of Islam, because the British viewed Islam then as a threat to the population of the South. The Muslims with fanatical tendencies were immediately kicked out of the South. The South was then demarcated off the limits, and only those with permission could be allowed in. For example, the official policy from the governor of Bahr el-Ghazal region of Southern Sudan was:

> The government does not want to make more Muslims, it wishes to technically instruct the natives, through the medium of their own language teaching them certain amount of English...religious education can be given to those whose parents desire it in the missionary schools...[66]

The British policy of keeping out Arabic and Islamic influence from the South was very clear. In one of the British memoranda, it reads, "the Government policy has been to keep the Southern Sudan as free as possible of Mohammedan influences."[67] To justify the action of the missionaries in Southern Sudan, the Sudan Governor-General, Wingate, wrote:

> ...we must remember that the inhabitants of both...Provinces are not Muslims at all, that the whole Uganda accepted

Christianity almost without a murmur, and that furthermore English is a very much easier language to learn than Arabic…[68]

The British had convincing evidence to pursue anti-Islamic and anti-Arabic policies in the South given the fact of history of slavery as well as the brutal invasions by the Turko-Egyptian rule as well as that of Ansar of the Mahdi revolution, which the Southern Sudanese resented very much to this day.

The Presbyterian

The British found Christian missionaries as allies to implement the anti-Islamic and anti-Arabic policies in the South. They allowed the United Presbyterian Church of North America to start its work in Khartoum but to concentrate a bulk of its work in the South. The Church had maintained a minimal work in the North with exception in the Nuba area where they enjoyed followers. In the South, the Presbyterian sphere of influence was in the Upper Nile region. Its work was concentrated among the Shilluk, Nuer, Dinka, Anuak, and Murle people. The first indigenous Sudanese to be ordained as a Presbyterian pastor was in 1942, in Doleib Hill. Today Presbyterian Church in Sudan operates independently under the name Presbyterian Church of the Sudan. It draws its members largely from the areas the missionaries first had huge impact on, and among the tribes in those areas.

The Anglican

Church Missionary Society (CMS) was the most enthusiastic group led by Llewellyn Gwynne, Dr Frank Harpur and Archibald Shaw. They began their work in Omdurman in 1899 and Khartoum in 1900. The group came to Sudan with specific aim to Christianize the Muslims who killed the popular British General, Chinese Gordon. Their expedition was supported by funds collected in Britain in memory of General Gordon. Their missionary work would have been done in the North; however, they were advised by the Anglo-Egyptian administration to proceed south and warned not to temper with the blood boiling Muslims of the North. As such, their work in the North remained minimal that can merely be identified with institutions that included dispensaries and schools with a few Christian followers.

By 1905, the group entered the South and from there they proceed to do work in areas of Dinka at Malek and Akot, the Nuer at Ler and Zeraf Island, the Azande at Yambio and Maridi and among the Bari at Yei, Loka, Juba and Kajo-kaji. The missionaries embarked on pastoral and evangelization work as well as providing education and medical services among the tribal areas in which they operated on. It would be until 1941 that the Anglican Church in Sudan would witness ordinations of its indigenous people and not until 1955 the first Sudanese bishop, Daniel Deng was ordained.[69] Today the Anglican Church operates out of twenty-four dioceses throughout Sudan with equal number of bishops heading those dioceses. It commands a considerable number of followers in Southern Sudan and is considered to be the second largest church in Sudan. Its members are concentrated largely in areas that the missionaries initially started its work. For those dioceses in the North, they mainly serve the Southern Sudanese Christians who are displaced by the war to the North and few Nubas who are Christians.

The Catholic

The Roman Catholic Church has been the oldest in the country. The Catholic first work started in 1842 in Khartoum and by 1850, the Catholic missionaries proceeded deep south to Jebel Lado (Rejaf) where three years later they established a church in Gondokoro. From that time, it would take the passion, dedication, and vision of one young Italian priest by the name Daniel Comboni to reinvigorate and sow the seed of Catholicism not just in Sudan but the world beyond. Daniel Comboni was born in 1831, in a small town of Limone in Italy to poor parents. The only surviving child of eight siblings, Comboni manifested earlier on to become a priest. While in the seminary, he was drawn to the missionary of Central Africa by passionately listening to the stories of the missionaries who came from Central Africa. Three years after his ordination, which took place in 1854, Comboni joined five other missionaries and set for Africa where his mother who was always being supportive, showed him off with the blessings, "go, Daniel, and may the Lord bless you."[70]

As they were deep inside Sudan on expedition to the South of Sudan to what would now be Rumbek, they were faced with tropical diseases, which decimated all of Comboni's colleagues. The superior of the team in his dying moments said, "if it should happen that only one of you be left, let him not give up or lose confidence…Swear to me that you will not turn back."[71] In response to his superior, Comboni, assured, "Africa or death."[72] Comboni ended up to be the only survivor of that treacherous journey where he had to go back to Italy for health reasons. While in Italy praying at the Tomb of St Peter, Comboni was struck by inspiration, which let him to draw his plan of "Save Africa through Africa." He would write, "the regeneration of Africa by means of Africa itself seems to me the only possible means to Christianize the continent."[73] His plan included building of institutions where Africans would learn not just religion but secular education including craftsman. To support his mission, he went on begging in Europe to kings, queens, bishops, nobles, and even to the poor people who could help the African mission. He went on to plea his case in the first Vatican Council and got seventy bishops to sign a petition for his plan of evangelization of Central Africa. In addition, he founded his missionary order, the Comboni Missionaries Father and the Comboni Missionary Sisters also known as the Verona Fathers and the Verona Sisters. By 1877, Comboni was ordained Bishop of Central Africa with its headquarters in Khartoum. There, Comboni added another mission to his work of fighting slavery. He was actually provided with an army of his own to combat slavery. Overwhelmed by hard labor and so many deaths surrounding him, Comboni himself was finally struck by sickness, and shortly after, he died of it in 1881. He was only fifty years old. As he was dying, he said, "I am dying, but my work will not die."[74] He was right, few years later his missionary is among the biggest and his impact went beyond and spread throughout several continents. From its small mission in the Sudan, today the Comboni missionary or community numbered in thousands, spreading the gospel of God and providing services in forty-four countries in Africa, the Americas, Europe and Asia. By 2003, Bishop Daniel Comboni was canonized as Saint by Pope John Paul the II. In his homily of canonization, Pope John Paul II, prayed for the Continent of African through Comboni by pleading:

> Africa, a land rich in human and spiritual resources, continues to be scarred by many difficulties and problems. May the international community actively help it build a future of hope. I entrust my appeal to the intercession of St Daniel Comboni, an outstanding evangelizer and protector of the 'Black Continent.'[75]

When the Mahdi revolution forcefully swept into power in 1880s, Comboni's work was briefly put into halt, but by then he already assured his missionaries of his long-term strategy as he laid it: "The missionaries have to understand that they are stones hid under the earth, which would perhaps never come to light, but which will become part of the foundation of vast, new building."[76] When the British re-colonized Sudan in 1899, those missionaries came back again, this time they spread beyond Khartoum deep into the South. They work almost among all the tribes of Southern Sudan. Today Catholic had the largest followers of Christian in Sudan. They managed to establish some of the best schools including seminaries where they ordained indigenous priests. Sudan's first native bishop, Ireneo Dud was ordained in 1955, to head the dioceses of Rumbek.

Missionaries as Scapegoats

During the independence, the Northern Sudanese Arabs messed up big time in dealing with the Southern Problems. They started with systemic marginalization of the Southern Sudanese in government representation. When the Southern Sudanese managed to get into the first and second democratic elected parliament and began to present their case of power sharing. The Northern Sudanese Arabs felt threatened, therefore, disbanded the parliament citing that Sudan was "not yet ready for democracy," simply because democracy would guarantee high level of Southern Sudan participation in the government.[77] To them, democracy was not the option; therefore, the Sudan must be ruled by the military who were all Arabs from the North. The problem was, the military could not manage to resolve the South Problems by its use of force. As such, they turned their frustration to missionaries and Christians as the British were not there to be blamed anymore. They enacted the Missionary Act of 1962, to kick all the Christian missionaries from Sudan, restrict Christian activities, and spread Islam to replace Christianity. By 1964, they finalized by kicking all the missionaries out of Southern Sudan. The native clergymen were left with the enormous task that they could not manage given the fact that they were few in numbers. For example, only thirty-one Catholic native priests were left in the entire Sudan. Moreover, they were harassed, and others such as Fr. Saturnino Lohure were forced out of the country, and the likes of Paulino Doggale were imprisoned for bogus charges. The aim was of course, to destroy Christianity so that Islam can reign over. They enacted a permit system where any Christian activity would require a permit before it is carried out. The powers to grant, revoke, or decide the terms of the permits solely rest with the council of ministers all of whom were Northern Sudanese Arabs. As such, the Christian activities were crippled completely. For example, the law forbids, "any missionary act towards any person or persons professing any religion or sect or belief thereof other than that specified in its license."[78] This hinders the Church from carrying out its fundamental and sacred duties such as the baptism, which is an initiation to the Christian Church. To the Christians, baptism is essential and is best that people are baptized at a younger age, but in this case, one had to wait until they turn eighteen years of age and then they will apply for permits, which in most cases they would not get. The act restricted Christians from maintaining orphanage, bookstores, and libraries or building new houses or even repairing the older ones. It also forbids the Christians as they could not also teach or propagate the Christian faith without risking jail or expulsion. The Christian were trapped as they could hardly do anything that could not be interpreted as "beyond the limits of their sacred mission."[79]

Bogus Reasons for Expulsion of Missionaries

The Arabs Northern regime came up with unfounded reasons for the expulsion of the missionaries, the restriction of Christian activities, and spreading of Islam. First, they alleged that Christian missionaries were responsible for the Southern Sudan sentiment for separation. In their policy statement, it alleges that Christian Missionaries had:

> Exploited the name of religion to impart hatred and implant fear and animosity in the minds of the Southerners against their fellow countrymen in the North with the clear object of encouraging the setting up of a separate political status for the southern provinces thus endangering the integrity and unity of the country.[80]

This was a misplace argument and no wonder they could not provide a shred of evidence to support such bogus claim. Perhaps the Khartoum government should have better reflect on who was responsible for the Northern Sudanese Arabs sentiment in demanding impendence from the British before they could go any further making wild unsubstantiated allegations against the people of South Sudan in their relationship with the Christian missionaries. If the government in Khartoum failed to reflect on themselves, they should have then reflected on other countries including their neighbors who demanded for their independence, and then from there conclude if at all the missionaries have anything to do with it. Better yet, the missionaries are now gone out of Sudan, did that in anyway stop the Southern Sudanese demands for separation and struggle for justice? If the Northern Sudanese Arabs could not figure out that the concept for self determination is the basic natural human right that applies to human beings universally, then they better be ready for more surprises to follow. Now they have the Muslims from the Nuba Mountains, the Furs from Darfur region, and the Beja people from Eastern Sudan demanding for the same rights of self-determination as the

Southern Sudanese were, could the missionaries also be responsible for that as well? They should go figure.

Another equally false alleged reason was that the missionaries were meddling in the internal affairs of the Sudan, therefore, must be kicked out. Of course, here they mean Fr. Saturnino Lohure and his fellow priest Fr. Poulino Doggale who both participated in the democratically elected parliament of 1958. What they forgot to acknowledge was that both of those priests were not missionaries, but Sudanese nationals. Fr. Saturnino Lohure was from a Lotuko tribe coming from the district of Torit while Fr. Poulino Doggale was a Bari from Juba. Both were democratically elected to the parliament by their native people from their respective districts. Even though they were priests, they were representing their people and their platform was not to rule Sudan with the Christian's Ten Commandments, but through a secular democratic federal Sudan where power was shared equitably and every citizen's rights including religious rights were respected. Fr. Saturnino Lohure made these points very clear while in parliament and continued to make it until his death. Another thing these Sudanese Arab Muslims failed to say was that while they falsely accused Christians for involving in the internal politics of Sudan, they did not acknowledge their Muslims involvement in the internal politics of Sudan. Matter of fact, they have Islamist such as the *al-Ikhwan al-Islamiah* (Muslim Brotherhood), which formed an umbrella political party, the National Islamic Charter, representing the interest of Islam in the parliament or government in this matter. Not only that, but also all the other Northern political parties, with exception of the Communist party, supported and are still continuing to support the creation of Islamic constitution to govern the multi-religious Sudan. As Abdullahi Ahmed An-Na'im, an Islamic scholar explains that under Islamic law, "non-believers may be allowed to stay under the terms of a special compact which extremely restricts their civil and political rights. Believers who are not Muslims, mainly Jews and Christians, are allowed partial citizenship under Shari'a...and are disqualified from holding any position of authority over Muslims."[81] If there was anyone against the unity of the country, it would have been those who were championing for Islamic law which would completely isolate non-Muslims. Actually, Ali Abdel Rahaman, Minister of Interior, in the parliament of 1958, made this point very clear when he declared, "the Sudan is an integral part of the Arab World, and as such must accept the leadership of the two Islamic religious leaders of the Sudan. Anyone dissenting from this view must quit the country."[82] One thing also they did not mention, was the fact that there were other Northern political parties such as the National Unionist Party (NUP), which were puppets of Egypt, a foreign Islamic Arab country. The allegation of missionaries' or in other word, Christian involvement in the internal politics of Sudan had no basis or it was hypocrisy at its low level.

Ironically, the Northern Sudanese Arabs had the audacity to denounce the missionary schools that those schools were providing low quality of education. This was also false and another hypocrisy. The first missionary schools were built in the North and the last functioning missionary schools standing after destroying the ones in the South were also in the North. The Northern Arab Muslims were the beneficiaries of the missionary schools. The products of those schools are the likes of Sadiq al-Mahdi who became the Arab Islamic leader. What they also failed to mention here is that missionary schools were bad for the Southern Sudanese because it would create Southern Sudanese leaders with a high qualities such as Fr. Saturnino Lohure. It is not any wonder they continued to cite Fr. Saturnino Lohure in their reasons of expelling the missionaries countless times and holding him as a justification for expelling the missionaries.[83] The fact was that to them, Fr. Saturnino Lohure was actually a threat because of his superior intellect, which was the result of the missionary school. It is Francis Deng who wrote, "the stronger the South grows, the more Northerners feel threatened and the stronger their attachment to Arab Islamic identity becomes."[84] So, it was only logical for them that to stop more of Fr. Saturninos, the missionaries' education should be banned from the South. K.D.D. Henderson was right to argue that the intention of Northern Sudanese Arab government in destroying missionary schools in the South was because, "the influence of the existing intelligentsia would be weakened by cutting away its feeder system, the missionary schools from which it was recruited."[85] They then moved forcefully with their anti-missionary schools plan as one observer noted, "interestingly, just one year after independence, the government nationalized all Christian missionary schools in the South, causing them to lose their Christian character while allowing missionary schools in the North to continue to provide education to mostly Muslim students, albeit without proselytizing Christianity."[86] What an irony or contradiction this was?

In their reasoning to Islamize the South, one author explains:

> Many northern Sudanese had the notion that there were but a bunch of uncivilized tribes in the South, and very condescendingly, Northerners regarded themselves as guardians of these, their backward brethren. Finding themselves in charge of the government of an independent Sudan, northern Sudanese politicians and administrators sought to replace the colonial regime in the South with their own. Arabic was naturally to replace English and what better religion than Islam could replace Christianity?[87]

In 1965, at the Round Table Conference, Sadig al-Mahdi stressed the importance of Arabic and Islamic culture as "a bright and civilizing side which tried to spread the religion and Arabic language."[88] The leader of People's Democratic Party concluded, "the homogeneity of Arabism constitutes our common feelings" as Sudanese.[89] Commenting on the government effort of Islamization, the minister of interior reported. "it is my government concern to support Religious Affairs Department and the development of the *Mahads* (Islamic religious schools) under its aegis."[90] Rallying the Muslim public behind the government Islamization effort, the daily Ra'i al-ʿAmm newspaper of April 8, 1960, urged, "there is no doubt that many in this country know how much need Islam has in the South of efforts on the part of the government. The administrative authorities and men of the Ministry of Education and of the Department of Religious Affairs continue to make gigantic efforts; but this by itself is not enough."[91] As evidenced by these facts, there was no doubt on the clear intention of the Northerners, both the government and public alike. If they can even institutionalize the efforts of Arabization and Islamization by having a government Department of Religious affairs to carryon with these efforts, it clearly shows not only the seriousness but the consequences of those efforts. The aim of course was and is still the destruction of African culture by way of introducing Arabic culture and the destruction of Christianity by chasing the missionaries out, and then Islamize the Southern Sudanese.

The Southern Responses

The British colonialists were the first ones to notice the Northern Sudanese Arabs failure to successfully convert the Southern Sudanese and also to notice the Southern Sudanese resistance against the force Islamization. Some of those British colonial officials could not help it but express doubt whether there was really sizable population of Southern Sudanese who were truly and sincerely converted into Islam in the centuries of their interactions with the Muslims.[92] According to Francis Deng, the South Sudanese reactions to the Arabization and Islamization are actually swift, making Christianity as "both a religion and a political weapon against Islamization and Arabization."[93] He added, "in the South, going to church is encouraged as both an act of faith and a political statement."[94] This is an absolutely right observation, because today in Sudan at the public rallies if the Muslims perform their usual ritual of shouting '*Allah Ahkbah!*' (God is Great!), the Southern Sudanese Christians would counter with a loud shouting back of '*Alleluia!*' In reality, the Northern attitude is actually backfiring. The Southern attitudes toward Arabs and Islam could be described as follows:

> They resent anything Arabic in nature. It is interesting that lighter skin is something that some circles enjoys, but in other parts of the South, people of lighter skins are scorned, simply because they resemble the Arabs. Speaking proper Arabic is viewed as a betrayal. Instead, they corrupt the Arabic language to form *Arabi Juba* to suit them. Studying Arabic in some parts of the South is an equivalence of illiteracy. Circumcision is an Arabic culture, and those who are circumcised are looked down at. Wearing *jallabia*, (an Arab Muslim attire), guarantees you a hall of shame in the best of clowns. Every Muslim is an Arab, even if one of them is your own son. Those Southerners who serve in the Khartoum armed forces are considered Arabs. The Southerners who work with the Khartoum government are

Arabs too. And, yes, those foreign countries who support Khartoum government are Arabs too.[95]

The attempt to institutionalize force Arabization and Islamization is met with fierce resistant from the Southern Sudanese Africans. For example, a Dinka elder with renowned spiritual powers spoke of resisting the Arabs influence as follows:

> I don't speak Arabic. God has refused my speaking Arabic. I asked God, 'Why don't I speak Arabic?' And he said, 'If you now speak Arabic, you will turn into a bad man.' And I said, 'Isn't there something good in Arabic?' And he said, 'No, there is nothing good in it.[96]

With the use of forced Arabization and Islamization, the successive regimes in Khartoum miserably failed as they did not manage to convert or assimilate the Southern Sudanese by use of force and other bizarre methods. They rather achieved the opposite by widening the gap between the Southerners and Northerners. The most interesting example of a failed attempt to convert Southern Sudanese is illustrated in a story widely narrated among Southern Sudanese of the internally displaced persons in a refugee camp in Northern Sudan. The war, which is largely concentrated in the South, has displaced over four millions of Southern Sudanese to the North of the country where they live in horrendous situations in cramped unsanitary camps. The Islamic charitable organizations use those camps as the ground for converts by taking advantage of the suffering of the displaced persons. Those who are interested to get assistance from those Islamic charitable organizations must register as Muslims, therefore, many Southern Sudanese register for the sake of getting assistance. To the surprise of the officials of those charitable organizations, they find that the Southern Sudanese who register with them actually go to church every Sunday. When those Islamists finally confronted those Southerners, the Southerners response was: *the Islamic religion, in which they register for, is the religion for food, while their real religion is Christianity.* The bottom line is that religion is not something that can be coerced or forced onto others. It is a matter of personal consciousness, where individuals choose to follow or not follow, and the only judge in this matter is their creator or divine ruler, or in some cases, perhaps God or even Allah.

Chapter Endnotes

[43] Gilli Aldo, MCCJ "Daniel Comboni: Africa Or Death" *New People*, March-April, 1996.

[44] Dunstan M. Wai, *The African-Arab Conflict in the Sudan*, New York: Africana Publishing Company, 1981. p. 27.

[45] Edward Gibbon, *The History of the Decline and Fall of the Roman Empire*: Chapter LI: Conquests By The Arabs. Part VIII.

[46] Francis Deng, "Green is the Color of the Masters: The Legacy of Slavery and the Crisis of National Identity in Modern Sudan" Yale University. [online] http://www.yale.edu/glc/events/cbss/Deng.pdf

[47] Marit Magelssen Vambheim "Making Peace While Waging War:—A Peacemaking Effort in the Sudanese Civil War, 1965-1966" MA thesis in history, University of Bergen, Spring 2007.

[48] Ibid

[49] Ibid

[50] Douglas Hamilton Johnson, *The Root Causes of Sudan's Civil Wars*, Bloomington: Indiana University Press, 2003. p. 23.

[51] Petition to United Nations by Sudan African Closed Districts National Union (SACDNU), 1963.

[52] Francis Deng, *War of Visions Conflict of Identities in the Sudan*, Washington, D.C.: Brookings Institution Press, 1995.

[53] Francis R. Wingate, *Mahdism and the Egyptian Sudan*, London: Macmillan & Co., 1891.

[54] Ather Joseph Ohrwalder, *Ten Years Captivity in the Mahdi's Camp—1882-1892*. London: Meinerann and Kalestier, 1893.

[55] Ibid

[56] Francis Deng, *War of Visions Conflict of Identities in the Sudan*, Washington, D.C.: Brookings Institution Press, 1995. pg. 72.

[57] Ibid

[58] Francis R. Wingate, *Mahdism and the Egyptian Sudan*, London: Macmillan & Co., 1891.

[59] Muriel Mirak-Weissbach "Why The British Hate Sudan: The Mahdia's War Against London" Printed in The American Almanac, September 4, 1995.

[60] Ather Joseph Ohrwalder, *Ten Years Captivity in the Mahdi's Camp—1882-1892*. London: Meinerann and Kalestier, 1893.

[61] Ibid

[62] Ibid

[63] Ibid

[64] Ibid

[65] Ibid

[66] Gabriel Warburg, *The Sudan Under Wingate: Administration in the Anglo-Egyptian Sudan (1899-1916)*, London: Routledge, 1971.

[67] David Sconyers "British Policy and Mission Education in Southern Sudan—1928-1946" Unpublished Dissertation, University of Pennsylvania, 1978.

[68] Gabriel Warburg, *The Sudan Under Wingate: Administration in the Anglo-Egyptian Sudan (1899-1916)*, London: Routledge, 1971.

[69] Church Missionary Society Archive, Africa Missions: Sudan, *Adam Matthew Publications Ltd.* [online] http://www.ampltd.co.uk/collections_az/cms-4-07/description.aspx

[70] Daniel Comboni, 1831-1881, Roman Catholic, Sudan [online] http://www.dacb.org/stories/sudan/comboni1_daniel.html

[71] Ibid

[72] Ibid

[73] Ibid

[74] Daniel Comboni 1831-1881, Vatican, [online] http://www.vatican.va/news_services/liturgy/saints/ns_lit_doc_20031005_comboni_en.html

[75] Homily of John Paul II, "Canonization of the Three Blesseds" Sunday, October 5th, 2003. [online] http://www.vatican.va/holy_father/john_paul_ii/homilies/2003/documents/hf_jp-ii_hom_20031005_canonizations_en.html

[76] Daniel Comboni, 1831-1881, Roman Catholic, Sudan [online] http://www.dacb.org/stories/sudan/comboni1_daniel.html

[77] Joseph Oduho & William Deng, *The Problem of Southern Sudan*, London: Oxford University Press, 1963.

[78] *The Black Book of the Sudan on the Expulsion of the Missionaries from the South Sudan: An Answer*, Milano: Istituto Artigianelli, 1964. pp. 16-17.

[79] Ibid

[80] Ibid

[81] Francis Deng, "Sudan—Civil War and Genocide: Disappearing Christians of the Middle East," *Middle East Quarterly*, Winter 2001.

[82] Petition to United Nations by Sudan African Closed Districts National Union (SACDNU), 1963.

[83] *The Black Book of the Sudan on the Expulsion of the Missionaries from the South Sudan: An Answer*, Milano: Istituto Artigianelli, 1964.

[84] Francis Deng, "Sudan—Civil War and Genocide: Disappearing Christians of the Middle East, Middle East Quarterly," Winter 2001.

[85] K. D. D. Henderson, *Sudan Republic*, New York: F. A. Praeger, 1965. p. 183.

[86] Francis Deng, "Sudan—Civil War and Genocide: Disappearing Christians of the Middle East," *Middle East Quarterly*, Winter 2001.

[87] Bona Malwal, *People and Power in Sudan*, London: Ithaca Press, 1981. p. 17.

[88] Marit Magelssen Vambheim "Making Peace While Waging War:—A Peacemaking Effort in the Sudanese Civil War, 1965-1966" MA thesis in history, University of Bergen, Spring 2007.

[89] Ibid

[90] Fr. Neno Contran, *They Are A Target: 200 African Priests Killed*, Nairobi: Catholic Publishers in Africa, 1996. p. 145.

[91] Francis Deng, "Sudan—Civil War and Genocide: Disappearing Christians of the Middle East," *Middle East Quarterly*, Winter 2001.

[92] Mohamed Omer Beshir, *The Southern Sudan: background to conflict*, London: C. Hurst & Co., 1968.

[93] Francis Deng, "Sudan—Civil War and Genocide: Disappearing Christians of the Middle East," *Middle East Quarterly*, Winter 2001.

[94] Ibid

[95] Steve Paterno, "Dilemma of Sudan's CPA to the Question of Identity" *Sudan Tribune*, July 16, 2007 [online] http://sudantribune.com/spip.php?article22863

[96] Francis Deng, "Green is the Color of the Masters: The Legacy of Slavery and the Crisis of National Identity in Modern Sudan" Yale University. [online] http://www.yale.edu/glc/events/cbss/Deng.pdf

Chapter Three
Off Leaping into Parliament

"Father Saturnino had fired the imagination of the Southerners by his heroic stance in the Constituent Draft Committee" (The Vigilant).

The Constituent Assembly

Fr. Saturnino Lohure career in the Sudanese parliament of 1958, was relatively short but remarkably memorable given spectacular display of his performance and historical significance of that parliament. The parliament of 1958, was historic in the sense that it was the second parliament since Sudan's independence and was the last genuine parliament in the history of Sudan whereby the Sudanese people through a political process came closer in resolving the political, economic, and social structures of the country by attempting to establish a constitution for the entire Sudan. That parliament was specifically referred to as Constituent Assembly because of its role to presumably establish the constitution for the entire Sudan. This is however, not in away to ignore the fact that the attempts of restructuring Sudan's political power, economic base, and social system, has its historical background way back during the colonial rule and is still to this day a matter of debates and arms struggle. Decades have passed with millions of lives lost in the struggle, but yet, finding the formula for restructuring and transforming Sudan into a viable constitutional state has been a miserable failure.

A Separate South Sudan

On arrival to Sudan in 1899, the British were immediately faced with the realities of the Sudan. These realities included cultural diversity, multi-ethnicity, geophysical differences, economic disparities, racial distinctions, ethnic conflicts, religious tensions, bloody history, and a host of all other issues, which made it difficult to constitute a colony; and which naturally separated the South and North of Sudan from each other. These distinctive differences presented the British with an urgent challenge to establish ruling structures for the colonial power to reap the benefit of their colonialism. In that effect, the British came up with a series of policies, at least, suitable for the British to govern Sudan under a modern state system. To illustrate the problem of Sudan, a British inspector general from the Lado Enclave (the present day, Equatoria region), argued:

> Little can be done for the Negro provinces whilst they are starved so as to turn over all available funds to the Arab provinces, and whilst they are subject to the laws and regulations made for the benefit of the latter...So the Negro provinces should be put in a class by themselves, under a vice-governor...and allow to work their own salvation...[97]

Not only that, the British had more other reasons to worry about as far as administering the South of Sudan was concerned. As evidence, K.D.D. Henderson explained:

> The Northerner for…the British administrator was either a raider or a trader. Up till the middle 'twenties the Baggara were still lifting slaves south of the river and disposing of them to inaccessible markets far to the north. When not slave raiding they were poaching elephants or hunting giraffe or lifting cattle. When they condescended to do a little trading, they usually swindled the unsophisticated Nilote or paid him with counterfeit coins. As for the professional trader, the Jellabi, he in baronial eyes was an equally undesirable immigrant, battering on the villages, selling rubbishy goods at a vast profit, and introducing venereal disease. He had always preyed upon the Southerner and now he threatened to interfere with progress, as the Indian was doing in East Africa, by monopolizing petty trade and cash farming.[98]

Thus, the British instituted a separate policy for the South of Sudan. One of such policies, the first in the series, was the *Closed District Ordinance* introduced in early 1920s. The Closed District Ordinance and the policies, which followed thereafter, practically created two separate Sudanese colonies of British. The Southern Colony and the Northern Colony. In a more practical sense, the South was more of a protectorate of the British rule as all attempts were made with intention of protecting it from the Northern Arabs. The policies instituted for the South of Sudan restricted the movement between South and North. Passports and permits were to be used to cross from South to the North. It prevented the Northerners from working in the South, vice versa. Commerce activities were restricted and were only possible through having permits and licenses. Arabic language was completely abolished in the South. English was introduced and local indigenous languages were encouraged to flourish in through school systems and at some administrative levels. Separate school system with curriculum resembling the ones in East Africa was established for the South and the Christian missionaries were the only ones allowed to run the schools in the South. Students from the Southern Sudanese schools were instead admitted in East African schools for further studies as opposed to getting admitted in Northern schools. Islam was prevented from spreading southward whereas Christianity was allowed to take deeper roots in the South. A separate military unit of Equatoria Corps was specifically established for the South. The development plans for the South were designed differently than the ones in the North. Customary laws were incorporated into the penal code system with local chiefs presiding over legal matters. In essence, the colonial power ran the South Sudan as a separate colony more in tune with the other of its East African regions.

By 1940s, the colonial power was debating the status of the South on whether it would be "cast with the Northern Sudan or with East Africa, or partly with each" as the notion of self determination was gaining momentum throughout the British colonies.[99] For the British, the idea of South Sudan having its own independence was out of the question based on the view that "the Sudan, though a vast country in area is small in wealth and population, and if the Sudan is ever really to become self-governing and self-dependent it must not be divided up into small weak units."[100] This is also supported by the fact that the Southerners where yet to develop economically and educationally not just if they want to stand on their own but even when they would be thrown with the Northerners or with the East Africans.

This claim true it may sound did not make sense just like the other absurd claims being made against the people of South Sudan. First of all, freedom of human kind does not have a price tag for the people of South Sudan to be sold out base on their lack of economic worth and low educational level as the British made it their justification to hand the South to the North. Second of all, the fact that the Southerners did not develop in the same pace with the Northerners economically and educationally should not be used to punish the Southerners as it was not their fault. To clarify this point even further, it is not true that the North of Sudan had more economic potential than the South, even though rich the North might have been. The North is a dry desert not suitable for anything, but the colonial British poured huge sums of money to develop the Northern economy by building projects such as the Gezira Scheme, which boosted the Northern economy. As for the economic prospects for the South, its potential surpassed that of the North. South Sudan could produce most of the crops grown in tropical Africans such as coffee, cotton, sugarcane, sisal, rice and other cash crops. The South is also suitable for growing food crops such as sorghum, millet, sesame, cassava, groundnuts etc. Other fruits such as oranges, pawpaw, pineapples, bananas, and mangoes could also be produced in the South. These could all be done without large scale of irrigation schemes such as the ones in the North where the British pour huge sums of money to get the system running. This is not to mention the huge herds of cows, goats and sheep, the South rear. The South also seats on a large deposit of minerals and natural resource. In an official British report submitted in 1947, it revealed that there was already "fear that in the South might subsequently be discovered the wealth which could guarantee the Sudan's independence."[101] Then, how true is the claim that the South was poor? The problem was and is still today that economics and politics go hand in hand, which means the political subjugation of the people of the South contributed into the economic degradation of the people of the South. Hence, the British justification of handing the South to the North was not reasonable by any standard of imagination.

The Closed District Ordinance might have been intended for the betterment of the South Sudan and undoubtedly had its positive aspects. However, it also had negative repercussions. One of the negative aspects of these policies was that the British failed to build an indigenous South Sudanese capacity in governance. Equally devastating, they failed to build Southern Sudan economic development base in the same way they did for the North. The economic schemes the British had for the South never materialized. The proposed scheme to grow sugar and build a refinery at Mongalla was later to be transferred North by the Northern Arab regime. A paper project factory at Malakal was later to be ignored. And the proposed fish-canning plant in Malakal was to be moved north to Jabal al-Awliya. The British also failed to build social structure suitable for modern statehood system. Through their indirect rule policy, they instead created societies along the regional, ethnic, cultural, and tribal lines, which made it difficult to forge national identity. Even with the commerce restriction of the activities of the Arab Northern merchants in the South, the British failed to encourage and promote Southern Sudanese to build their own businesses. The commerce was still dominated and exploited by the Northern Arabs which made Southerners to resent the Arabs even more. The presence of the Northern Arabs merchants in the South created unfavorable competition to the disadvantage of the Southerners. For those were the lack of progress the British would use later as excuses to justify for the South to be under the colonial yoke of the Northern Arabs who were already advanced then during the independence.

On the positive side, one of the things that happened during the Closed District Ordinance period was the prevention of the adduction of slaves who were mainly drawn from the South. Even though the British mandate was to abolish slavery in the entire Sudan, they were not able to manage to do so even in Khartoum for the fear that a rapid abolition of slavery would in turn lead into shortage of labor, therefore, economic decline and would also agitate the slave masters, the so called Arabs. By the time the British took control of the Sudan in 1899, it was estimated that twenty to thirty percent of the population in North of Sudan were slaves.[102] Even with the presence of the British, slavery was still well and alive in the north of Sudan. A leading Islamic religion figure warned the British by writing, "no slave should be allowed to leave his master before proving that he is badly treated by him."[103] The British reluctantly complied by declaring, "slavery is not recognized in the Sudan, but as long as service is willingly rendered by servants to masters it is unnecessary to interfere in the conditions existing between them."[104] But unfortunately, who would have imagined that the abduction of slaves, which was prevented during the Closed District Ordinance of 1920s, could revive itself in a government sponsored militias raids in the supposedly independent Sudan of the twenty first century where the Southerners once again are targets of slave abductions.[105]

The prevention of Islamic religion and Arabic culture from penetrating deep in the South is also one of the positive aspects of the Closed District Ordinance. Had the Arab North managed to Islamize and Arabize the Southerners, it would have destroyed the Southerners' resolved to struggle against the Arabs, and by now the Southerners would have completely submitted to the whim of the Arab North just as the Nubians and Furs were subdued for centuries. The intention of the Arabs is to create an inferior society who would "accept their inferior position as inevitable."[106] And even worse, the notion of using South Sudan as a springboard in spreading Islamic religion and Arabic culture to the south of Sudan would have come a reality and devastating for the entire Africa south of Sudan. The African countries south of the equator must the Southern Sudanese people to thank for being their shield and protector. Also thanks to the missionaries and their schools, otherwise, the Southerners would have been inadequately treated with only Koranic schools and their brains would have been crammed with verses of Koran but nothing else, and the product of which would have been, "ignorance rather than knowledge," just as Ahmed Alzobier a Sudanese writer correctly puts it as he tries to analyze the declining educational standard promoted by the Islamist government in Khartoum.[107]

The Closed District Ordinance is actually one of the historical realities that provide political, legal, and even natural justification for the separation of South Sudan from the North Sudan. Those realities were as valid then and are even more valid today than ever before as Southerners have built their capacities in governance, manage economically viable region, and having a social system with national consciousness which encourages formation of national identity. Chief Cir Rehan, speaking on the Juba Conference of 1947, doubted on participating in Sudan government in the North on the basis that "the South was distinct from the North."[108] The first ever Southern Sudanese political party established in the exile by the Southern Sudanese politicians led by Fr. Saturnino Lohure adopted its name after the Closed District Ordinance to justify the political, legal, and natural separation of the South from the North. The Arabs decried such a move by the South Sudanese nationalists. One of Arabs sarcastically wrote that the South Sudanese leaders "found no appellation more suitable to adopt than the Sudanese African Closed District National Union (SACDNU)."[109] In his speech at the Round Table Conference of 1965, Aggrey Jaden, who was then the president of southern political party, Sudan African National Union (SANU), declared that "there are in fact two Sudans and the most important thing is that there can never be a basis of unity between the two."[110] Even William Deng who was in favor of unity of Sudan in the Round Table Conference of 1965, suggested that there are only two solutions for the problems of South Sudan, and those solutions are "separation or federation," because South and North Sudan are distinctively different to be ruled by a unitary government.[111]

The Path to Re-colonization

By mid 1940s, Sudan as a whole was preparing itself for the art of self-governing. In the exclusion of the Southerners and on the advice of the British, the Northerners established an Advisory Council, a body that consulted with the government on issues of governance. By 1946, the Governor-General of Sudan, Sir Hubert Huddleston convened a conference in Khartoum. The conference came to be known as Sudan Administrative Conference. The aim of it was to engage Sudanese so as they increase their participatory role in the government. Unfortunately, South Sudanese were neither represented in that conference nor were they consulted, but yet, their fates were tragically decided in that conference by the British and the Northern Arabs in collaboration with the Egyptians. The resolution of that conference managed to answer the question on where the South should belong in the event of independence or self-governing. The resolution states:

The policy of the Sudan Government regarding the Southern Sudan is to act upon the facts that the peoples of Southern Sudan are distinctly African and Negroid, but that geography and economics combine (so far as can be foreseen at the present time) to render them inextricably bound for future development to the Middle East and Arabs of the Northern Sudan and therefore to ensure that they shall be educational and economic developments be equipped to take their places in the future as socially and economically the equals of their partners of the Northern Sudan in the Sudan of the future.[112]

After tragically decided on the future status of the South, a nice Briton by the name B.V. Marwood who was then the governor of Equatoria became a little bit sympathetic to the Southerners. He hosted a conference in Juba on the instruction of James Robertson, the then Civil Secretary. The conference involved the Southerners and Northerners as well as some British officials some of whom were sympathetic to the Southerners plight. The conference was a historic event and it came to be known as the *Juba Conference of 1947.* The aim of the conference was to "gauge Southern reactions to and feelings about the recommendations" made in the previous conference, the Sudan Administrative Conference that took place in Khartoum, which the Southerners were not represented or consulted.[113] When asked on why the Southerners were purposely excluded from the Sudan Administrative Conference that took place in Khartoum, the answer was, the "Southerners had not reached a standard of education which would enable them to represent their compatriots in such a Council."[114] When the Juba Conference kicked off, the question on the status of the South was not on the agenda of the conference, even though the issue is touched on briefly during the discussion. The proposed agenda were more to do with the administrative structures and with the southern representation in the future government of Sudan. More specifically and officially, "the main item on the agenda was whether the Southern Sudanese would send representatives to the proposed Sudan legislative Assembly or whether they would like to have an Advisory Council of their own, similar to the one established for the Northern Sudan in 1944."[115]

The False Myth of Juba Conference

The most interesting myth about the Juba Conference of 1947, is that the Northern Sudanese Arabs view the conference as a final affirmation of the unity of Sudan, by arguing, "Juba Conference had taken the final decision on the question of unity, and that Southerners at that conference had then opted for this solution."[116] In trying to downplay the Southern Sudanese sentiment for separation, the notorious governor of Equatoria, Ali Baldo argued, for the interested of the South, it was firmly decided that it must unite with the North during the Juba Conference of 1947.[117] After the Torit Mutiny, Ismail al-Azhari, who was then Prime Minister, stated, "Sudan should be one unit on the basis of the decisions arrived at during the Juba Conference in June 1947."[118] This view is as much misleading as it is very wrong. First of all, the status of the South was not decided in the Juba Conference but a year earlier in Khartoum at the Sudan Administrative Conference where the Southerners were deliberately excluded and were neither represented nor consulted. Secondly, the aim of the Juba Conference was not to discuss or resolve issues patterning on the future status of South Sudan. Instead, it was as the official records rightly put it, to "gauge Southern reactions to and feelings about the recommendations" that was already been agreed upon at the Sudan Administrative Conference.[119] Those decisions made at the Sudan Administrative Conference, were by the way, irreversible as far as the British were concerned. Both, Marwood, the Governor of Equatoria and James Robertson, the Civil Secretary, confirmed this fact during the Juba conference. Marwood explicitly stated that the Juba Conference was in "no way a continuation of the Sudan Administration Conference."[120] In his closing remarks, Robertson who was the chairman of the conference said he could not "promise that every suggestion would be carried out, nor when it would be carried out."[121] Even more to the point, Robertson later on disputed the claimed that the Juba Conference resolved the issue of unity when he wrote:

> I thought that before advising the Governor-General in Council about this matter I ought to satisfy myself about the capacity of the Southerners to sit in a Legislative Assembly and play a constructive part in the discussions and deliberations...I looked upon the conference solely as a means of finding out the capabilities of the Southerners, and it was therefore quite inaccurate for some people to say later that at the Juba Conference the Southern representatives agreed to come in with the North...The only decision resulting from the conference was taken by myself. I decided that I could, after what I had seen of the Southerners who attended, endorse the recommendation of the Administrative conference, and ask the Governor-General-in-Council to accept its proposal that the new Legislative Assembly should be representative of the whole Sudan.[122]

One cannot need more evidence than this, but if so, this view is further supported due to the fact that the status of future South Sudan was not in the agenda of the Juba conference to begin with. During the discussion of the Juba Conference, the issue of the unity of Sudan came, but only briefly. It was Sheik Serur Ramli who brought the issue of unity up as he was wondering on whether the principle of unity of Sudan was settled. Judge Mohamed Saleh Shingeiti, who was the head of the Northern delegation, deplored such a question, calling it "outside the meeting's terms of reference."[123] The chairman of the conference, Robertson asked whether anyone had objection on the principle of unity of Sudan. The chairman then concluded that since nobody spoke on the subject then the assumption was that there was agreement on the principle of unity.[124]

That was the closest the Southerners ever came into agreeing to the united Sudan during the Juba Conference. If some of the Southerners who were at the conference did agree on this subject inadvertently since it was not part of the agenda of the conference or the discussion, then the agreement was not unanimous or legally binding by any standard known by human beings. However, there were those Southerners who had a changed of minds on the second day of the conference not on the issue of unity, but of sending Southern representatives to participate on the Sudan Legislative Assemble. There were only two individuals who explicitly said they changed their minds from the day before and decided that it was in the best interest of the South to send representatives to the Assembly. Those two individuals were Clement Mboro and James Tombura. It is said, "the change of attitude of certain educated Southerners who had first spoken against any participation in the legislative assembly and later changed their minds was due to the efforts of Mohammad Shingeiti."[125] Such allegation is further corroborated by Robertson who wrote, "I guessed at the time that my friend Mohamed Shingeiti, one of the Northern Representative I took with me, had been busy during the night persuading the Southern officials that Northern rates of pay would surely come to the South, if they agreed to come in with the North. This apparently persuaded Clement Mboro and others."[126] This does not only show that the Southern Sudanese officials were susceptible to bribes but that the Northern Sudanese Arabs were very corrupt, and they are still corrupt to this day. An honest Northern Sudanese Arab published an article on El Rai el-Aam newspaper dated December 11th, 1957, recounting his experience as an administrator in the South confirmed:

> The legacy of the Northerners is a great enterprise and to my great sorrow very few understand it. Here in the South, the Northerner is either the governor or a merchant; they look for gain, a dirty gain and drink the blood of naked bodies as if they were half English...and the young employee is addicted to satiate his instinct to spread corruption among people who are ignorant; this is the condition of the Northerners, except for a few by the mercy of God.[127]

It also goes to show that the Northern Sudanese Arabs were so desperate that they could do just about anything to force Southern Sudanese for the unattractive unity that history had proven was impossible and experience continues to prove that it is impossible. So, how legitimate and genuine this unity of South with the North is with the fact that the Northerners claim Juba Conference was a final affirmation of unity of Sudan, while bribery was involved? But even assuming that the Southern Sudanese who participated in the Juba conference agreed on the principle of unity, it would still not be legally binding as they had no mandate from the Southern Sudanese people, but were rather hand picked by the colonial government.

Actually, most of the Southerners who participated in the Juba Conference were of the conviction that if there was any arrangement of unitary government in Sudan at the time, it would be temporary, because the status of the South would be decided on a later date when the Southerners were ready for self-government, and so they would decide on that time on their own accord. Even the British officials who made the decision of uniting the South and North were of this view as well, rendering this view a prevailing one. In the middle of the text for the decision they reached with respect to the unity of Sudan, the British officials, parenthesized the phrase, "so far as can be foreseen at the present time."[128] This phrase implies that as far as the British were concerned, the decision was only good at that time, but is this decision good today, over sixty years later? Chief Lapponya who participated in the Juba Conference stressed this issue clearly when he stated, "the principle of unity could only be decided later when the Southerners were grown up, by which time they would be in a position to decide whether to join the North or go to the Belgian Congo or Uganda."[129] On the same subject of unity, Chief Lolik Lado another participant of the conference, said, "an immediate decision could not be taken now."[130] He then added with a warning, "a hurried union might result into unhappy home, likely to break up in a violent divorce."[131] Another participant of the conference, Chief Buth Diu even went far by suggesting that if there was going to be any genuine unity on Sudan, it must be on the conditions that the Northerners were not allowed to settle in the South without permission, Northerners should be stopped from interfering in Southern local governments, and Northerners must be punished for calling Southerners slaves.[132] T.R.H. Owen, then Deputy Governor of Bahr El Ghazal, who also participated in the conference, warned the Northern Sudanese Arabs by saying, Southerners "had not forgotten the days of oppression even if the North had done so, and even today the Southerners view was dominated by fear and suspicion."[133] He went as far as concluding that "the Southerners would never willingly join the North until the latter should prove by their acts, not merely by their words, that they had undergone a change of heart."[134] Prior to the Juba Conference, Owen seriously challenged the British decision of the unification of the South and North of Sudan in a confidential corresponding among the British officials in Sudan by highlighting the obvious differences between the South and North of Sudan.[135] Owen actually was among the British officials serving in Sudan who would remain criticizing the unification of the South and North of Sudan, and rightly so.[136]

In the bloody history of slave ownership and capturing, the Arabs hold a record in being the most cruel and brutal slave masters. It is reported that the slaves transported by the Arabs had a highest death toll than any other slaves. It is said that for every slave who reached Cairo, several died on the way. In a letter by an Ottoman official in 1849, it reference of 1,600 black slaves dying of thirst on their way to Libya.[137] Worse yet, from leaving slaves lingering in the desert to their death was the practice by Arabs of throwing slaves overboard from their ships to be drawn in the water as a means to dispose evidence from the British sailors who were patrolling the waters to stop transportation of salves. One such brutal example is depicted below:

> The worse that could befall slaves was when the slaver was overhauled by a British cruiser, and they might then be flung overboard to dispose of all evidence. Devereaux mentions a case where the Arabs, when pursued by an English cruiser, cut the throats of 24 slaves and threw them overboard. Cololm also states that Arabs would not hesitate to knock

slaves on the head and throw them overboard to avoid capture.[138]

In some instances, the Arab traders would just sink their boats and flee away, leaving the slaves to be drowned in the deep waters. They did not in anyway value slaves as human. Another graphical example of such brutality against the slaves was:

> When the Daphne's cutter captured a dhow with 156 slaves on board many were found to be in final stages of starvation and dysentery. One woman was brought out of the dhow with a month-old infant in her arms. The baby forehead was crushed and when she was asked how the injury had happened she explained to the ship's interpreter that as the boat came alongside the baby began to cry. One of the dhowmen, fearing that the sailors would hear the cries, picked up a stone and crushed the child's head.[139]

In another example, David Livingston recounted an incident of "one woman who was unable to carry both her load and young child, had the child taken from her and saw its brains dashed out on the stone."[140] Many who witnessed the brutality of the Arabs slave trades where shocked including the hardcore military commanders such as Mohammed Ali who ruled Egypt. In the case of David Livingston, he was to have nightmares for weeks after his encounters with the slave traders and their victims.[141] When Sir Samuel Baker went to South Sudan in the year 1869, on a mission to abolish slavery, he was surprised to discover, "the population was fled. Not a village was to be seen" because of the settlement of traders from Khartoum who "kidnap the women and children for slaves and plunder and destroy wherever they set their foot on."[142] Another eye witness, Fr. Ather Ohrwalder, who spent ten years of captivity in Mahdi's camp among the black slaves, remarked, "the dhurra ratio of a slave is generally so small and so small that numbers of them die of starvation long before they are fortunate enough to be sold."[143] One can fill pages of books with these example, but in all, these to the Southern Sudanese people, means in the words of one author, ". . .nothing less than the total destruction of their society. Oral history in Sudan refers to this period as the time when the world was spoiled."[144] Despite this brutality and trauma the Arabs caused the black Africans they have never "undergone a change of heart," not even in the twenty-first century. The uneasiness dealing with the Arabs is actually increased ever since. Dustan M. Wai sums it all when he argues, "Africans perceive Arabs as cunning, crafty, dishonest, untrustworthy, and racially as well as culturally arrogant."[145] He goes on to conclude, "many Africans do not feel at ease dealing with Arabs."[146] In 2005, when the Sudan People Liberation Movement (SPLM) signed the Comprehensive Peace Agreement (CPA) with the government in the North, the phrase "making unity attractive" has to be emphasized and stressed because for decades the Northerners were not making unity attractive given their cruel and brutal attitude.[147]

The Re-colonization of the South

So, it could not have been the Juba Conference, but the Sudan Administrative Conference, which became the basis for the formation of the fragile united Sudan, which is still bleeding today as a consequence of such fragile unity. As a result of the resolutions of Sudan Administrative Conference, the first mock Legislative Assembly of

Sudan opened its session in the end of 1948. In that Assembly, thirteen Southerners were handpicked to represent the South. By 1951, a Constitution Amendment Commission was formed under the British supervision to provide guidelines and recommendations as away forward for Sudan self-government. A Southern member of the commission was frustrated in his effort as his proposals for separation or unity with constitutional guarantees to the South was vehemently opposed. He was reported to have walked out of the commission, leaving Southerners unrepresented.[148] The commission, however, later on recommended that the Governor-General "shall have executive and administrative powers in the South" as a safeguarding measure.[149] Unfortunately, the Northern Sudanese Arabs opposed such measures referring to it as an "imperialist plot" that carries "a hidden scheme for partition."[150] They took their complaints to the Egyptians who also had stake on Sudan per Anglo-Egyptian condominium rule. Budging to the pressure, the Egyptian finally replaced that provision with a more vaguely worded provision that reads, "the Governor-General shall have a special responsibility to ensure fair and equitable treatment to all inhabitants of the various provinces of the Sudan."[151] In addition to removing this safeguarding measure, the ministerial posts for the Southerners was also limited into just two. A sound minded British civil servant in dismay wrote:

> Without protection the Southerners will not be able to develop along indigenous lines, will be overwhelmed and swamped by the North and deteriorate into servile community hewing wood and drawing water. To pretend that there are not fundamental differences between them is like covering up a crack in the tree trunk with moss. Such process, like any obscuring of the truth, is unsound.[152]

Some British press and members of parliament criticized this provision. Despite this, it was formally promulgated into law in March of

1953 as the Anglo-Egyptian Agreement, officially known as the Cairo Agreement. It paved way for Sudan's independence. The agreement set a transnational government for the period of three years whereby Sudan would then decide for its own independence. During the promulgation of this agreement into law, the Arabs North went hysterical in celebrations while the Southerners were angrily saddened by it. In their celebratory victory against both the colonial rule and the Southerners, it is said that the Northern Sudanese Arab traders in Southern towns were mocking the Southerners on how they were going to rule them as soon as the British departed the Sudan. This let into clashes in some parts of the South. For example, in Torit town some Arabs were reported to be severely beaten by the locals who resented their celebration and mocking of the Southerners. When the Arab administrators arrested the perpetuators, the locals stormed the prison with their full traditional attires which included spears, helmets, and shields to free the prisoners.[153]

In 1954, a Sudanization Committee was appointed of a five member committee where three of whom were supposed to be Sudanese, but unfortunately Southerners were not represented as the three Sudanese positions were filled with the Arabs. When the committee completed its task, 800 civil servant positions were to be filled by the Sudanese, but yet only four low level positions went to the Southerners. Such a move was nerve-racking to the Southerners as it affected all segment of the Southern Sudanese communities. The concern was not anymore confined to the Southern politicians as every Southerner was disappointed with their Arab counterparts whom they were supposed to share a country with. For example, a Southern Sudanese merchant by the name Gregory Deng Kir wrote in disappointment to the Southern members of parliament:

The result of Sudanization have come with disappointing results, i.e. four Assistant District Commissioners…Well as it appears, it means our fellow Northerners want to colonize us for another hundred years.[154]

It was not only the Southerners who were concerned with the negative effects of Sudanization. The report of Commission of Enquiry also acknowledged the dangers with Sudanization. The report states:

Since the Southern Sudanese benefited very little form Sudanization they found little or no difference between conditions now and conditions previously; and independence for them was regarded as merely change of masters. We feel that the Southern Sudanese by finding themselves holding secondary positions in the Government of their country have a genuine grievance.[155]

The Southerners were infuriated by this Sudanization policy which tended to exclude them deliberately from any meaningful participatory role in the government of Sudan. The Southern political party, the Liberal Party, immediately held a conference in Juba where they developed a Southern position, and they resolved that the Southern position should be a federal system of government where they would have more saying in their own affairs. They also concluded that if they failed to obtain federalism, then the "alternative would be to seek complete independence by asking the popular will of the Southerners" in a plebiscite.[156] They developed certain strategies to send their message of disapproval of Sudan transitional government dominated by the pro Egyptian party of National Unionist Party (NUP) of Ismail al-Azhari.

When Prime Minister Ismail al Azhari visited Juba, the Southerners boycotted to meet with him or attend his meetings. He was only left to listen to the Arabs who were in Juba. When it came time for the declaration of independence, the Southerners, snubbed. For them, an independent that could not contain safeguards for the South was unaccepted as it would amount to re-colonization. Instead of voting for the declaration of independence, the Southerners proposed that a plebiscite be held in the South under the auspicious of the United Nations (UN) or that the Red Cross should study the deteriorating situation in the South and report back to the government before any action is taken. As they reached a deadlock, they compromised on the condition that the Southerners vote for the declaration of independence and in return "the claims of the Southern members of parliament for a federal government for the three Southern provinces be given full consideration by the Constituent Assembly."[157] That compromise was the only way the Northern political parties got the Southerners to vote for the declarations of independence. After this compromise reached, they declared independence, which was officially took place in January 1st, 1956. The British then departed the country leaving a vacuum in the position of Governor-General. That position which is equivalent to the head of state was conferred on a five-man commission as a measure of interim government. A fragile coalition government was formed under the Premiership of Ismail al-Azhari who was still commanding a slim majority lead with his National Unionist Party (NUP) party.[158] Al-Azhari coalition government never survived longer as he suffered defection from the coalition which tilted the power to the Umma Party. By July of 1956, Abdallah Khalil, the secretary-general of the Umma Party replaced al-Azhari as Prime Minister.

The Father as a Parliamentarian

It is at this juncture that Father Saturnino Lohure emerged into political prominence demonstrating his oratory skills, sheer eloquence, and fluency in clearly articulating the Southern cause to the amazement of the Arabs. His first appearance in political scenery was in 1956. The Father was elected by the Christian Churches to represent the interest of the Church in the National Committee which was to issue recommendations in drafting the constitution for Sudan. The committee was drawn from all sections of the communities and from all walks of life. Among those were members of political parties, doctors, lawyers, Islamists, Christians, university students, trade unions and many more others. It was an attempted representation of Sudan's diversity at its best. The committee was composed of forty-six members. However, the Southerners were grossly underrepresented in this committee of forty-six members with only three members were Southerners, two of whom from the Liberal Party, and the Father representing the Christian Churches. In the end, the three Southerners could not match the majority Arabs as they were swallowed in. The committee's rule of business was based on the majority vote. The Southerners' complaints and proposals were completely ignored. The three Southerners even maintained a minority status in the smaller subcommittees that was created for specific issues such as the Southern Committee. In frustrations, the Southerners had to pull out of the committee, relinquishing their roles to the majority Arabs.[159] The committee went ahead with its proceedings not feeling shameful of its Southern members' pulling out. They made the recommendations for Sudan constitution along Islamic lines. Those recommendations were later to be tabled for the next parliament of 1958, for discussion and final approval.

The 1958 was the critical moment in Sudan's history. By then the first ever census of Sudan was announced. The census was used in redrawing the voting districts and it also provided vital data such as the compositions of ethnic and racial groups and their demographics. The Father never took the frustrations from the previous experience as a defeat. Instead it reenergized him to do even more. The best forum to take the fight, according to him will be in the parliament, and the Father was willing to go that far for the sake of the South Sudan. With the permission of the Holy See, the Father and a fellow priest, Fr. Paulino Doggale ran for elections in March of 1958. For priests to run for parliament was something unheard of. This unprecedented maneuver would later haunt the Christian missionaries and the Christians of Sudan in general. However, it is not surprising in an environment where religion tension is very high that each religion would try its best to assert itself. If Islamists can be represented in the government, there is no reason why Christians would not be represented. Fr. Doggales represented Juba while the Father represented Torit. They both won and went on to the parliament as members of the Liberal Party, a Southern political party.

In this parliament, the Southerners were once again deprived despite their population. They were disproportionally represented in parliament. Out of thirty percent of the entire population of the Sudan, only forty-six were sent to the parliament compared to 173 Northerners. The Umma party alone sent sixty-three members in parliament almost doubling the entire Southern Sudanese members. To even make this worse, some Arabs were allowed to contest in the South. One such example was in Renk, and another was in Kapoeta where an Arab was let to run while a Southern member of Liberal Party was denied to run. When the Southerners complained, they were ignored. Therefore, the Southerners were not only disproportionally represented but also deprived in their own constituencies.

While in parliament, the Father quickly captured the leadership of Liberal Party. He dismissed the notion of Southerners standing on positions based on party affiliations or independently. Instead, he created a bloc of Southern members of parliament irrespective of their party affiliations. The Southern bloc was to speak on one voice when it came to issues affecting the South Sudan. The platform for the Southern bloc was federation for the South. The Father became the leader and spokesperson for the Southern bloc. He discouraged other Southern Sudanese members of parliament from getting bribed by the northern political parties. When it came time for debating the drafting of the constitution the Father took over representing the Southern cause in a most outstanding fashion. *The Vigilant* newspaper remembering the Father during his times in parliament as a man who:

> Had fired the imagination of the Southerners by his heroic stand in the Constituent Draft Committee. Here was a man incorruptible, here was one brave enough to speak his mind; here was one so articulate enough to present the Southern viewpoint in the Constituent Assembly in 1958, as none other before him had done."[160]

Another individual, Rogato Ohide recounting the Father's performances during that period wrote:

> Fr Ohure's parliamentary contributions were particularly superb, as they were remarkable. He was known for his oratorical capacity, eloquence and fluency. This development left northern political adversaries to doubt his origin as a Southerner and might have mistaken him for a black

American. Furthermore, between Otuho and among Southern supporters he gained the name of "Ohure, iwahatic Arabi ahas ahide" (Lotuko language translation for, Ohure, the Arabs throw their hands up), in amazement of course.[161]

And of course the Father won the admiration of the Southern Sudanese students at the time. Besides the serious business in the parliament, the Father also had a lighter side of it as he enjoyed his time in parliament to the fullest. Later on while he was traveling with a group of young boys on the back of the lorry the Father jokingly said, "standing among the children on the top of the lorry was like standing in the Parliament."[162] Despites all these efforts in debates and counter debates, the Southerners and Northerners could not reach into agreement. The Northerners were not living to their promised of considering the federal system, which they made as a condition for the declaration of independence. In a last ditch effort, the Father went and stood up, and he delivered what was going to be the last and decisive position of the Southern Sudanese in the Constituent Assembly. The speech he delivered, read in part:

> Mr. President, Sir, the South has no ill-intentions whatsoever towards the North; the South simply claims to run its local affairs in a united Sudan. The South has no intention of separating from the North, for had that been the case nothing on earth would have prevented the demand for separation. The South claims to federate with the North, a right that the South undoubtedly possesses as a consequence of the principle of free self-determination, which reason and

democracy grant to a free people. The South will at any moment separate from the North if and when the North so decides, directly or indirectly, through political, social and economic subjection of the South.[163]

After delivering this speech, the Southerners withdrew completely from the Constituent Draft Committee. They fallback and waited to asses the effect of this speech. Amazingly, this speech had a ripple effect far deeper and farther away to the peripheries of the Sudan and deep to the marginalized regions of the Sudan. The message of the speech resonated pretty well with the people of the peripheries and the marginalized of the Sudan. It was for the first time the phenomenon of viewing the concentration of power from the center and in the hands of the Arabs is seriously challenged. With the benefit of data provided by the census, the Southerners knew that the African population was the largest in Sudan and the Arabs were the minority. The so-called marginalized, those in the peripheries, did not start to challenge the power of the center, which is concentrated in the hands of Arabs in the twenty-first century nor did they did it with the emergence of the New Sudan ideology envisioned by John Garang of Sudan People Liberation Movement (SPLM). The first time they actually did it was in 1958 after studying the position of the Southern Sudanese on the Constituent Draft Committee. For example, in August of 1958, the Beja people invited the then Prime Minister, Abdallah Khalil to Port Sudan and made a host of demands among which was that the Beja people would want to have a government where they have more saying in their own local affairs and less being subjected into the power in Khartoum. In effect something similar to the one the Southerners wanted. When the Prime Minister Khalil came back to Khartoum from his trip in Port Sudan, he was ambushed by the

Darfurians and the people of the provinces of Kordofan who invited him for their celebration, which was taking place in El-Obied. There, they also demanded a government system where they will have more saying in it.[164] It is worthy remembering that these are the people Judge Mohammad Shingeiti, a leader of the Northern delegation at the Juba Conference of 1947, referred to "as backward as anyone in the South Sudan."[165] Overwhelmed by these challenges and not knowing what to do, Prime Minister Khalil turned to his advisors who then advised him to give up the power to the military instead of giving it to the people, the marginalized people of the Sudan. He accepted the advice and let the military took control of the democratically elected parliamentary government. One observer wrote, the Father "nearly single-handedly brought South Sudan federation courtesy of his insistence on self-determination" in the parliament of 1958.[166] Writing for the Journal of Modern African Studies, Alexis Heraclides, wrote, "in 1958, the Southerners appeared to be nearer to success than ever before, but their hopes were dashed unceremonious by General Abboud's coup d'etat, which apparently had the blessing of the two predominantly Muslim orders, the Khatmiyya and the Ansar."[167]

Indeed, through the leadership and performance of the Father, the Southerners were closer than ever before in getting federal system of government, however, in November 1958, the military came in under the leadership of Major-General Ibrahim Abboud. In a radio announcement, the military declared the takeover of the government. They then declared the state of emergency, the political parties were banned, and some key government figures were briefly detained. General Abboud now the president justified the takeover "in order to save the country from the political chaos of opportunistic politicians."[168] Mistakenly, the Northern Sudanese Arab military regime thought they would impose unity to Sudan through the military discipline by use of force. When the Southern parliamentarians were packed into the boat and shipped to the South, those who arrived in Juba were immediately summoned by the government and there they were warned that the new military government did not tolerate dissents. They were told specifically not to involve in any political activity or utter the word 'federal' again or else they will face the wrath of the law.[169] Unfortunately, for the Northern Arab successive regimes, fifty years later, they still failed to impose their unity through the use of force. The country now is even more fragile than ever before. Those fights, which were waged in parliament, are transferred in the jungles of Southern Sudan and in the desert of Darfur as well as in far eastern part of the Sudan. The war is transformed in away that it is resulting in tilting the power toward the peripheries. It is the war of mouth as well as the war of bullets fought in battle fields. It cost the oppressed as much as it also cost the oppressors. The Southerners already gained much of their powers; the Darfurians would probably take a little bit longer and others would probably follow as well. It seems those who have been deprived of power for so long are gearing to get it with whatever means necessary including arms struggle.

The Betrayal of the Southerners

As for the Prime Minister Abdallah Khalil, the fellow who voluntarily gave power to the military, he invited three Southern Sudanese parliamentarian right after the coup to his place of residence. And below is what he confided to them in their ensuing conversations:

> My experience has shown me that this country is not yet ready for democracy; I have therefore decided, at the suggestion of my advisors, to hand the reins of this country to the army; though political parties have now been banned

I still believe that the Umma people and the people of the South will work in close cooperation.[170]

It is very interesting that the people like Khalil who wanted independence so bad will eventually give up a civilian elected government to military rule just because they were not willing to agree on a simple formula of power equation where power lies with the people. After all, the governments supposed to be for the people. What were they thinking, really?

And for the British, if they were genuinely concerned of a nation that is not "divided up into small weak units," then, they should think again, because they just created one big, weak, and monstrous nation called the Sudan.[171] From its creation, it has been at war with itself and the war continues to rage with no prospect for a total stoppage. Speaking of lives, over three millions innocent souls have been lost just in the last two decades, not to mention the ones from the previous decades. Worse yet, many more lives are continued to be lost in a senseless act of genocide, which seems to have no ending in sight. Famines and diseases are rampantly complementing each other, and the people are the targets and ultimately victims. People in millions fled the country and millions more are displaced from their homes to be languished in horrible and unbearable conditions in foreign countries and in the internally displaced persons' camps. As far as the current numbers stand, a total of a million Sudanese are refugees in neighboring countries plus a total of six millions who are internally displaced.[172] This is almost the exact number of the entire Sudanese population from the last time the British checked before they left the country. Perhaps it is time they check again. The economy of the country is in shambles and the only available opportunities for economic growth are squandered by poor, incompetent, and corrupt leadership. And yes, the River Nile is still there running in pretty good conditions as it was half a century ago, despite the threat of global warming. However, the fear is, with the current trend of turmoil, the river may loose its inhabitants including those ones referred to in the bible "whose land is divided by rivers."[173]

The least that is expected of the British is sympathy and a feeling of guilt for the decisions that they took in uniting the South with the North of Sudan knowing that it was not going to work since they, the British were ruling the South and North separately. By then, the British had more options; all of which would have been favorable to the South. But for whatever reason, they chose the wrong option. The best option would have been for the British not to rush with the independence for Sudan. If the Northerners were desperately in need of independence they should have gone ahead and have it by themselves without involving the South in it. After all, they have been separated since time immemorable.

Even if assuming that the South and North of Sudan were to be administered as one nation during the colonial rule, it would have still been possible that they could be separated in their independence. There are examples of countries which were administered as one under colonial rule and then separated during their independence. One of such examples is the British Indian Empire. However, it is ironically interesting that Mansour Khalid, one of the most respected Northern Sudanese Arab intellectuals, uses India as "the most obvious example in order to prove that real national interests can be served and problems solved even in a country with much greater diversity and scale than those prevailing in Sudan."[174] If the Northern Sudanese Arab intellectuals of Mansour Khalid caliber would used India as a perfect model for Sudan unity, then one wonders what the rest of the ignorant and illiterate Northern Sudanese Arabs would use as a perfect model for the unity of Sudan. In the contrary of those of Mansour Khalid's view, India actually provides a good example for separation of South Sudan. If those of Mansour Khalid would care of history or at least learn history, they would have known that India never existed until a junk of its Muslim territory were carved to form a separate nation of Pakistan. This is not to mention the further partition between the Muslim Pakistanis, which further created the countries of Pakistan and Bangladesh. So, a country that was under one colonial rule can even become not only two countries but three during independence as case of British Indian Empire clearly illustrates. The question then, why shouldn't the South then become at least two separate countries?

Even without these historical facts, one still wonders why India with its constant sectarian violence, terrorist activities, secessionist movements, and insurgencies would be a perfect model for a country like Sudan, which has a potential for peace and prosperity if it must to be separated once and for all.[175] Anyway, it is not surprising that people of Mansour Khalid's intellectual conviction would reach into such erroneous conclusion of presenting India as a perfect model for Sudan's unity.

Whatever the case could have been, the British would have let the North of Sudan get loose on its own, and the British would then take this opportunity in building the South for its own independence, and until then, the South should have remained under a British colony or in other words, the South would have remained under the British protectorate. There was nothing wrong or shameful to be under a British colony a little bit longer. After all, all the black African countries obtained their independence after the Sudan did obtain its independence. Hence, there was no reason for the South to rush for independence, especially when they were not ready for it. Even the nation of Israel which is one of the powerful states today had to ask the British to extend its colony over them a little bit longer until they felt they were ready for self-government. More to the point, even the Northern Sudanese Arab powerful groups were appealing to the British in the 1920s to continue colonizing Sudan and especially not to tie Sudan's fate to Egypt in case Egypt was granted independence. In one of such appeals, a letter written to the Governor-General read in part:

> All natives of the Sudan are conscious of the benefits conferred by the British government upon the Sudan, and desire that the government continue her work of developing the Sudan of guiding her and of assisting her along the path of national progress, until she reach the standing which she hopes for among the cultivated nations of the world.[176]

Another letter by a different group with a similar tone and appeal reads:

> If the British government intends to grant Egypt its independence and wishes to include us also under the terms of that independence, please let us know because we firmly believe that our interest, the interest of our country and our rights and conditions in general differ vastly from those of Egypt and we should like to be prepared to safeguard these interests in event your wishing to leave the matter in the hands of Egyptians.[177]

If the Sudanese Arabs could beg the British to colonize them so as to avoid unity with Egyptians who are just Arabs and Muslims like them, who are they to stop the Southern Sudanese from deciding their own fate?

In other words, if the Northern Sudanese Arabs could reject unity with their cousins, the Egyptian Arab Muslims, and then what on earth would stop the Southern Sudanese Africans from rejecting unity with the Northern Sudanese Arabs? One observer was right to assert:

> The problem of the Southern Sudan is the biggest human difficulty in the country. Educated Sudanese (*meaning the Arabs*) regard the South as the Egypt regards them. The loss of it would become a matter of prestige and to some extend of anxiety, but there is also a fear that in the South might subsequently be discovered the wealth which could guarantee the Sudan's independence.[178]

If it is because of the prestige, one wonders whatever happens to the exaggerated Arab prestige that the Northern Sudanese always boast about. It was Ismail al-Azhari who enthusiastically declared their pride in "Arab origin."[179] Another one of them, Sadiq al-Mahdi, proudly bragged of "brightest and civilized" Arab culture.[180] Is it that the Northern Sudanese Arabs have a low self confidence in their Arabism when they are with their Arab cousins, but have a lot of Arab pride to show to the non-Arabs? At least, that is what they demonstrated thus far by showing that they can only boast about Arab pride with the Africans but when dealing with their Egyptian cousins, they shrink. One cannot understand this irony, but one of those Northern Sudanese Arab intellectuals, provides a plausible answer by saying:

> The reason [for northern identification with Arabism] stems from an inferiority complex really. The Northern Sudanese is torn internally in his Arab-African personality. As a result

of his Arabic Islamic cultural development, he views himself in a higher status from other Sudanese not exposed to this process. Arabism gives him his sense of pride and distinction and that is why he exaggerates when he professes it. He becomes more royal than the King, so to speak.[181]

The overemphasis in professing Arabism by the Northern Sudanese Arabs is a widespread phenomenon with deeper psychological implications to them. Another one of those intellectuals, Al-Baqir al-Afifi Mukhtar argues that the evocation of this Arabism phenomenon is "repeatedly issued by the political and cultural entrepreneurs. Unlike the elite of the Arab world, who do not need to state the obvious, Northerners feel the need to complement their lack in features by words."[182] So, it is the lack of Arabic features among the Northern Sudanese, which prompt the Northern Sudanese to pretend to be more Arabs than the Arabs, sort of compensating what they don't have. Even more sickening psychologically, Mukhtar explained:

This inferior position has undoubtedly had its impact on the psychology of the Northern individual...The understanding was that the lighter the color of the skin, the closer the person is to the center, and the more authentic his or her claim to Arab ancestry. Failing to comply with the standard color, as is the case with most of the Northerners, the individual seeks a second resort in the hair, in order to prove his or her Arab identity; the softer the hair the closer the individual to the center.[183]

Given this overwhelming evidence, it is obvious that the Northern Sudanese Arabs are covering up their inferiority by falsely professing Arabism when in fact they lack the right Arabic features. Unfortunately, they find themselves tangle in between the middle, hence creating conflict within thyself—the conflict that they spread onto others. But again, that is their problem to deal with, after all, nobody force them to associate with the Arabs. They choose it and they should live with it.

Some scholars and intellectuals made some attempts in explaining the psychological root causes of the Sudanese Arabs inferiority complex, which often led them to exaggerate their Arabism. These root causes had its tracks in the history. The first Arabs who came to Sudan were predominantly male as they settled in Sudan; they had no options but to marry to the African beautiful black women, therefore, producing offspring who are mixture of Arab blood with a Black African blood. That became a root cause of not only the dilemma of identity but a source of inferiority complex as Mukhtar further explained:

> Northerners live in a split world. While they believe that they are the descendants of an 'Arab father' and an 'African mother', they seem to identify with the father, albeit invisible, and despise the mother who is so visible in their features. There is an internal fissure in the Northern self between the looks and the outlook, the body and the mind, the skin color and the culture, and in one word, between the 'mother' and the 'father'…a misfit.[184]

The reason Northern Sudanese detested their African mothers and turned to their Arab fathers, according to Muhammad Omar Bashir, another Northern Sudanese Scholar, was because, "the Africans in the

Southern Sudan, who were among the most backward peoples on the continent, could hardly inspire their Arab compatriots with any desire to identify with Africa."[185] To even worsen their status, the British came in and showed them what a real humiliation and defeat was by conquering and colonizing them. As such they "...passionately attached to the glorious past of Islam, which, together with the richness of classic Arabic culture and thought provided the necessary psychological prod."[186]

As clearly indicated here, the Northerner Sudanese Arabs are seriously suffering from inferiority complex with serious psychological consequences. If the other intention of the Arabs to claim the stake of the South so as to exploit the wealth of the South Sudan for their advantage, then they are just equally making a fatal mistake by creating more animosity with the Southerners. The animosity now reaches its climax, given the fact that the South pretty much controls its territory and is poised to partition.

The Water Worshipers

The awful predicament the South Sudan finds itself in is a clear demonstration of the African proverb which says, "if the elephants fight, it is the grass that suffers." In this illustration, British, Egyptians, and Sudanese Arabs are symbolic of the elephants while the Southern Sudanese people are the representation of the grass. From the onset one could see the creation of this problem when the British and Egyptian signed Anglo-Egyptian condominium to jointly rule the Sudan. One analyst describes such colonial rule made out of a convenience as "clumsy and unsatisfactory form of government devised as a solution to a delicate and international problem."[187] If this is true, then one wonders how come for years the issue of the South Sudan is always considered as internal affairs, if in fact it has an international dimension to it. Anyway, that should be left for those who doubt the international dimension on the issues affecting Sudan to figure it out.

Of course, when the British came in the Egypt, they were to control the Suez Canal and when they go further south into the Sudan, their intention was to control the entire Nile Valley. For one reason the control of the Nile Valley would ensure stability in Egypt—the stability which was very much needed. For another reason, the flow of Nile waters could contribute to unabated import of cotton and other materials into Britain as the Nile was important source for irrigation and farming that greatly benefit British industrial revolution. Also, the British interest in controlling the Nile was so that they could use it as gateway to the African heartland. Matter of fact, the British managed to control the Nile from its source in Uganda all the way to its ending in Egypt. They fought and negotiated deals to secure the flow of the Nile and its tributaries. The British were willing to blow the French up when in the process of trying to conquer the Nile they met with the French at Fashoda, in the Upper Nile region of Southern Sudan. After securing the Nile for itself, one of the British geo-strategist, Lord Cromer, boasted by stating, "when, eventually, the waters of the Nile, from the lakes to the sea, are brought fully under control, it would be possible to boast that man—in this case, the Englishman—has turned the gifts of nature to the best possible advantage."[188] For the Englishman, the River Nile was as much valuable as the gold. Not surprisingly the British worshiped the Nile and eventually punished the Southern Sudanese for it.

On the other hand, the Egyptian wanted to unite with Sudan so as to have a complete control of the Nile valley from downstream to upstream. To the advantage of the Egypt, it could easily link with the Arab and Muslims of the Sudan to form a one nation. However, such unity of Egypt and Sudan could threaten British leverage in both the Nile valley and in the Suez Canal. Instead, the British used its control of the Nile valley as a leverage of carrot and stick to control Egypt and maintained its presence at the Suez Canal. A confidential memorandum issued in 1923, from British foreign office declared, "the power which holds the Sudan has Egypt at its mercy, and through Egypt can dominate the Suez Canal."[189] Wingate even puts it succinctly when he said, "as long as we hold the Sudan we hold the key to Egypt because we control her water supply."[190] When Egypt finally gained full independence in 1920s, its impact had far reaching effects on the Nile politics, which lasted to this day. First, the independence of Egypt undermined the British rule in Sudan and encouraged anti-British sentiment as well as strengthened the idea of nationalism in Sudan. Until then, Egypt was still maintaining that Sudan is its province and since Egypt is independent, British had no legal claim in Sudan. As such, both Egypt and Britain had to woo the Northern Sudanese Arabs to maintain their own competing interests. As for the Southerner Sudanese Africans, they were completely ignored because the Egyptians and British viewed them irrelevant in these competitions. Interestingly, it was the Northern Sudanese Arabs who later in the game made serious attempt to woo the Southern Sudanese Africans, such as demonstrated in the Juba Conference of 1947. Of course, they did it also for the interest of Northern Sudanese Arabs not for the Southern Sudanese interest. In the end, the interest of the South was left at the mercy of these three competing parties.

When Sudan first political parties emerged in late 1930s, Egypt got hold of National Unionist Party (NUP). The National Unionist Party (NUP) drew its major support from sufi-brotherhood, the Khatmiyya and Ashiqqa. The main platform for the party was Sudan union with Egypt under the slogan of 'Unity of the Nile Valley.' Egypt became the main sponsor of the party. Not surprisingly, the party was hostile toward the British rule in Sudan. On the other hand, the British got hold of the Umma Party. The Umma Party had the support of the Ansar with traditional strongholds in rural areas in the North and Western Sudan. The al-Mahdi family controlled the leadership of the party. The al-Mahdi family, interestingly enough, had a long tie of collaboration with the British and the family gained enormously from the British support, making the family rich to this day.

These two major political parties became important players leading to the independence of Sudan. Matter of fact, the expedited process of Sudanese independence was partly due to the fact that each of the countries, Egypt and Britain, tried to gain favoritism from the Sudanese Arabs by doing whatever it took to please the Sudanese Arabs. Douglas Johnson corroborated this fact by arguing, "both the timing and terms of Sudan's independence were less a product of nationalist mobilization than international diplomacy, arising out of the Sudan's *de factor* status as a colony of two countries."[191] In this ensuing fight to gain over a mere favoritism from the Sudanese Arabs, South Sudan became a bargaining chip. For the Egyptians, they preferred the unity of the South with the North of Sudan on the condition that the Northern political parties will agree on the unity of Sudan and Egypt. While for the British they agree on the unity of the South Sudan to the North of Sudan on the condition that the Northern political parties agree on separation with Egypt. As for the Northern Arabs, it was a win-win situation as they had to do nothing other than just wait and see their goal of uniting the South of Sudan to the North being delivered to them by both Egypt and British who were both wooing for them. The Northern Arabs emerged as winners in this fights. The British lost as they had to leave the country and the Egyptian lost too as their objective of Unity of the Nile Valley was not realized. As for the Southern Sudanese, they were not only losers but ended up suffering by being used as a pawn for other people's interest. The British had to abruptly abandoned its policy of letting "Southern Sudanese progress on African and Negroid lines" by handing the South to the North of Sudan.[192] From there the British left and never to be seen again. That is the political history of South Sudan tragedy, which is more completed today than ever before.

Chapter Endnotes

[97] Gabriel Warburg, *The Sudan Under Wingate: Administration in the Anglo-Egyptian Sudan (1899-1916)*, London: Routledge, 1971.

[98] K. D. D. Henderson, *Sudan Republic*, New York: F. A. Praeger, 1965. pp. 162-63.

[99] Juba Conference "Proceeding of the Juba Conference on the Political Development of the Southern Sudan" June, 1947.

[100] Ibid

[101] Petition to United Nations by Sudan African Closed Districts National Union (SACDNU), 1963.

[102] Amir Idris, *Conflict and Politics of Identity in Sudan*, New York: Palgrave Macmillan, 2005.

[103] Ibid

[104] Ibid

[105] Human Rights Watch, "Slavery and Slave Redemption in the Sudan" March 2002 [online] www.hrw.org

[106] Petition to United Nations by Sudan African Closed Districts National Union (SACDNU), 1963.

[107] Ahmed Alzobier, "The Intellectual Degeneration in Sudan" Sudan

Tribune, April 3rd, 2007 [online] http://www.sudantribune.com/spip.php?article21140&var_recherche=higher%20education

[108] Juba Conference "Proceeding of the Juba Conference on the Political Development of the Southern Sudan" June, 1947.

[109] Amir Idris, *Conflict and Politics of Identity in Sudan,* New York: Palgrave Macmillan, 2005. Pg. 47.

_____ Abdelwahab El-Affendi, "Discovering the South: Sudanese Dilemmas for Islam in Africa" (written in 1990). [online] http://www.islamfortoday.com/sudan.htm

[110] Marit Magelssen Vambheim "Making Peace While Waging War:—A Peacemaking Effort in the Sudanese Civil War, 1965-1966" MA thesis in history, University of Bergen, Spring 2007.

[111] Ibid

[112] Juba Conference "Proceeding of the Juba Conference on the Political Development of the Southern Sudan" June, 1947.

[113] Ibid

[114] Ibid

[115] Petition to United Nations by Sudan African Closed Districts National Union (SACDNU), 1963.

[116] Marit Magelssen Vambheim "Making Peace While Waging War:—A Peacemaking Effort in the Sudanese Civil War, 1965-1966" MA thesis in history, University of Bergen, Spring 2007.

[117] Joseph Oduho & William Deng, *The Problem of Southern Sudan*, London: Oxford University Press, 1963.

[118] Ibid

[119] Juba Conference "Proceeding of the Juba Conference on the Political Development of the Southern Sudan" June, 1947.

[120] Ibid

[121] Ibid

[122] James Robertson, *Transition in Africa: From Direct Rule to Independence: A Memoir,* New York: Barnes & Noble Books, 1974. p.107.

[123] Juba Conference "Proceeding of the Juba Conference on the Political Development of the Southern Sudan" June, 1947.

[124] Ibid

[125] James Robertson, *Transition in Africa: From Direct Rule to Independence: A Memoir,* New York: Barnes & Noble Books, 1974. p.108

[126] Ibid

[127] Petition to United Nations by Sudan African Closed Districts National Union (SACDNU), 1963.

[128] Juba Conference "Proceeding of the Juba Conference on the Political Development of the Southern Sudan" June, 1947.

[129] Ibid

[130] Ibid

[131] Francis Deng,, *War of Visions Conflict of Identities in the Sudan,* Washington, D.C.: Brookings Institution Press, 1995.

[132] Juba Conference "Proceeding of the Juba Conference on the Political Development of the Southern Sudan" June, 1947.

[133] Ibid

[134] Ibid

[135] Mohamed Omer Beshir, The Southern Sudan: background to conflict, London: C. Hurst & Co., 1968.

[136] David Sconyers "British Policy and Mission Education in Southern Sudan—1928-1946" Unpublished Dissertation, University of Pennsylvania, 1978.

[137] Thomas Sowell, *Black Rednecks and White Liberals,* San Francisco: Encounter Books, 2005. pg. 137.

[138] Ibid

[139] Ibid

[140] Ibid

[141] Ibid

[142] Francis Deng, *War of Visions Conflict of Identities in the Sudan*, Washington, D.C.: Brookings Institution Press, 1995.

[143] Ather Joseph Ohrwalder, *Ten Years Captivity in the Mahdi's Camp—1882-1892*. London: Meinerann and Kalestier, 1893.

[144] Deng, Francis, "Sudan—Civil War and Genocide: Disappearing Christians of the Middle East" Middle East Quarterly, Winter 2001.

[145] Amir Idris, *Conflict and Politics of Identity in Sudan*, New York: Palgrave Macmillan, 2005. p. 46.

[146] Ibid

[147] Comprehensive Peace Agreement (CPA), signed between Sudan People Liberation Movement (SPM) and National Congress Party (NCP), January 9th, 2005.

[148] Joseph Oduho & William Deng, *The Problem of Southern Sudan*, London: Oxford University Press, 1963.

[149] Ibid

[150] Ibid

[151] Ibid

[152] Ibid

[153] Ibid

[154] Oliver Albino, *The Sudan: A Southern Viewpoint*, London: Oxford University Press, 1970.

[155] Joseph Oduho & William Deng, *The Problem of Southern Sudan*, London: Oxford University Press, 1963.

[156] Petition to United Nations by Sudan African Closed Districts National Union (SACDNU), 1963.

[157] Oliver Albino, *The Sudan: A Southern Viewpoint*, London: Oxford University Press, 1970.

[158] Robert Collins, (forthcoming publication in 2007): "Chapter Five:

Parliamentary and Military Experiments in Government, 1956-1969" *The History of the Modern Sudan,* Hollywood: Tsehai Publ.

[159] Joseph Oduho & William Deng, *The Problem of Southern Sudan,* London: Oxford University Press, 1963.

[160] The Vigilant, "Fr Saturnino is Dead but His Soul Liveth," February 7th, 1967.

[161] Rogato Ohide "Otuho Leadership in the Context of Modern Sudan Governance: The State of Its Sabotaged and Undermined Credentials" A paper presented at Otuho Speaking Community of North America Historic Conference, December 24-25, 2005, Erie, Pennsylvania, USA.

[162] Adriano Bonfanti, "Padre Saturnino ha Compiuto la Sua Missione" *Nigrizia,* Aprile, 1967 Translate by Fr. Hilary Boma.

[163] Joseph Oduho & William Deng, *The Problem of Southern Sudan,* London: Oxford University Press, 1963.

[164] Ibid

[165] Juba Conference "Proceeding of the Juba Conference on the Political Development of the Southern Sudan" June, 1947.

[166] Rogato Ohide "Otuho Leadership in the Context of Modern Sudan Governance: The State of Its Sabotaged and Undermined Credentials" A paper presented at Otuho Speaking Community of North America Historic Conference, December 24-25, 2005, Erie, Pennsylvania, USA.

[167] Alexis Heraclides, "Janus or Sisyphus? The Southern Problem of the Sudan" *The Journal of Modern African Studies,* 1987. pg. 218.

[168] Robert Collins, (forthcoming publication in 2007): "Chapter Five: Parliamentary and Military Experiments in Government, 1956-1969" *The History of the Modern Sudan,* Hollywood: Tsehai Publ.

[169] Oliver Albino, *The Sudan: A Southern Viewpoint,* London: Oxford University Press, 1970.

[170] Joseph Oduho & William Deng, *The Problem of Southern Sudan*, London: Oxford University Press, 1963.

[171] Juba Conference "Proceeding of the Juba Conference on the Political Development of the Southern Sudan" June, 1947.

[172] United States Commission on International Religious Freedom "Policy Focus: Sudan" Winter 2006 also visit www.uscirf.gov

[173] *The Holy Bible*, Old Testament: Isaiah 18:6-7:

[174] Gabriel R. Warburg, "Sudan: 1898-1989, The Unstable State. (book reviews)" Middle Eastern Studies, January 4th, 1993.

_____ Mansour Khalid, *The Government They Deserve, the Role of the Elite in Sudan's Political Evolution*, London: Kegan Paul International, 1990. pp. 139-42.

[175]*BBC*, "Country profile: India," [online] http://news.bbc.co.uk/2/hi/south_asia/country_profiles/1154019.stm

_____The Central Intelligence Agency, *World Fact Book* [online] https://www.cia.gov/library/publications/the-world-factbook/geos/in.html

[176] Francis Deng, *War of Visions Conflict of Identities in the Sudan*, Washington, D.C.: Brookings Institution Press, 1995.

[177] Ibid

[178] Petition to United Nations by Sudan African Closed Districts National Union (SACDNU), 1963.

[179] Marit Magelssen Vambheim "Making Peace While Waging War:—A Peacemaking Effort in the Sudanese Civil War, 1965-1966" MA thesis in history, University of Bergen, Spring 2007.

[180] Ibid

[181] Francis Deng, *War of Visions: Conflict of Identity in the Sudan*, Washington, D.C.: The Brookings Institution, Washington, DC, 1995. p. 43—31.

[182] Al-Baqir al-Afifi Mukhtar, "The Crisis of Identity in the Northern Sudan: A Dilemma of a Black People with a White Culture," a paper

presented at the CODESRIA African Humanities Institute tenured by the Program of African Studies at Northwestern University.

[183] Ibid

[184] Ibid

[185] Francis Deng, "Green is the Color of the Masters: The Legacy of Slavery and the Crisis of National Identity in Modern Sudan" Yale University. [online] http://www.yale.edu/glc/events/cbss/Deng.pdf

[186] Edward Atiyah, *An Arab Tells His Story: A Study in Loyalties*, London: John Murray, 1946. p. 158

[187] Petition to United Nations by Sudan African Closed Districts National Union (SACDNU), 1963.

[188] Terje Tvedt, *The River Nile in the Age of British: Political Ecology and the Quest for Economic Power*, London: I B Tauris & Co Ltd, 2004.

[189] Ibid

[190] Gabriel Warburg, *The Sudan Under Wingate: Administration in the Anglo-Egyptian Sudan (1899-1916)*, London: Routledge, 1971.

[191] Douglas Hamilton Johnson, *The Root Causes of Sudan's Civil Wars*, Bloomington: Indiana University Press, 2003

[192] Petition to United Nations by Sudan African Closed Districts National Union (SACDNU), 1963[192] Petition to United Nations by Sudan African Closed Districts National Union (SACDNU), 1963.

Chapter Four
Fleeing into Exile

"At the news of his disappearance, the governor of Equatoria, Ali Baldo, spread the word that he had been devoured by a beast of the forest" (Fr. Neno Contran, They Are A Target)

Military Takeover

After the military takeover of the government in 1958, and the parliament was disbanded, Fr. Saturnino Lohure moved to Yei Catholic mission in South Sudan to serve there as a priest. By now, the new military regime of General Ibrahim Abboud is asserting its supremacy and control to gain legitimacy as a military ruler. Of course the first official business of General Abboud dictatorial regime was to declare a successful coup, and like all other coup makers do, to scare of the elected officials to abandon the government. Historian, Robert Collins summarizes the immediate actions of Abboud as follows:

Major-General Ibrahim Abboud ('Abbud) ordered the army to secure the Three Towns and announced in his radio address that the military had assumed power in order to save the country from the political chaos of opportunistic politicians. A state of emergency was declared, political parties dissolved, ministers briefly detained, and trade unions abolished. The Transitional Constitution was suspended, and the Heads of State, the five-man Supreme Commission, summarily dismissed. The Sudan was declared a "democratic republic" in which sovereignty was held by the people, but real power, reminiscent of the Egyptian model, was invested in a twelve-member Supreme Council of the Armed Forces which, in turn, delegated "full legislative, executive, and judicial powers" to General Abboud. A subordinate council of ministers was established consisting of seven military officers who sat on the Supreme Council and five civilians including two ministers from the dismissed coalition government. Abboud declared himself prime minister and shortly thereafter president and minister of defense.[193]

While all this was taking place, the situation was getting tense in the South. The Southern politicians were being harassed here and there. On the arrival of the Southern Members of Parliament to Juba, they were summoned to the government and warned that the new military regime would not tolerate politicians who utter the word federalism.[194] During that time the Catholic Church was also trying to establish its somewhat uncertain future in the Sudan—the future, which was threatened by the Khartoum government anti Christian policies. A proposal was put forward by the Catholic Church for Fr. Saturnino Lohure to become bishop of the new Vicariate of Juba. But the Father had a different goal for himself than the church intended. He declined the proposal of becoming a bishop by citing, "what is the use of baptizing babies, if in the future, it would become impossible to instruct them? Or if to get a job or employment they must become Muslims."[195] To the Father, the church cannot operate under oppressed political system and it is only under the free society that the church interest can be safeguarded. It was there that the idea of launching a Southern Sudanese resistance movement from abroad began to float around. It is said, the Father must have been responsible for that idea and that must have been the reason on why the Patronage of the Southern Sudanese resistant movement was conferred on him in line with his role as a leader of the Southern Sudanese Bloc in the parliament.

The Escape to Exile

Now the government is not happy with the Father and it was just a matter of time before they could catch up with him. On the evening of December 23rd, 1960, rumors spread that six Southern Sudanese leaders disappeared, and among them was Fr. Saturnino Lohure. Just informed on time by a friend about an imminent arrest to be carried against him, the Father never wasted anytime. On the pretext of visiting a sick, he slipped away from his house in Yei, and on the way to Kajo-Keji waiting for him was a catchiest with a bicycle. There, they rode off to the obscurity of the future awaiting them in the foreign land. Under the cover of darkness, the Father quietly slipped through the Ugandan border and entered into Uganda. The only witness to the escape was the shaded dark night. Fortunately, those Arabs who would later be responsible for spreading rumors were not witnesses.

On the aftermath of his escape, the news spread throughout the South to the disappointment of the government. The Khartoum government countered such news with propaganda hoping to discourage others from following suit of escaping and also for the people not to remember the Father anymore. They began to spread false news that the Father was severely devoured by the wild beast in the forest as he was trying to escape. However, their propaganda was not taken seriously by the Southerners, as many prominent Southern Sudanese leaders began to trek to the neighboring countries for safe haven.

Six months later, the Khartoum government has no choice but to face reality, and that was when they acknowledged that the Father escaped safely into Uganda. The acknowledgement only came through issuing of an arrest warrant for the Father on the allegation that he exited the country without permission, the very country that is trying to eliminate him. However, neither the spread of propaganda nor the threat of the arrest warrant actually deterred the South Sudanese determination to escape into the neighboring countries and launch a resistance movement against this oppressed government. And for that matter, neither was "a beast of the forest" an obstacle to escape as the people who escaped actually had to walk on foot through the wild forest. For example, at one point, Ugandan authorities reported over 7,000 refugees crossing into the border within a matter of ten days. By that early 1960s, the U.N. reported the Southern Sudanese refugees in the neighboring countries of Uganda and Zaire (Congo) numbering over 60,000.[196] However, the Father put that figure even more higher to about 100,000.[197] Beside this huge exodus of refugees, the prominent South Sudanese leaders such as Joseph Oduho, Aggrey Jaden, Alexi Mbali, William Deng, to mention just a few, all escaped the country around that same period, confirming the Southern Sudanese determinations to not let any obstacle stand on their way.

The Difficulties in Exile

While in Uganda, the Father registered as a refugee, but unlike any other regular refugee, his activities were restricted. He was only allowed to maintain his refugee's status in Uganda if he could abide by the restrictions and conditions imposed on him by the British colonial government of Uganda. He was not allowed to leave the capital and was to report to the police headquarters regularly. He was not allowed to participate in any political activities, whatever that meant, because anything could be determined as political activity, given the fact that such determinations were made arbitrarily. And he was not to conduct any media interviews. These plus other restrictions crippled his ability of doing anything meaningful for South Sudan. It was then that he confirmed that the British, which was still running the colonized Uganda, was against the cause of South Sudan. He hinted in opting out of Uganda for a country that would sympathize with the cause of the suffering people of South Sudan. He then applied for asylum in Tanganyika, currently Tanzania. The government of Tanganyika, which was still heavily under the cloud of imperial power accepted his application, but there also, he was imposed with the same restrictions and conditions like the ones in Uganda. He declined the offer of the Tanganyika. Never discouraged by these, the Father went on and approached Nigeria for the same purpose, but unfortunately he never went through with a plan to stay in Nigeria as it will prove to be far from Sudan for him to conduct his activities effectively. But nevertheless, he maintained a pretty good relationship with the Nigerians who were sympathetic to the cause of South Sudan.[198]

The last resort for the Father to remain effective in Sudan's affairs was to cross into Congo. In the beginning of 1962, he managed to cross into Congo (Leopoldville), using a provisional pass. It was there that he was joined by other Southern Sudanese leaders such as Joseph Oduho, William Deng and a host of others. Congo, though a little bit freer than Uganda because of its independence from the colonial power, it was not safe either. The risk of anyone of them Southern politicians to get killed, captured or imprisoned was very high. By then, Congo was in state of turmoil characterized with emergence of secessionist movement, struggle for power, and foreign interventions. After obtaining its independence in June of 1960, a province of Katanga declared independence of its own, then power struggles emerged within the first ever elected government of Congo, and in the midst of these, the coup was declared. To worsen the crisis, the Cold War warriors, the United States of America (U.S.A) in particular meddled in the middle by supporting one of the actors, which tangled the fate of Congo in the web of Cold War confrontations. Belgian, another foreign power was on the other hand, supporting a secessionist Kantangese movement. So, Congo was not only destabilized by its own internal turmoil but also became a ground for foreign powers confrontations.

Trying to elude capture in such security risky environment, the Father juggled between here and there, and at times taking refuge in Congo (Brazzaville), which was not safe either by any security standard. One time crossing into Congo (Brazzaville), the Father wrote a letter saying, only by a grace and miracle of God he escaped the Congolese (Leopoldville) police who were collaborating with Khartoum government to have him captured. At one point in 1964, the Father risked getting captured by the Simba, a rebel movement in Congo (Leopoldville), which was willing to trade him off to the Khartoum government for a truckload full of weapons or food, but fortunately he narrowly escaped the capture.[199] Others were not so lucky. For example, Joseph Oduho could not elude capture as he was captured and imprisoned. While in captivity, a guard informed him of a plan to extradite him to Khartoum by air. Worried of the potential danger, Oduho managed to use his broken French to convince the guard that he was going to be thrown out of the plane before the plane could reach Khartoum. Fortunately, the guard was convinced, he facilitated Oduho's escape and let him free on the very day that he was supposed to be flown to Khartoum.[200] The art of throwing prisoners out of flying planes has some basis in the history of Khartoum government. So, Joseph Oduho was not making it up. Also, the Congolese (Leopoldville) press on May 15th, 1962, reported an attempted kidnapping of the Father, Joseph Oduho, and William Deng by the Khartoum government from the Congo.[201] In short, the situation of the Father and his colleagues in exile was precarious and the Arabs were not ready to let them free, even after fleeing the Sudan.

The Wonderful Work of Exile

Despite these risks, the Father and his colleagues immediately got into business. Among the first things, they embarked on was the establishment of Sudan Christian Association (SCA) of East Africa. The Sudan Christian Association (SCA) was created for the purpose of catering for Sudanese refugees, but in practical sense, the outfit was a front organization for the political party, the Sudan African National Union (SANU) and its military wing, the Anyanya. With its headquarters in Kampala, the organization operates clandestinely raising funds, facilitating contacts among the groups, providing accommodations of members, and promoting the political and military objectives of SANU, and Anyanya. The members of the organization are planted covertly in strategic locations where there were South Sudanese communities. They were encouraged to take regular jobs in their places of residence so as to support the movement as well as not to put more burdens on the movement in sustaining them. In other words, it was John F. Kennedy's appeal of "ask not what your country can do for you; ask what you can do for your country"[202] put into practice by these dedicated members of Sudan Christian Association (SCA).

The system of SCA was good such that it encouraged every citizen of South Sudan to contribute to the movement according to their own capacity and in any way possible. It also encouraged individuals to build their professional capacity in their places of residence while helping the movement at the same time. If one thing the Southern Sudanese politicians in exile succeeded in, it would be the establishing and maintaining of a system such as the SCA in addition to the scholarship programs that they also established. Those politicians were visionary in a sense that they were building a next generation of leadership through education. They did not only encourage scholastic programs but they managed to secure scholarships for the Southern Sudanese students, especially in Uganda where they managed to have churches to sponsor students. Their scholarship programs were very successful that it produced most of the Southern dreSudanese leadership who took over after the signing of Addis Ababa Agreement among whom was Dr. John Garang who went on to lead a successful liberation movement of Sudan People Liberation Movement/Army (SPLM/A) from 1983 until his tragic and mysterious death in 2005. At the time, youngsters of school age were literally discouraged from participating in war as they were pushed to study. Even those students who were old enough and were capable of carrying out combat operations could not be allowed to fight. Instead, they were rather encouraged to finish with their studies before they could join the fighting in the bushes of Southern Sudan.

First Political Party in Exile

Under the leadership of the Father, this exiled group went on to establish the first ever South Sudan political party in exile. Joseph Oduho an ex-parliamentarian and the school headmaster was made the president. Marko Rume also an ex-parliamentarian was the vice president. William Deng who was an administrator was the Secretary General with Aggrey Jaden as his deputy. The Father was the National Patron for the South Sudan movement, the position that he held until his death. The Father won the respect of all, especially, his former colleagues in the parliament of 1958, some of whom were the likes of Joseph Oduho, Marko Rume, Ferdinand Adyang, Pancrasio Ocheng, and others. For them, they were convinced that they were "given mandate by the people of South Sudan to fulfill the pledge given by the Southern members of the last parliament (1958) that if federation were turned down, the alternative would be to seek a complete independence" for South Sudan.[203] The Father was the head of the Southern Sudanese bloc in that last parliament of 1958. He was also well connected with the outside world. It was agreed that the political party be named Sudanese African Closed Districts National Union (SACDNU). A "Closed District" is a reference to the historical colonial act that divided the southern part of Sudan to be governed separately from the north. This is an indicative of the objective of this group, which was "independence for South Sudanese within the framework of Black African Unity."[204] When the headquarters of the party was moved to Kampala, they changed the name to Sudan African National Union (SANU) so as to reflect the inclusiveness of other Africans who are in the north of Sudan. The reasoning was that there were actually more Africans in Sudan than Arabs, therefore, SANU should not exclude them on that basis. Practically it was only a symbolic gesture of inclusiveness of all the Africans in Sudan as the reality was the participants of this organization were all Southerners who were struggling for the independence of South Sudan.

By then, the Father had already established his headquarters in Congo (Leopoldville) at a place called Aru, which is strategically located closer to both Sudan and Uganda. That strategic location provided him with proximity and ability in reaching out to the population of Southern Sudanese people in all these three countries of Sudan, Congo, and Uganda. The Father coordinated his activities from there and he travel extensively throughout African and European countries. It was from there, the Father immediately began to raise his concerns regarding the leadership problems affecting SANU. Some of his concerns regarding the leadership of SANU was that he did not appreciate the fact that the leadership of SANU were not in one location to coordinate their activities affectively. His reason was that if they were in one place their effort would have significant impact. He blamed William Deng for his overstaying abroad while blamed Joseph Oduho for refusal to stay with him at Aru for the love of a lavish city life in Kampala. Joseph Oduho defended himself by saying that if he moved to Aru, a rural remote area, he could not be effective with things such as media campaign, which require facilities of city settings. Instead, Oduho blamed William Deng for not tending to his duty as secretary general of the party. That the position of secretary general is very essential to the party and the absence of William Deng crippled the party's activities and performance. By then, Aggrey Jaden, the deputy Secretary General, who would have assumed the duties of secretary general, was living in Nairobi.[205] Joseph Oduho appointed Severino Fuli who had just arrived in Kampala Secretary of the Administration so as he performed the necessary task of the secretary general.[206] These differences of views among the Southern Sudanese politicians were to mark the beginning of the South Sudanese political party both in exile and at home degenerating into squabbles, personal ambition, and greed for power.

The Birth of Anyanya

Despite this political weakness within the party, the Father was enthusiastic about the military prospect to probe the Khartoum government militarily. He proposed to move ahead with a major and wide spread military strike against Khartoum solders targets in the South, which would mark the birth of Anyanya movement. He set the D-Day of a first military strike to coincide with the anniversary of the Torit Mutiny of 1955. By then, they have already organized the soldiers on strategic locations inside Sudan and along the Congo and Ugandan borders. He proposed that the name of the military wing of SANU be Sudan Pan African Freedom Fighters (SPAFF) so as to attract Pan-Africanist sympathizers throughout Africa. However, members of SANU executive who preferred a name that have local meaning opposed the name and after deliberation came up with the name Anyanya, which means poison in a local Madi language. The Father accepted it all the same.

The group coordinated what was going to be their declaration of armed resistance against Khartoum government. Orders were relayed to the command centers on various locations to strike on the D-Day and an all-ready signal was sent back. The plan was going well as expected. The Father didn't expect so much of a military victory on the D-Day but to alert the whole world that there are problems going on in Sudan. He also expected that the attack would send a signal to Khartoum that the Southerners are ready to confront them militarily. On the D-Day, the attacks went as planed. As expected the world media picked up on the news. News spread that a group calling itself Anyanya attacked several locations in Sudan. SANU in Kampala was delighted, but they had more work to do with the media. They braced for media showdown. Joseph Oduho, President of SANU, instructed the Secretary of Information to keep up following the news through all the media outlets. Oduho went on issuing a press release denouncing the Anyanya so as SANU should not be implicated in an armed violence. However, the Ugandan government did not believe him. The Ugandan security forces went on raiding the houses of SANU officials, SCA officials, and all their affiliates. Joseph Oduho and many Southern Sudanese were apprehended and thrown in a notorious Ugandan prison, Luzira. Their documents were seized on those raids and used against them in court trail. They were charged with inciting violence in a foreign land. In the case of Oduho, he landed eight months in jail for his part in supporting a violent action against a foreign country, the Sudan.

Father, the National Patron for South Sudan

Of course, the Father was as active as usual. In around the same time, he completed writing a book, a first book about South Sudan written by a Southern Sudanese. Because of his position as a catholic priest, he could not publish the book under his name, which will implicate him. He instead asked two of his compatriots, Joseph Oduho and William Deng to publish the book under their names. The book is entitled *The Problem of the Southern Sudan*. It is part of his literally campaign to alert the world of the problems affecting the people of South Sudan. The book contains detailed historical accounts on the subjection of the people of Sudan, in terms of politics, economic, social, religion, and education. The book calls for impendence of South Sudan.[207]

When the heads of African states were meeting in May of 1963 in Addis Ababa, Ethiopia, in what was going to be the founding of Organization of African Union (OAU), the Father had an opportunity to present to them a petition, explaining the problems of Southern Sudan. The petition was calling for the declaration of South Sudan into an independent state. He wanted the problem of Sudan to be taken seriously at the international level as those of other African countries like South Africa, Mozambique, and Rhodesia. In 1963, the Father also presented a petition to the United Nation (U.N.) alerting the world leaders of problems in Sudan. He appealed that the U.N. investigate the problems of Sudan and supervise a plebiscite for independent South Sudan. In the same year, the Father traveled to Rome to make known the situation of South Sudan to the African bishops who participated on the Second Ecumenical Council of the Vatican also known as Vatican II.[208]

Changes in Leaderships

By 1964, a series of developments took place both in exile and in Sudan. In exile, Joseph Oduho, the president of SANU completed his eight month sentence in the Ugandan notorious prison, Luzira. By then, SANU was already plagued into personal petty politics of squabbles and power struggles. Relationship between Joseph Oduho, the president of SANU and William Deng, the Secretary General of SANU was already strained. Oduho had already written several letters for Deng, asking him to report to Kampala but received no response. Not just most, but all of the members of the executive at that time wanted to see a change of leadership in SANU. They demanded that Oduho called for a national convention. At any rate, Oduho, set a date for the convention, which was on October of 1964. During the convention, they deliberated on a lot of issues and fourteen members voted for new SANU leadership. To Joseph Oduho surprise, he lost the election to Aggrey Jaden. Jaden quickly assembled his cabinet and moved on to perform business. The Father retained his position as a Southern Sudan National Patron. He is the only person who cannot be sidelined or ignored by any of those who are trying to get to power given his reputation and abilities to collect funds for the South Sudan cause and ability to articulate the cause of South Sudan clearly and effectively. William Deng, perhaps knowing that he could not win any position decided not to show up at the convention all together. Instead, he came from Europe and went straight to Kinshasa. While in Kinshasa, he declared himself the president of SANU and announced that he was planning to go to Sudan transferring along with him SANU to Khartoum. As for Joseph Oduho, even though he accepted the new SANU leadership, he went on forming his own party called Azania Liberation Front (AZL) as rival to the SANU. That was the worse episode of political split among the Southerner Sudanese politicians in exile which was later to be transferred home. This occurred at critical juncture when the South was to mount a strong Southern front against the North. One observer of Sudanese politics notes, "if the breakdown of parliamentary government in the North was a failure of leadership, the failure to forge viable political organizations in the South was much the same."[209]

Southern Sudan Political Party in Khartoum

Back home in Khartoum, Southern Front, the only genuine Southern political party was established as a result of the fall of General Abboud, which brought back political parties. The Southern Front drew its members among the intellectuals, mainly Southern civil servants and students who were living in Northern Sudan. The Southern Front was first established under Gordon Abiei as president, but when it was later officially registered, Clement Mboro became the president, Gordon Muortat its vice president and Hilary Logali, the secretary general. Some of the prominent members of the party included Abel Alier, Ezbon Mondiri, Othwon Buogo, Othwonn Dak, Natale Olwak, Lubari Ramba,

Bona Malwal and Romano Hassan. The party later ended up cooperating with the SANU from exile in number of policy issues and its members were to actively participate on the Round Table Conference of 1965. Some of the Southern Front activities were effective, especially the publication of its informative newsletter, the, *The Vigilant*, which became an effective voice of the South Sudan cause including the voice of Anyanya from inside Sudan. The party also managed to push for their own candidates for high government posts such as securing a post of minister of communication and transport to Ezbon Mondiri. However, in the later years, some prominent members of the party left to join the Anyanya rebellion in the bush when their efforts to work from within were systematically sabotaged. Example of those would be Gordon Muortat and Ezbon Mondiri.

The Collapse of General Abboud Regime

By now, the Anyanya is numbered in thousands strong combatants. They were carrying major raids, capturing more automatic weapons, and generally making their presence in the South felt. More significantly, Anyanya unit from Bahr el-Ghazal led by Captain Bernardino Mou Mou made a daring attempt to capture war. The result of the attack was devastating for the Anyanya as they were beat back, several killed, and many including Mou were captured. This, however, demonstrate to Khartoum and the outside world that the Anyanya movement was a serious threat. The whole event was widely publicized. The strength of Anyanya could not be ignored anymore. One historian notes that the effectiveness of Anyanya could best be "measured by the embittered Sudanese army officers serving in the South who staged a short-lived mutiny" in 1965, in Juba protesting lack of effective equipment and incompetent senior officers.[210]

From the perspective of the Northerner Sudanese public opinion, the failure of Abboud government to crush the Anyanya militarily brought into question Abboud's ability to rule, especially the ability of military rule. Abboud could not ignore such strong public opinion. In an attempt to find solutions in resolving the situation in the south, Abboud regime permitted public discussions among the Northerner Sudanese on issues affecting the South Sudan. Such was a miscalculated move, which inadvertently drew hostility, especially from the university students toward Abboud's government. The student union from the University of Khartoum met in October of 1964, and resolved that as long as the military regime is in power, the Southern Problems would not be resolved. The students intensified their opposition against the government, and suddenly, feeling the heat, the government revised its decision and banned all public discussions on Southern Problems. The government action to ban public discussions, however, never stopped the students resolved to storm the streets. Even in a larger numbers, the students poured on the streets of Khartoum. There, they were joined by their faculty members, and together, they managed to paralyze the businesses in the city. As a result, few were wounded others were killed in their confrontations with the police force, but as the numbers of the students on the streets surged, they were soon joined by a political umbrella group calling themselves National Front of Professionals who included teachers, engineers, lawyers, and doctors. Soon, they were calling for a general strike that would include virtually all sections of the Sudan political societies. The military intervened to maintain order in the capital Khartoum, but even the military discovered that it was divided. It immediately became obvious and interesting that the military could not save the military regime.

Therefore, the solution was for the military brass to convince Abboud that his time was up, and the military must once again become a real military by returning to the barracks, where the military rightly belong. Convinced, Abboud dissolved the Supreme Council, an act that sent jubilation and ululation on the streets full of cheering crowds. This act was to follow with intense negotiation that resulted into setting up of a Transitional Government where Abboud was its lame duck president. By November of 1964, Abboud left the palace after successfully securing himself generous pensions and obtaining permission for his son to stay in Great Britain. He left the government in the hands of a Transitional Government under the five-man commission and Sirr al-Khatim al-Khalifa as the Prime Minister. An enthusiastic beginning of Abboud's regime which took power military showed its way out reluctantly through the pressure of civilian streets demonstrations, largely due to the Southern Problems. If Abboud came to power with a notion that he was going to resolve the Southern Problems once and for all, especially applying military discipline as a measure, then he miserably failed. And that would have served a better and bitter lesson for his successors in Khartoum.

In the ensuing mess plus the changed of power from military into civilian, William Deng, on behalf of his splitter group of SANU, wrote a letter to the Transitional Government, right after its formation, demanding a political negotiation among Sudanese political parties on resolving the issues affecting South Sudan. To implicate the matter even more, by December 6th, 1964, Clement Mboro, the first South Sudanese who has ever been given the highest post of minister of interior was due in Khartoum from a tour in the south. But for some apparent reasons, his arrival to Khartoum was delayed. Soon, rumors spread and tempers flared among the enthusiastic Southern Sudanese supporters who were waiting to welcome and receive Clement Mboro at the airport. As a result, the

Southerners took to the streets of Khartoum causing huge destructions with a highest death toll of over a hundred people dead. Many Southern Sudanese were shackled and in chains thrown into jails. Ezbon Mondiri, who was then the minister for communication and transportation, helped to facilitate the shipping of many Southern Sudanese from Khartoum into the South, where most of them were very compelled to join the people of the bush.

This incident also compelled the Transitional Government of al-Khalifa to make an attempt in addressing the Southern Problems in a more serious way—through what was going to be known as the *Round Table Conference of 1965*. Therefore, the Prime Minister, al-Khalifa, could not ignore the Southern Problems anymore. On December 10th, 1964, he finally responded to William Deng's letter by guaranteeing amnesty to any Southerner who left Sudan after 1955. The Prime Minister also dispatched a delegation for Uganda to negotiate the return of thousands of the refugees including the SANU officials. However, the SANU officials in Kampala rejected any political negotiation that would take place inside Sudan. They hinted that they will be willing to participate if such a negotiation would take place in a neutral ground. The Father was the first to show pessimism on any positive prospects on a political negotiation with the northern political parties. He wrote to the East African Standard a long article warning, "if the political parties of the North do not take to heart in a more realistic manner the Southern Problems, the perspectives of reaching a positive final solution in a democratic way are extremely remote, if not impossible."[211]

However, not all Southern politicians were as pessimistic on the prospects of political negations with the Northern political parties as the Father was. The Father went ahead and warned them by dismissing this seemingly convincing ploy on a political negotiation. Through his analytic insight, the Father prophesized, "for us to be under a Communist Government led by the Arabs or to remain subject to the North under any other form of Government does not spell any difference. What happens in the Sudan today is nothing other than the North changing of tactics in order to remain in the South."[212] The Father prophecy was to be proven right. Nonetheless, some Southerners neglected all the signals and ignored all the warnings by moving ahead with arrangement to convene a political negotiation with the Northern political parties in Khartoum.

The Round Table Conference

In the preparation for the Round Table Conference, William Deng with eight others who claimed to be representing SANU departed for Khartoum on February of 1965, a move that Southern politicians in exile considered a desertion and a betrayal to the cause of South Sudan. As such, the SANU in Kampala needed nothing than a little convincing to join the Round Table Conference since William Deng already claimed to be representing SANU. A delegation of Southern Front party members who already made unsuccessful several trips to Kampala was finally able to successfully convince members of SANU in Kampala to participate in the Round Table Conference. Their response was more of an attempt to maintain their entity, since William Deng already usurped the party and threatened to have transferred it to Khartoum. In such, the members of SANU quickly resolved their rivalries in Kampala and picked a unified exiled delegation for the conference, which included Aggrey Jaden, the president of SANU. The Father was not enthused by any of these maneuvers. Instead, the Father was frustrated. In an effort to convince the Father, a delegation of Southern Front headed by Abel Alier tracked the Father down and eventually caught up with him while he was in Nairobi. They briefed the Father on the internal political situation and changes, which have just taken place in Sudan. In response, the Father gave them a long historical lecture on why the Northern Sudanese Arabs should not be trusted with any agreement and why it was not worthy to pursue any political negotiation with them, especially in Khartoum. The Father specifically emphasized on how the Northern Sudanese Arabs don't honor agreements, interestingly to someone like Abel Alier who will take almost three decades later to write a book with a thesis of *South Sudan: Too Many Agreements Dishonoured*.[213] The Father pessimistically concluded by expressing great deal of doubt on the safety of Southern Sudanese political leaders and refugees who may opt to return to Sudan.[214] He went on to warn, "we are entering the most difficult period of our struggle. With the introduction into Sudan of a false appearance of democracy, the Southerners who are weak and thinking only about themselves are tempted to surrender."[215] The Father then added, "there are many roads to find freedom. Ours seems to be the most difficult. Therefore we must accept this reality and do only what we can."[216]

At any rate, the convening of the conference seemed to be gaining momentum and the preparations went ahead as it was decided that the conference would take place on March 16, 1965 and to last until March 30th of the same year. Even though the Southerners who participated in this conference claimed to be representing Southern interest, from the onset, lack of solidarity among them crippled any positive outcome of this conference. There were four political parties representing South Sudan. There was the two factions of SANU one headed by William Deng, representing those from inside and another headed by Aggrey Jaden representing those in exile. There was also the Southern Front party which its members are educated professionals working inside Sudan. And the Arabs added two spoiler parties to even divide the Southerners more. Those were Sudan Unity Party (SUP) and the Free Southern Front (FSF), which were unified under the coalition of *Other Shades of Opinion*. In total, there were about twenty-seven Southern Sudanese represented in the conference compared to only eighteen Northerners. In the North, all the major political parties participated. They included, Sudan Communist Party (SCP), the National Unionist Party (NUP), the Umma Party, Peoples' Democratic Party (PDP), the Islamic Charter Front (ICF) and the Professionals' Front. In addition, there were foreign observers from Uganda, Kenya, Nigeria, Tanzania, Algeria, Egypt, and Ghana.

The opening speech for the conference by the Prime Minister al-Khalifa was conciliatory in tone, showing a little bit of seriousness from the transitional government. The speech states, "there is complete and absolute agreement between all sincere Sudanese whether they come from the North or the South, or from the East or the West—as to the necessity of hard and consistent work for the advancement of this country and for the happiness of all the Sudanese people irrespective of their differences in religious belief, tribal dialects or racial origins."[217] The speech goes on to blame the Problems of Southern Sudan on "an organized part of an evil policy which was evolved by the imperialists for the purpose of destroying all human cultural and economic links between Northern and Southern Sudanese."[218] It also acknowledges the weaknesses of the previous Northern governments in failing to resolve the issues of South Sudan.

Luckily enough, the Southern Front and the SANU in exile agreed on all their positions. The spoiler parties of Sudan Unity Party (SUP) and the Free Southern Front (FSF) disappointed their Northern masters by having no positions of their own other than the ones of the Southern Front and the SANU. Therefore, they were kicked out of the conference. One of the members is quoted as he conceded, "I am now just considered as a Northerner, because I have been chosen by the North. But I have to go to the South."1 m[219] The Southern Front and the SANU in exile demanded among other things a plebiscite on federation, union, or independence. They also demanded that the South must have a full control of its finance, foreign affairs, and military. While the SANU inside demanded a united federation of Sudan among other things. The Northerners rejected outright separation, however, they did agree on a regional government where the power resides in the central government to conduct foreign affairs, control the armed forces, regulate taxes, and maintain natural resources. After intense days of disagreements, the parties reached a deadlocked; therefore, the conference had to be abruptly terminated. To impress the foreign observers, they resolved that a twelve-man committee should be selected to follow up with the negotiations. They selected a twelve-man committee which included six from the North and six from the South. They purposely excluded the SANU in exile from participating in the twelve-man committee despite the fact that the Southern Front pleaded for their inclusion. This is partly because Aggey Jaden, the president of SANU in exile had actually left the conference abruptly on noticing that the demand for separation was not forthcoming.

For the next several months the twelve-man committee deliberated, but the deliberations were single-handedly sabotaged by Hassan al-Turabi who used his persuasive powers, legal skills, and voting power within the twelve-man-committee—the attributes that seemed to match none of the Southerners in the committee.[220] On the issue of security Andrew Riang Wieu of SANU inside, suggested that the committee condemned the violent activities of both Anyanya and that of the government armed forces. Lubari Ramba of Southern Front defended the military activities of Anyanya as "nothing but a group of men who have resorted to arms when all other means have failed."[221] In response, al-Turabi said that the committee cannot condemn the Sudanese armed forces as they are acting to defend the integrity of the country. His view was supported by the Northerners who labeled Anyanya as "terrorists."[222] On discussing the principles of self determination, members are asked to submit proposals within the term of reference where the power resides with the central government and autonomy to the regional government of the South. Abel Alier of Southern Front presented a proposal and al-Turabi countered it with one of his own. They then, both dismissed each others' proposals as not meeting the requirements of the terms of reference. In the case of al-Turabi's proposal, Alier argued that it supported the maintenance of status quo while al-Turabi counter argued that Alier's proposal called for separation of the South. In the end both proposals were rejected on the grounds that Alier's proposal indeed supported separation and al-Turabi's one did not only maintain status quo but took powers away from the South. Both were asked to rewrite their proposals for further consideration. The shrewd and intelligent al-Turabi responded by declaring that he supported the proposal of National Unionists Party (NUP), therefore, no need to rewrite one again. As for Alier, he failed to rewrite his proposal as he could not beat the dateline for submission. Just another prove of al-Turabi's effort to frustrate the process of the negotiation for the Southern Sudanese. In the end, the Round Table Conference and everything that was associated with it, was turned out to be a sham that did not worth any effort to start with. The ploy failed completely, the fact that proved Northerners uncompromising nature, incompetence of the Southerners who participated in the conference, and the hostility of the Khartoum government toward the South.[223] In retrospect, the failure of the Round Table Conference confirmed Southern determination to rather resolve the Southern Problems through military option as oppose to negotiations.

The Father on the Tour Abroad

As all these things were happening, the Father was busy as usual touring the world, especially the European world pleading for Southern cause. In those tours, the method the Father presented the cause of Southern Sudan and the ideas he presented were as relevant then as they are today, or they will continue to be relevant so long the South continues to exist. The Father was very realistic assuring the donors and those who sympathize with the cause of South Sudan that the people of South Sudan "know very well that the major responsibility for the emancipation of the Southern Sudan lies with" the South Sudanese.[224] Such realistic view was in the heart of Father's conviction in his dependence on military force as a resolved and in the unification of Southerners for one cause. He was to say, "it is my personally conviction that the solution now lies in the interior of the Sudan and not in political decision taken abroad."[225] The most powerful statement by the Father along this line showing his determination for the struggle for the cause of South Sudan is when he stated, "on our part, neither the external pressure nor the divergences among the Southerners will change our attitude, as we prefer to die fighting rather than to serve the Arabs of the Sudan or the international community policy."[226]

In warning the world, especially the Christian world, with respect to the Khartoum government intentions of spreading and imposing Islamism and Arabism into the Southern Sudan, the Father stated, "it is well known that the policy of the Sudanese government to eradicate Christianity in the South has a double objective: one immediate and one long-term."[227] The Father went on to explain those plans as he understood them:

> The complete destruction of the Church in the shortest possible time is the immediate objective. To carry it out, all

means are put to work, from intimidation and torture to massacre. This was determined years ago by the creators of the policy. It succeeded in presenting to the external World its policy of duplicity. It denies that there is persecution, proclaiming the existence of utmost freedom of religion for all the citizens, feigning to grant concessions and to accept the mediation tactic. But in reality they have no intention of reversing their decision. What the Sudanese government needs is time to implement its object...[228]

For the long-term intentions of the Khartoum government, the Father had this to say:

Its second objective is that the Southern Sudan, once Islamized and Arabized, would at last become springboard for Islamizing the whole of Black Africa south of the Equator. This policy is backed by the whole Islamic World. The efforts made by the Sudanese government to carry out this policy have cause the loss of thousands of human lives and exodus of more than 100,000 refugees who have fled from Southern Sudan to other African states: Uganda, Kenya, the Congo, Central African Republic and Ethiopia. Whole villages have been reduced to ashes by the Arab soldiers in retaliation. The survivors had to settle in distant places where they suffer from lack of everything.[229]

The Father went further by substantiating these explanations with some of the statements the Northern Arab politicians were making both secretly and publicly. One such statement was made by Ali Abdel

Rahman, a graduate of Cairo Islamic University and Minister of Interior. The Father said, Rahman was reported to have said, "Sudan is an integral part of the Arab world and as such must accept the leadership of the two Islamic religious leaders of Sudan; anybody dissenting from this view must quit the country."[230] Of course, most of these plans and intentions for Arabization and Islamization were not made in secret rooms. In the Father's words, "the Arabs became more daring" with their approach and determination in sending their message across.[231] For example, one of the Northern political parties, the Democratic Unionist Party (DUP) to be exact, released its political declaration, which states:

> It is our top priority to speed up the spread of the Arabic language throughout the South and in the Nuba Mountains. In this era of modern national identities the importance of language as a means of consolidating the Arab and Islamic culture is obvious. We regard the spread of Arabic in these areas as part of Jihad (wholly war) for the sake of Allah and Arab nationalism. Our policies toward the South thus outlined must be followed very soon by similar ones towards the Nuba Mountains and Darfur.[232]

The Repressive Northern Arabs Regime

One cannot understand these statements in isolation without understanding the full background of the situation that the Father was referring to. By then, in early 1960s, the government of General Abboud was already waging a complete war of destructions against the Southern Sudanese and Christian Missionaries. According to the government, anything that was wrong in the country, including the problems of Southern Sudan, was the fault of the Christian missionaries. Therefore, missionaries were as much legitimate of targets as the Southern Sudanese were. Sunday as a day of rest for the Southerners was abolished instead Friday was observed as a day of rest partly because majority of the officials in South were Northern Arab Muslims. Missionary schools were taken over by the government. Islamic schools were built throughout the South. In places where there are schools closer to the Christian missions, the schools have to be transferred far away to avoid the Christian influence. Arabic language replaced English in Southern Sudanese schools. Islamization was put into a full motion. All the missionaries were expelled from the South Sudan. The government organize meeting under the ministry of interior with the remaining indigenous church officials and requested that the churches should be nationalized in similar manners it was done in China. The government insisted that it was willing to help the church with nationalization effort. Places of worship were burnt down. Many good Christians were killed, imprisoned or intimidated to the point that they leave the country. Worse, the Church officials were address as "Dogs of the Sudan Church."[233] Writing for the Dakar, newspaper, *Afrique Nouvelle*, a Southern Sudanese priest testified:

> I have spent five years in prison. I was arrest in 1960 under the military government of Abboud and sentenced into twelve years imprisonment. This term was reduced to five. I was released in January 1965. Compelled to leave the Southern Sudan, we followed our Christians who had fled the country because of the atrocities perpetrate in the South by the government troops.[234]

Torture and inhumane treatment for those held prisoners was rampant. Recounting on those ordeals reveals despicable acts such as the following encounter of Chief Stephen Thongkol Anyijong of the Atwot:

> I stayed jailed for about two years. I just lay there. I did not bathe. I had no clothes to change. And I lay on the floor. It was…a house full of insects, dead insects, and all kinds of dead things… My cell was the place into which people were brought when they died. When bodies rotted, they were taken to be thrown wherever they were thrown. Another man would be killed the following day and would be brought into my cell… They beat me and beat me. Hot red pepper was put into my eyes. I said, "Why don't you shoot me, kill me and get it over with? Why do you subject me to this slow death?" They said, "You have to talk." I said, "What do you want me to say?" They said, "You have to say that this idea of the South wanting to be a separate country is something you do not believe in and that you will never support it….You have to swear to that…You will not be left alone until you swear by both the Bible and the [Sacred] Spear. "I said, "How can I swear when the whole South is angry? When so many southerners are in jail? How can I swear that the South will not be separate when this is what everybody wants? This cannot be.[235]

After his release from the prison, Chief Anyijong had no option but to join the people of the bush, the Anyanya rebellion. However, his joining Anyanya never helped things for him and for his family either. It actual gotten worse as he explains:

Because of my going to the forest,…they destroyed my things…in a way that never happens. If you were to know about them you would cry with tears. First of all, they took my small child who had only a common cold. When they heard he was the son of a rebel, they killed the child…I suffered through that. They came and took 28 goats and sheep from my place. Then they went looking for my other home. They took eighty sheep and goats and burned the village. Then they…went to my cattle camp and took one hundred cows and three girls…My wives went and built another home at a distant place… They came and broke down the home…They caught my little girl and took her away. The women they threw into…a big fire. You know those big Dinka huts that are raised on high platform. They put fire under the hut. The hut was turned into an oven in which the women burned.[236]

The violence toward the innocent Southerners was only intensifying, because these repressions, torture, and inhumane treatments were to follow with more rigorous act of violence toward the Southern Sudanese with the coming of Muhammad Ahmad Mahgoub as a civilian Prime Minister in mid 1960s. Mahgoub was an epitome of what the Sudanese Arabs could be, sort of a perfect representation of a Sudanese Arab. In the words of one author, Mahgoub is "personification of Northern Arab Sudanese conservatism."[237] An accomplished poet, and a qualify lawyer and architect, Mahgoub spoke and write Arabic language with such perfection in grammar and fluency. He poetically depicted how he cherished the glorious past of Islam and Arabic culture and its impact in the civilization of the world and how all that would be translated into the glorious future and changing the world. His love for the Arab World was so ever conspicuous. At one point acting as Arab delegation spokesman in introducing a draft resolution of the situation in the Middle East, Mahgoub declared, "I am not speaking...in the name of the delegation of the Sudan...It is my honor and privilege to speak in the name of all...the ten Arab states which are related not only by a common language or a common heritage of history and culture, but also by blood."[238] Of course no one would doubt Mahgoub Arabness even though he was a black Arab like all his Sudanese Arab causins who are blacks. His problem was that the African leaders have no trust in him for acting too much of an Arab than the Arabs themselves.

Through his literary skills, he played a pivotal role in the independence movement where upon independence; he became the first ever Sudanese foreign minister. An epitome of the Northern Sudanese Arab that Mahgoub was, he was widely admired in the North and described as "democrat, in temperament, style of government, as well as in his private life."[239] Of course, the man enjoyed such flatteries very much. He lived under illusion that he was an indispensable leader. However, when it came to Southern Sudan, Mahgoub was a real monster. He considered the issue of Southern Sudan as a matter of law and order while he viewed the Anyanya movement as "the terrorist gangs which abuse security."[240] He came to power convinced that the "only language the Southerners understand is force."[241] He never delayed in implementation of his policies. His first order of business "...to the Army were to destroy rebel camps and hunt the rebels."[242] The Northern media came into his support. For Example, the Al-Ayam newspaper launched a series of articles criticizing the Transitional Government of Prime Minister Sirr al-Khatim al-Khalifa for being soft on the Southern Sudanese. The paper also launched serious attacks against the Northern political parties who participated in the Round Table Conference of 1965, as those parties were viewed to have been supportive of the Southern cause.[243]

Enjoying these flatteries and high public support from his Northern Sudanese supporters, Mahgoub wasted no time. He went on to unleashing a full use of force against the innocent Southern Sudanese civilians. Just in one night in Juba of July 8th, 1965, the Khartoum soldiers went on rampage killings. They burned down the civilian quarters. In the morning, a total count for the dead was reported at 2,000 including 6,00 lepers and the sick who could not escape the ensuing massacre. They were short on their beds and others born while laying on their beds. The corpses were dumped along the Juba-Yei road. They were burned including those who were still alive, but hanging for their lives. Two days later in Wau, the soldiers hatched similar plan, but this time around the target was a wedding celebration at a house of a famous and well respected Chief Cyer Rihan. There, they opened fire, killing the guest most of whom were Southern Sudanese intellectuals. Unlike the corpses in Juba, these ones, three trucks loaded, were dumped in the river, also limiting the hope and chances of those who might be still alive. Communication and travel were restricted within the Southern Sudanese towns. The massacre continued onto places like Rumbek and Tonj were two of Father's colleagues, Fr. Ali Archangel and Fr. Deng Barnaba were massacred in cold blood killings.[244] The brutality toward the Southern Sudanese civilians was incomprehensible as it spread throughout the entire South Sudan in both rural and urban centers. At the time, the government policy toward the Southern Sudanese was such as follows:

> The Government declared that it would henceforth authorize the army and other security forces in the South to do whatever they saw fit for the maintenance of law and

order in the South. This meant in practice that if the southern guerilla army attacked a town, all the Southerners within it were suspects and could be killed for not reporting the presence of the rebels. If the army went outside the town for patrol and were ambushed by the guerillas, all the villagers in the surrounding areas were condemned to death and their villages burned down.[245]

In all, it was estimated that the number of the Southern Sudanese who were massacred by the Khartoum armed forces from 1963 through 1966 was more than half a million.[246] SANU in exile pleaded for the United Nation (UN) intervention so as to protect the Southern Sudanese civilians. However, the plea was met with neglect. The Southern Front sent in an investigation team from Khartoum to the affected areas in the South Sudan. Those investigators were harassed and beaten while they try to conduct their investigation. Their investigative report which was sent to Organization of African Unity (OAU) and the head of states of sympathetic African countries were equally ignored. The *Vigilant*, the only Southern Sudanese newspaper in Khartoum ran reports into some of these atrocities, but it was ordered to close and its editor was ordered to be prosecuted.[247] In away, the Southern Sudanese were left to the mercy of the ruthless Khartoum armed forces and repressive regime in Khartoum.

This policy of massacring the urban settlers was complemented with the inauguration of "peace villages," the internally displaced camp designated for rural population. The rural populations were forcefully removed from their respective villages and herded into peace villages erected in the surroundings of big towns. The peace villages were not actually peaceful as its name suggested. The camps were congested and diseases were rampant, killing people in hundreds. There was hardly any service provided, whether it was medical or education. The food was insufficient and malnutrition took its significant toll, especially on the little ones. There was no clean water in the camps. According to historian Robert Collins, "the IDPs were literally held hostage in return for information as to the whereabouts of the Anyanya."[248] Even worse than the peace village, the government organized militias to exploit the old history of ethnic rivalries, differences and conflicts to the disadvantage of the Anyanya rebels and civilians. Government organized militia became one of the most effective and potent tools that the Khartoum government will continue to use against the Southern Sudanese resistant movements to this day.

In response, the Southern Sudanese took on their feet, fleeing by thousands to safety in neighboring countries to languish there as refugees, a phenomenon that is too well familiar to the Southern Sudanese even today. Some of the educated Southern Sudanese, those in the Khartoum army, police, prison warders, and game wardens were compelled to join Anyanya movement and with strong resolve and determination to resist oppression. This policy of repression inadvertently created more enemies for Khartoum, strengthened the Southern Sudanese cause, and increased the Anyanya recruitment pool. Such harsh policy and treatment of the Southern Sudanese was the background on which the Father was speaking on. This was a clear policy, strategically designed with intentional aim of systematically destroying the African identity through Arabization, replacing Christianity by means of Islamization, and a policy of silencing and wiping out populations with the repressive use of force. It is a policy applied by successive regimes in Khartoum, both military and civilians who are either elected or otherwise. And it is the policy that is still in place to this day. From Khartoum's perspective, the state of emergency that was declared in the South Sudan during the Torit Mutiny of 1955, is still in full force today. And from the Southern Sudanese perspective and life experience, they are used to living under heightened state of insecurity and fear due to the state of emergency imposed in the South Sudan by Khartoum government since 1955.

The Father on Offense

In his part, the Father was a keen intelligent observer who understood too well not just the political strategy but the military strategies and tactics of the Khartoum government. At one point, the Father revealed to the world that the Sudanese minister for defense "went to West Germany to beg arms, cars, lorries, planes to smash the South."[249] The Father went as far as confirming that the lorries given by West Germany had actually arrived in Sudan. He accused the West Germany in participating for the genocide of Southern Sudanese and for supporting a reckless government in Khartoum. He also blamed other countries, both the West and the East for ignoring the plights of the South Sudanese people. He said, "the African of South Sudan are not so lucky" as their plights are considered internal affair that does not deserve international attention or intervention.[250] He also disclosed that Nasr Hassan, the minister for defense was quoted in public saying, "poor we have found the South and poor we shall leave it."[251]

The Father approached and tackled the situation of South Sudan from every angel imaginable and did not seem to spare any possible actor or player in Sudanese affairs. A missionary bishop wrote to the Father saying for South Sudanese "to raise too loud a voice means getting the worst. Instead if we discuss openly and ask for comprehension, we easily get a compromise."[252] This is pleading to someone who not only knew the Arabs too well but tried in many occasions to work peacefully with them.

In his response, the Father begged to differ sharply with the missionary bishop. He wrote:

> The worst that can happen to your congregation in the South is to lose the confidence of the people in general and of the upper class in particular. To admit with me that the peace tactics followed up to now by the Church in Sudan did not bear good results; but rather the opposite: the Arabs became more daring. They reached their objectives: the systematic destruction of the Church with the new anti-missionary law. The blacks of the South, on the other hand (I refer to a common feeling as expressed by intellectuals of the South, Catholic and Protestants alike), have the impression that the missionary societies in the South are more interested in saving their presence in Sudan than in any other thing.[253]

The irony of expulsion of Christian Missionaries from Sudan was that the missionaries, especially the Catholics who were in the North were left to continue with their activities mostly of running schools. To make this even more interesting there were no Christians in the north to minister to. And second of all, there was no potential population in the North to convert from. Even though the missionaries were in a way supporting the Southern Sudanese liberation movement, there actions and dealing with the Northerners could also be construed as appeasing the Northern Sudanese. And this was what the Father was alluding to in his response to a missionary bishop who seemed to take an appeasing tone toward the Northern Sudanese government as he expressed it in his plea to the Father.

However, the Father's response to this missionary bishop was actually in a broader sense of Christians as whole. It was neither the only time the

Father addressed the negligence of the Christians of South Sudan nor was it the first time he was speaking on behalf of all Christians, Protestants included, given that he was a Catholic priest. He had criticized some of the Christian countries for their cooperation with the Khartoum government. The Father said, "Christianity has disappeared from North Africa" and then he asked, "will it also disappear from Central Africa?"[254] He said the answer will pretty much depend on the Christian world. And for those who could listen, he plead, "if the Christian world will not show sympathy with the persecuted Church in the Sudan, our Christians will reach the false conclusion that Christianity sides with those that are powerful and not with those who are persecuted for the reign of Christ."[255] This was a clear challenge to the core of Christian's belief. He then predicted, "this conclusion would be more dangerous to the Church than the threat of the Islamic religion itself."[256] With those Protestants who constantly accused him of trying to handover the South to the Catholic Church in Rome, he assured them even more, "if they did not help us from Rome, we shall turn communist."[257] This was not in away an endorsement of communism, but to show that the plight for the Southern cause is too greater than one religion denomination and Rome was not the only place the South can turn to for assistance. Any help the Southerners will get would certainly be appreciated. The Father understood the problem of the South as "not political in the usual meaning of the term, as it is for one of the satellite states of the communist world."[258] The problem, according to him is rather "something greater: actually it is the question of life or death, of racial slavery."[259]

The Father Is Gone

By late 1966 while in Entebbe, the Father was to say, in what seems to be his premonition, "we are now crossing a decisive moment. We don't want to give up. The Arabs also don't want to give up."[260] From there he got into the plane and took off for abroad. On his way back while in Nairobi, the Father was informed of Ugandan plan to seal the borders and intercept the Anyanya and Southern Sudanese refugees who would be crossing the borders. Ugandan troops were being deployed in the borders, more specifically, the troop that was in Jinja was ordered to move to Ugandan border on January 15, of 1967.[261] While n the borders, the Ugandan soldier mangled freely with the Khartoum government troops. The Father quickly rushed to the border so as he could cross and go inform the Southern Sudanese people of this plan. What happened next is an account of an eye witness:

> On the evening of January 21, he was hungry and tired. That Saturday he had already cycled eighty kilometers. Nevertheless, accompanied by two friends, he walked to the border forty kilometers from Kitgum. On reaching Padibe (sixteen miles beyond Kitgum) they learned that Ugandan troops controlled the border. They then detoured toward Lokung which they reached at one a.m. The rested until seven a.m. 'I keep on going,' said Fr. Saturnino. 'I must reenter Sudan.' His companions told him that it was dangerous to cross the border at that moment. They said they were ready to go before him into Sudan to inform the people of what was happening. He retorted that he thought it cowardice to stay in a safe place while they risked their lives. They asked young students who lived nearby to find out whether the path on which they were to travel was safe to pass. Fr. Saturnino and the other two remained on the road waiting. The Father took his camera for some photos.

Suddenly, the silence was broken by gunshots. On the border, some few hundred meters from them, the Ugandan soldiers were firing at some refugees: three dead and many wounded. As they listened in order to make out the meaning of the shouts that came with the shots, they noticed that behind them a platoon of Ugandan soldiers was coming from Lokung to the border. When they saw them, it was too late. Their officer gave the halt signal and ordered the three to drop what they had in their hands and to advance toward him with raised hands. They obeyed. He searched them and took away from the Father his watch and the little money they had. 'you are spies,' he said. A Nubian soldier came forward. He seemed to know the Father and called him by name. Father on his part answered by saying that he knew the soldier. They exchanged some words in Arabic, then the soldier said to his officer that he was a priest involved in politics. Among the papers found in Fr. Saturnino's pocket there was also a letter with his name and personal data. 'So!' commented the officer, 'you are ruining the people!' He commanded Fr. Satunino and the other two to carry the luggage of the soldiers on their shoulders. They walked for some hours. The order to stop was given at noon. The officer began to interrogate the prisoners. He asked the Father whether he was going to celebrate mass. Where? At that late hour? From where was he coming? The officer interrogated the other two. Then the Father again. At that moment, the young man sent ahead came back. At once he was stopped. He answered that he was a student and that for three days he had been on holiday in the district. 'You are spies sent by the

Anyanya to control the movements of the Ugandan troops,' said the officer. He sent the prisoner some distance off and spoke with those chosen to accompany the prisoners to the police station in Lokung. At 2:00 p.m. on Sunday, January 22. They set out for Lokung. They returned to the spot where they had left their bicycles and their belongings. The corporal examined Father's bag. He found his passport (a Congolese one) and looked closely at it. There was also some money. He tied the bag to the bicycle and ordered the Father to push it. Fr. Saturnino and his friends, really tired, kept on going. At a certain point, they fell to the ground. The soldiers gave each three lashes. The corporal kicked the Father on the head, and one of his friends did the same. Then they marched on. Later on, the small group stopped again. The corporal sat drinking beer and, then stood up and struck Fr, Saturnno's head three times. Then they resumed their journey to Lokung. Meanwhile, the two soldiers began to discuss between themselves in Acholi about the place where to kill one of the four. But the prisoners understood Acholi, and they tried with their eyes and half words to exchange some of their views. Fr. Saturnino said that it was necessary to get rid of the guards. The others replied that it was better to wait: once they reached the police station at Lokung, they would undoubtedly be set free. After all, they had done nothing wrong. They reached Alebi torrent, a mile from Lokung. The four were ordered to sit near one another facing the water. Fr. Satunino understood that it was the end. In fact, the corporal was going back a few steps so as to aim and kill the prisoners all together. Luckily, he was rather drunk, and he could not find the right position. The other soldier, by himself, was holding the bicycles. The Father hinted to the others that it was necessary to take hold of the two before the corporal could open fire. He jumped to his feet and followed by another prisoner, hurled himself on the nearest soldier, throwing him to the ground. But the soldier easily got free of the Father. Then he caught his gun and fired at his head, killing him. The second prisoner then ran into the high grass and disappeared. The other two prisoners had already escaped. It was a local Christian who, having heard of the murder went to that place the following day and found the body of Fr. Saturnino. He ran to inform the missionary of the station of Padibe and the police. The Fathers carried the body to Kitgum so that the superior of the mission could identify it and bury it. The Sisters of Kitgum tried in vain to dress him in a cassock; he was too deformed. They placed it over him. In a short time they prepared a coffin, and they nailed on it a great crucifix.[262]

That was the tragic ending for the Father. It had not been easy for him. He started it with a harsh experience and he ended harshly by facing a courageous death. He could have become the first ever bishop of Juba, but that was not as appealing as fighting along side his people of the South Sudan. While in Uganda he could have easily enjoyed the city life and employ his skills for other works there, which could be done in the city, but yet he chose the suffering of walking, cycling, and facing dangers of crossing the borders, traveling to unknown places and terrains, and facing the Arabs in the frontline. The other alternatives would have been for him to stay in Nairob,

Kinshasa or Rome but those options never seemed appealing for him. He instead risked it all by putting his very live on the line. A remark in his eulogy states, "he has been delivered to the God in untimely fashion through the wickedness of the world he talked of."[263] All the remarks that he used to say seemed to have come true. It seems he was making a premonition about his life when he said people of the South rather died fighting than serving the Arabs or the interest of the International community. He is among those Southerners who die fighting. He used to always say that the South can be saved by the sacrifice of the best of its sons. Indeed he is among the best of those sons of the South who sacrifice with their lives.

Joseph Oduho

As for the colleagues of the Father, Joseph Oduho and Aggrey Jaden, they ended up combining SANU under AFL where Oduho was the president and Jaden the vice president. Later on, Oduho dismissed Jaden on hearing the allegation that Jaden met with William Deng without informing him. AFL party disappeared in oblivion after Oduho moved inside South Sudan and trying to establish his base along the Imatong mountain ranges, in Dito. When the Addis Ababa Peace Agreement was signed, Oduho went on to serve in the autonomies regional government of Southern Sudan in various ministerial capacities. He later joined the Sudan People Liberation Movement/Army (SPLM/A) where he was made the chairman of SPLM. However, he was detained by Dr. John Garang who ended up taking both the SPLM and SPLA, consolidating both entities under his control. Joseph Oduho was eventually killed on March 27, 1993, in Kongor, Southern Sudan as he was participating in a conference that was trying to unite the SPLA splitter groups. In his case, his killers were Southerners. This is evidence proving that Southern

Sudanese political rivalry had never ended since the Anyanya times and have even grew deadlier.

Aggrey Jaden

For Jaden, after being dismissed from Oduho's AFL party, he was encouraged by others to form another party of his own. He went on to form a party called Home Front, which he later changed to the Southern Provisional Government (SSPG). He organized a convention in Angurdiri, Southern Sudan, which successfully attracted both Southern politicians and soldiers, where they able to form an inclusive Southern political party that reflects on the different nationalities and ethnicities of the South. At first, the party seemed to be operating effectively but it later suffered from desertions. The Bahr al-Ghazal and Upper Nile people objected the fact that SSPG was dominated by the Equatorians. And even worse, the Western Equatorians withdrew on their insistence of not acknowledging Emedeo Tafeng, who is a Lotuko from Eastern Equatoria, as the Cammander-in-chief of SSPG. By 1968, SSPG was left to the central Equatorians. Without any explanation, Jaden left for Nairobi. Depressed and frustrated, he could not listen for any pleas to bring him back and that marked an end to SSPG.

To fill the Vacuum Jaden left, another national convention was convened by Kamilo Dhol, a Dinka from Aweil who was Jaden deputy. The resolution of the convention resulted into the creation of Nile Provisional Government (NPG) with Gordon Muortat as its elected president. This time it was the Dinka who dominated the NPG, as such the Equatorians defected. Emedio Tafeng went on to found Anyidi Provisional Government (APG). By 1971, all the various groups including Sue Republic of Samuel Abu John were dissolved, and they came under Joseph Lagu's command and leadership. Lagu renamed the

Anya-Nya National Armed Force the Southern Sudan Liberation Movement (SSLM).

After the Addis Ababa Agreement signed in 1972, Jaden was convinced to come to Sudan. When he came back, he went to his people and declared that he brought back his bones to be buried home. It seemed that on his coming back to Sudan, he was not interested for anything other than to lay to rest. He led a poor life and miserably died shortly after. As poor that he was, Jaden ended up dying at a local hospital in Khartoum at a common people's ward. It was only after his death that the both the central government in Khartoum and regional government of Juba recognized him as one of the significant figures while completely ignored him when he was alive, wandering on his own.

William Deng

As for William Deng, he continued with his political activities from within. In several elections that he participated in, his SANU were out competed by the northern political parties in the South, his supposedly stronghold. For example, in a by-election of March 1967, to fill the thirty-six vacant for South Sudan, the Umma party captured fifteen seats, SANU only captured ten seats, and National Unionist Party (NUP) gained five seats, while the remaining seats were divided among the Sudan Unity Party and Liberal Party plus few independents. Part of the reason SANU inside was not successful in netting votes in the South was because the Northern Sudanese Arabs controlled the Southern Sudanese towns where elections were held, and the countryside was virtually controlled by the Anyanya where it made it impossible to conduct elections. Despite this reality, such disappointing election results were used against William Deng to undermine his claim to speak on behalf of the Southern Suidanese, because it showed that he had no support to back his claims up. According to one historian, when internal split developed from within the party, "SANU operated as the personal fief of William Deng."[264] And in March of 1967, William Deng was killed in an ambush in Behr el-Ghazal, presumably by the Khartoum soldiers who were always wary of him. For example, at one point, Prime Minister Mohamed Mahgoub shut down the Southern Sudanese politicians in a heated debate by pulling in front of him documents implicating William Deng in supporting the Anyanya soldiers. Mahgoub read out loud from one of those documents purported to be from William Deng addressed to the Anyanya, which reads in part:

> Hold on to your arms for the next five years beginning from now. We have proved to the Arabs we are strong politically and are not afraid to defend our land when necessary. The Arabs have learned a lesson and it is most unlikely they will resort to army rule again.[265]

Not surprisingly, the Southerners including William Deng went silent without even making any attempt to dispute the authenticity of the document, leave alone even to dismiss the claim.

General Joseph Lagu

As for Joseph Lagu, he was the luckiest one. He actually attributes luckiness as one of the contributing factors for his success as a leader.[266] Machiavilli would say Lagu came to power by "good fortune."[267] For one he had his work cut out for him. He gained loyalty and confidence of the Father's soldiers even before the death of the Father. By far, the soldiers loyal to the Father were the most strongest as they were better trained and equipped in comparison to the other Anyanya units. Another thing was, he also gained the confidence of the friends of the Father who opened the way for him to the outside world. Even though in his own words he said, he hated politicians, he had to become one by consolidating power under his Southern Sudan Liberation Movement (SSLM). He also brought different Anyanya groups under his control and was able to secure them unlimited supplies of weapons from Israel. He went on to negotiate a peace agreement with the government of Numairy in 1972. He was rewarded with a ceremonial rank of major general in Khartoum's Arms forces for having signed the agreement with Khartoum government. He served in the successive governments that took power in Khartoum at various positions including two times vice president of Sudan, president of Higher Executive Council in the autonomous government of Southern Sudan, and roving ambassador. Currently he resigned from government positions and leading a private life. He is contemplating to live and work privately among the communities with his permanent residence in his hometown of Torit.

Dr. John Garang

As for Dr. John Garang, he was a young student by 1960s. He gained from Anyanya's scholastic program which encouraged all the young Southern Sudanese to stay in schools in preparation for future leadership as oppose to fighting in the bushes. Garang is a success story of that program. Completing his high school in Tanzania, he went on to the United States of America (USA) for undergraduate in economics at Grinnell College where he completed in 1969. He declined scholarship to continue further education at University of California, Berkeley. Instead, he went on to do fellowship at the University of Dar es Salaam in Tanzania where he subsequently joined the Anyanya liberation movement. On the signing of Addis Ababa Agreement, John Garang was absorbed as a captain in the Khartoum armed forces. He was later to rise into the rank of colonel. He also managed to complete a master's degree and a Ph.D. in agricultural economics at Iowa State University in the USA. From 1983 through 2005, he led a successful liberation movement, Sudan People Liberation Movement/Army (SPLM/A). In January 9th, 2005, he signed a Comprehensive Peace Agreement (CPA) with the Khartoum government, which settled the Sudan's South-North civil war. Tragically, in July 30th, 2005, a Ugandan presidential helicopter he was traveling with from Uganda en route to Sudan mysteries crashed along Uganda and Sudan borders, killing everyone on board including him. The official investigation to the mysterious crash concluded that the cause for the crash was due to poor whether and inexperience pilot.[268] However, some people, especially the Southern Sudanese doubt the conclusion of the official investigation. Even Yuweri Museveni, the president of Uganda, on whom Garang was traveling in his helicopter has some doubts with the official version of the cause of the crash. For President Museveni, he is not ready in "ruling anything out" as a possible cause for the crash.[269]

The Southern Sudanese People

And as for the Southern Sudanese people, they are continuing on with the struggle despite the mounting challenges ahead of them. Hopefully, along the way, they will be able to produce leaders preferable of equal or higher qualities than the ones who have led them and sacrificed for them for all these years of struggle for freedom, justice, fairness and peace. These new warrior generations of leadership immediate task is to protect the Comprehensive Peace Agreement (CPA), which guarantees the people of South Sudan an alienable right for self determination. They must possess enough courage and ability to confront and ward off any obstacles real or imagine which will interfere with the South Sudanese rights for self determination. They must develop vision that resonates very well with the aspiration of the South Sudanese and develop a national consciousness along this very vision as a means of rallying all the people of South Sudan behind the same goal. This national consciousness must go beyond mere rallying together to face a common enemy but must rather be built on a basis of a shared common goal and destiny. Tribes, some people may suggest are evil, however that is not the case. There have to be ways where those various Southern tribes can live harmoniously. The South and North of Sudan have already proven beyond reasonable doubt not to live harmoniously with each other. Now the biggest challenge for Southerners is whether they can prove to live harmoniously among the varying Southern tribes. Nations institute constitutions, which guarantee harmony among diversity. For its more than fifty years of existence, the Sudan as a whole failed to do that and a free South can manage to have its own constitution, but the challenge remains on whether the Southerners can have the spirit in maintaining that constitution. Otherwise, the future is still turbulent for South Sudanese, which means, the struggle must continue.

Chapter Endnotes

[193] Robert Collins (forthcoming publication in 2007): "Chapter Five: Parliamentary and Military Experiments in Government, 1956-1969" The History of the Modern Sudan. *Hollywood:* Tsehai Publ.

[194] Oliver Albino, *The Sudan: A Southern Viewpoint, London:* Oxford University Press, 1970.

[195] Fr. Neno Contran, *They Are A Target: 200 African Priests Killed*, Nairobi: Catholic Publishers in Africa, 1996. p. 143.

[196] Robert Collins, (forthcoming publication in 2007): "Chapter Five: Parliamentary and Military Experiments in Government, 1956-1969" *The History of the Modern Sudan.* Hollywood: Tsehai Publ.

[197] Fr. Neno, Contran, *They Are A Target: 200 African Priests Killed*, Nairobi: Catholic Publishers in Africa, 1996.

[198] Ibid

[199] Ibid

[200] Severino Ga'le, *Shaping a Free Southern Sudan: Memoirs of our Struggle*, Nairobi: Paulines Publications Africa, 2002.

[201] Petition to United Nations by Sudan African Closed Districts National Union (SACDNU), 1963.

[202] John F. Kennedy, Inaugural address, January 20, 1961.

[203] Petition to United Nations by Sudan African Closed Districts National Union (SACDNU), 1963.

[204] Ibid

[205] Joseph Lagu, *Sudan: Odyssey Through a State: From Ruin to Hope*, Omdurman : MOB Center for Sudanese Studies, Omdurman Ahlia University 2006.

[206] Severino Ga'le, *Shaping a Free Southern Sudan: Memoirs of our Struggle*, Nairobi: Paulines Publications Africa, 2002.

[207] Ibid

_____ Fr. Neno Cpntran, *They Are A Target: 200 African Priests Killed*, Nairobi: Catholic Publishers in Africa, 1996.

[208] Fr. Neno Cpntran, *They Are A Target: 200 African Priests Killed*, Nairobi: Catholic Publishers in Africa, 1996.

[209] Robert Collins, (forthcoming publication in 2007): "Chapter Five: Parliamentary and Military Experiments in Government, 1956-1969" *The History of the Modern Sudan*. Hollywood: Tsehai Publ.

[210] Ibid

[211] Fr. Neno Cpntran, *They Are A Target: 200 African Priests Killed*, Nairobi: Catholic Publishers in Africa, 1996.

[212] Ibid

[213] Abel Alier, South Sudan: Too Many Agreement Dishonoured, London: Ithaca Press, 1992.

[214] Ibid

[215] Fr. Neno Cpntran, *They Are A Target: 200 African Priests Killed*, Nairobi: Catholic Publishers in Africa, 1996.

[216] Ibid

[217] Marit Magelssen Vambheim "Making Peace While Waging War:—A Peacemaking Effort in the Sudanese Civil War, 1965-1966" MA thesis in history, University of Bergen, Spring 2007.

[218] Ibid

[219] Ibid

[220] Robert Collins, (forthcoming publication in 2007): "Chapter Five: Parliamentary and Military Experiments in Government, 1956-1969" *The History of the Modern Sudan*, Hollywood: Tsehai Publ.

[221] Marit Magelssen Vambheim "Making Peace While Waging War:—A Peacemaking Effort in the Sudanese Civil War, 1965-1966" MA thesis in history, University of Bergen, Spring 2007.

[222] Ibid

[223] Ibid

[224] Fr. Neno Contran, *They Are A Target: 200 African Priests Killed*, Nairobi: Catholic Publishers in Africa, 1996.

[225] Ibid

[226] Ibid

[227] Ibid

[228] Ibid

[229] Ibid

[230] Joseph Oduho and William Deng, *The Problem of Southern Sudan*, London: Oxford University Press, 1963. p. 8.

[231] Fr. Neno Contran, *They Are A Target: 200 African Priests Killed*, Nairobi: Catholic Publishers in Africa, 1996.

[232] Marit Magelssen Vambheim "Making Peace While Waging War:—A Peacemaking Effort in the Sudanese Civil War, 1965-1966" MA thesis in history, University of Bergen, Spring 2007.

[233] Fr. Neno Contran, *They Are A Target: 200 African Priests Killed*, Nairobi: Catholic Publishers in Africa, 1996. p. 126.

[234] Ibid

[235] Francis Mading Deng, *Dinka Cosmology*, London: Ithaca Press, 1980. pp. 122-28.

[236] Ibid

[237] Cecil Eprile, *War and Peace in the Sudan*, Newton Abbot: David & Charles, 1974. p. 162.

[238] Muhòammad Ahòmad Mahòju¯b, *Democracy on Trial: Reflections on Arab and African Politics*, London: Deutsch, 1974. p. 97.

[239] Mansour Khalid, *The Government They Deserve: The Role of the Elite in Sudan's Political Evolution*, London: Kegan Paul International, 1990. p. 280.

[240] Robert Collins, (forthcoming publication in 2007): "Chapter Five: Parliamentary and Military Experiments in Government, 1956-1969" *The History of the Modern Sudan*, Hollywood: Tsehai Publ.

[241] Amir Idris, *Conflict and Politics of Identity in Sudan*, New York: Palgrave Macmillan, 2005. Pg. 52.

[242] Muhòammad Ahòmad Mahòju¯b, *Democracy on Trial: Reflections on Arab and African Politics*, London: Deutsch, 1974.

[243] Robert Collins, (forthcoming publication in 2007): "Chapter Five: Parliamentary and Military Experiments in Government, 1956-1969" *The History of the Modern Suda,*. Hollywood: Tsehai Publ.

[244] Fr. Neno Contran, *They Are A Target: 200 African Priests Killed*, Nairobi: Catholic Publishers in Africa, 1996. p. 133.

[245] Bona Malwal, *People and Power in the Sudan*, London: Ithaca Press, 1981. pg. 96.

[246] Amir Idris, *Conflict and Politics of Identity in Sudan*, New York: Palgrave Macmillan, 2005. P. 52.

[247] Francis Deng, "Green is the Color of the Masters: The Legacy of Slavery and the Crisis of National Identity in Modern Sudan" Yale University. [online] http://www.yale.edu/glc/events/cbss/Deng.pdf

[248] Robert Collins, (forthcoming publication in 2007): "Chapter Five: Parliamentary and Military Experiments in Government, 1956-1969" *The History of the Modern Sudan*, Hollywood: Tsehai Publ.

[249] Fr. Neno Contran, *They Are A Target: 200 African Priests Killed*, Nairobi: Catholic Publishers in Africa, 1996.

[250] Ibid

[251] Ibid

[252] Ibid

[253] Ibid

[254] Ibid

[255] Ibid

[256] Ibid

[257] Ibid

[258] Joseph Oduho and William Deng, *The Problem of Southern Sudan*, London: Oxford University Press, 1963.

[259] Ibid

[260] In an interview with Fr. Neno Contran, the Editor of Comboni Italian magazine, *Nigrizia.* Entebbe, July 1966.

[261] Ibid

[262] Fr. Neno Contran, *They Are A Target: 200 African Priests Killed*, Nairobi: Catholic Publishers in Africa, 1996.

[263] Ibid

[264] Robert Collins, (forthcoming publication in 2007): "Chapter Five: Parliamentary and Military Experiments in Government, 1956-1969" *The History of the Modern Sudan*, Hollywood: Tsehai Publ.

[265] Marit Magelssen Vambheim "Making Peace While Waging War:—A Peacemaking Effort in the Sudanese Civil War, 1965-1966" MA thesis in history, University of Bergen, Spring 2007.

[266] Joseph Lagu, *Sudan: Odyssey Through a State, From Ruin to Hope*, Omdurman: MOB Center for Sudanese Studies, Omdurman Ahlia University 2006.

[267] Niccolo Machiavelli, *The Prince*, Penguin Books, Translated with Notes by George Bull & Introduction by Anthony Grafton.

[268] BBC News "Garang's death is blamed on pilot" April 18th, 2006. [online] http://news.bbc.co.uk/2/hi/africa/4920322.stm

[269] BBC News "Sudan crash cause is 'not clear'" August 5th, 2005. [online] http://news.bbc.co.uk/2/hi/africa/4748061.stm

Chapter Five
Joining the People of the Woods

"If we cannot be disposed of funds, we will be compelled to abandon political activities and join the people of the woods. On our part, neither the external pressure nor the divergence among the South Sudanese will change our attitude, as we prefer to die fighting rather than to serve the Arabs of the Sudan or the international policy" (Fr. Saturnino Lohure)

Justification for Arms Struggle

Militant is perhaps not the right word to describe Fr. Saturnino Lohure, but he, in every respect, believed that the use of arms struggle is the only way the South will achieve its objectives of justice, freedom, equality, and peace. According to the Father, a physical liberation of the land would be an answer for the Southern Problems. This conviction is built and reinforced over a long period of time by a way of knowledge and experience. First, the Father did not only study philosophy and theology, but understood politics very well that one can only negotiate better when one is armed and begin to consolidate power through arms liberation struggle. The philosophical thoughts that the Father came across are loaded with heavy emphasis on the importance of arms as a means for maintaining peace, liberty, and power. Among the most notably on the list is Machiavelli. On his message to the princes, he advised, "Rome remained free for four hundred years and Sparta eight hundred, although their citizens were armed all that time; but many other states that have been disarmed have lost their liberties in less than forty years."[270] This is a clear indication that being strongly armed is a guarantee to liberty, freedom and power.

In the case of fragile Sudan this becomes the norm. Power, respect and recognition come with the strengths of bearing arms and waging a liberation struggle. For example, while in the bush, the Khartoum government offered John Garang, a rebel leader, cabinet positions for the Southern Sudanese. In response to their offer, Garang asked, "what about Darfur, Beja, and the Nuba? Do they have to take arms before their place is recognized?"[271] This goes to indicate that to pick up arms and fight for a cause cannot only guarantee attaining of one's objectives but also recognitions. There have been examples of this sort from allover the world; especially the 1950s through 1960s where it was the years of liberation struggle in most of the African countries. The Father took the arms struggle as a serious and personal business. By the time Anyanya was already active, the Father's book collection titles on warfare and guerilla tactics ranges from war tactics to instructions of blowing up bridges and to booby traps.[272] The Father was applying those intellectual warfare theories into practical work.

Secondly, the Father had witnessed first hand how coward the Arabs were as they were fleeing under intense armed fire during the Torit Mutiny of 1955. Whereby, had it not been of the Father, many of those

Arabs would have perished under the intense fire of the Southern Sudanese soldiers who mutinied in protest of the Arabs' oppression in 1955. The Father had to protect many of them at the mission in his own house as they were fleeing in desperation. And he could sense the inborn and natural fear in them. If Prime Minister Muhammad Ahmad Mahgoub said, "the only language Southerners understand is force," he was referring to the innocent Southern Sudanese civilians, but not those who were willing to pick up arms for struggle.[273] But the Father could speak the same language of Mahgoub with even a strong tone and credibility by directly referring to the Arab soldiers as he had seen them fleeing in disarray under intense fire coming from the brave Southern Sudanese nationals. Mahgoub who was a civilian did not only abuse the use of force but tend to measure Arabs military strength and might with the number of civilians they massacred and number of military equipments they possessed—the strength that seems like no match to the Southern Sudanese arms resistance movement. The Father was convinced that the arms struggle would drive the Arabs running from the South as they did run in 1955. Commenting on the military effort of the Southerners during the mutiny, the Father wrote, "Southerners nearly freed themselves using the very force preached by" the Arabs during the mutiny of 1955.[274]

Perhaps it is not a good idea to make several references to the 1955 mutiny as it would surely evoke terrible memory of fear and lost toward the Arabs. Surely, there were no cameras or news reporters to capture the terrifying atmosphere by which the Arabs found themselves in during the Torit Mutiny of 1955. However, what was there were the Southern Sudanese people whom through their singing and poetic skills, they graphically captured and depicted the entire terrifying atmosphere in their poetic words and warrior songs. Saleh who was a military officer in Torit and who had triggered the mutiny by cowardly shooting at a Southern

Sudanese soldier and Ismail Azhari who was the Prime Minister at the time had most songs dedicated to them for cowardice. As perpetrators and leaders, they may as well share the brunt with the rest of their brothers who were not able to make it to the North. For example, a song in Lotuko language entitle *Saleh Irwata* (Run Saleh), recounts how Saleh contemplated on his escaped by wishing for an airplane to come and fetch him to the North because the Lotuko people of Torit were bad, as they already killed many of the Arabs. So, he did not want to be the next victim as terrified as he was. Luckily, he managed to escape by a car as there was no plane to come and rescue him. Another song also in Lotuko language entitle *Owour Azhari Etoi* (Azhari broke the stick), speaks of the commander of the military whom on arrival to the headquarters in Khartoum, he refused orders from Azhari by breaking the stick as a promise of never wanting to come back to Equatoria or South Sudan given his encountered with the mutineers. The Arab commander was terrified indeed, and he had to swear in the name of Allah and his prophet Mohammad of never wanting to return to the South given the trauma he sustained during the 1955 mutiny. Such songs depict the atmosphere and the feelings of the Southerners and Northerners alike. The atmosphere and feelings of the Southerners is of courage, will, and victory whereas for the Northerners it is of timidness, reluctance, and defeat. For centuries to come, those songs will continue to remain inspirations for the Southern Sudanese generation for arms struggle against injustice and oppression inflicted by the Arabs and whoever foreign who will try to oppress them.

Thirdly, the Father experience in parliament whereby the South failed to secure a federal system through political process is enough prove that no political process will resolve the problems of South Sudan. Actually, the Arabs had to bring in the military to replace the democratically elected parliamentary government of 1958 so that the Southerners could not get the federal system of government through a political process. The Arabs continued to this day to sabotage any peaceful political process of resolving the Southern Sudanese issues by trying all means possible including use of force against unarmed civilians. Some of the good examples of their continuing efforts of sabotaging peaceful political process would include the Round Table Conference of 1965, the abrogation of Addis Ababa in 1983, and their ongoing effort in sabotaging the Comprehensive Peace Agreement (CPA) reached in 2005. The Arabs are also infamously known for being untrustworthy in keeping part of their deal and promises. They use all sort of tactics including delaying tactics, briberies, and false representation to renege and get out of the deals and promises.

Fourthly, the tactics by the Khartoum government, especially under the Premier, Muhammad Ahmed Mahgoub, in using military force in dealing with the Southerners was so compelling that it required to be countered with an armed resistance. These, plus other reasons reinforced the Father's believes in the use of armed struggle as the solution in resolving the problems of South Sudan as he declared, "we prefer to die fighting rather than to serve the Arabs of the Sudan or the international policy."[275] The element of arms struggle became an important component for the emancipation of South Sudan. As they say, to wage war is "nothing more than the continuation of politics by other means."[276] Lubari Ramba of Southern Front political party, put it more clearer in the discussions at the Round Table Conference of 1965, when in defense of the military activities of Anyanya, a Southern Sudanese rebel movement, he said, they were "nothing but a group of men who have resorted to arms when all other means have failed."[277] With these convincing reasons, the Southern Sudanese arms struggle was not only the ideal solution but was inevitable if the South was to liberate itself.

The History of Arms Struggle

The history of the South Sudan arms struggle has its roots into the institutionalization of the Sudanese into an organized army by the colonial power. In the beginning, the Sudanese armed forces were largely commanded by the British and Egyptian officers. However, that composition changed gradually. It all started when Egyptians recruited a special unit of Sudanese army known as *al-Awtirah* to serve within the Sudanese army in Anglo-Egyptian Sudan. This unit was loyal to Egyptian King Fuad and politically was pro Sudan unity with Egypt. In 1922, one of the officers among that unit, First Lieutenant Ali AbdalLatif, disobeyed the British orders citing that it violated the Sudanese sovereignty and undermined King Fuad's authority whom he took an oath to uphold. This led to his detention. Abdallatif went on founding a political party, the United Tribes Society where he demanded the removal of the British from Sudan and that power be given to the different Sudanese ethnic groups to be shared. He was then dishonorably discharged from the military and arrested for agitating nationalism. But later on he became even more instrumental in promoting nationalism. He went on to found the White Flag League in 1923, in an attempt to drive the British out of Sudan whereby his group conducted demonstrations and revolts against the British rule. His actions along with his Egyptian colleagues serving with him in Sudanese army destabilized the British rule. By then, anti British sentiment in Egypt was running very high as it could be evident by assassination of Governor-General and Sirdar Lee Stack, which took place in a broad daylight.[278] The British responded harshly by ordering the evacuation of all Egyptian troops and exiling Abdallatif along with his Egyptian counterparts where he ended in an Egyptian mental institution. This, however, marked the death of nationalism in Sudan because the nationalist leaders could not get the support from the Northern Arabs simply because of their origin and also because of the fact that the powerful Arab tribes were collaborating with the British instead. Amazingly, it turned out that Abdallatif was of a Southern origin. Born in Egypt around 1899 to an ex-slave of Dinka mother and a Nuba father, Abdallatif went on to study in Gordon College and Khartoum Military School where he graduated as a second lieutenant in 1914.[279]

In a modern day Egypt, it is not even imaginable to think that an action of a non-Arab was somewhat responsible for weakening Egyptians' enemy, the British, at the time when Egypt was struggling against the British rule in both Sudan and Egypt. Worse yet, the appreciation and acknowledgement Abdallatif received from the Sudanese Arabs for his heroic nationalism stand was a betrayal at its best. The prominent Northern Sudanese Arab leaders such as Sayyid Abd al-Rahman al-Mahdi and Judge Muhammad Saleh Shingiti all spoke contemptuously against Abdallatif. Judge Shingiti in particular was quoted in an interview as he was boasting of the fact that since Sudanese were of Arabic descents with their origin in the Arabian Peninsular, Abdallatif whom his mother was a negress and father unknown could not fit into Sudanese mainstream society.[280] The Sudanese first Arabic independent newspaper, *The Hadarat al Sudan*, went on as far as pressuring the British to "exterminate those wayward street boys" (a reference to Abdallatif and the company) and sarcastically asked, "what lowly nation is this that is now being led by people of ilk of Abdallatif? From what ancestry did this man descent to merit such fame? And of what tribe does he belong?"[281] To support this racial stereotyping, the British who had their racial supremacy and authority challenged, moreover by a black person, had this to say about abdallatif:

...a young savage...who found himself in military cadet at his teens and at the age of twenty-two became a commission office, and so was translated at bound from the dregs to the cream of the local society.[282]

This is an obvious indication that the Sudanese Arabs and their Egyptians counterparts plus their British masters could not appreciate, leave alone acknowledge a courageous act of nationalism and patriotism, which was demonstrated by a non-Arab, First Lieutenant Ali Abdallatif. In civilization of human beings, there is something known as honor whereby one is obligated to acknowledge his enemy's strength, but it seemed, the Sudanese Arabs, the Egyptians, and the British degenerated from this norm of human civilization, and yet in a daring act of hypocrisy they claimed to possess civilization. This, however, is not in away suggesting that the heroism, honor and dignity of the non-Arabs of Sudan is eroded by this lack of appreciation and acknowledgement by the very people who are impacted by these acts of heroism.

After this incident, came World War II, and during World War II, the British sought to recruit strong Sudanese armed forces manned by Sudanese people to assist them in their war. Unfortunately, the Sudanization of armed forces also meant the Arabization of the Armed forces. The British recruited the military officers from Gordon's High School where there was no Southern Sudanese attending, therefore, limiting the chances of Southern Sudanese from becoming military officers completely into zero. From 1938 through 1944, Sudan military college was graduating an average of fifty officers a year.[283] Such number was needed in boosting the British war effort in World War II. The Southern Sudanese were only to be lucky that the British instituted a separate policy for the South, which increased the opportunities for the

Southerners to be enlisted in the armed forces in the unit of Equatoria Corps, not as officers but regular low rank enlistments. A good number of Southerners were then recruited in the Equatoria Corps unit. Prior to the independence, almost all the enlisted men in the armed forces in the South were Southerners. However, their officers were Northern Sudanese Arabs. This was always resented by the Southerners, especially the fact that Northern Sudanese Arabs were also dominating political scenery, economics, and businesses in the entire South.

A Declaration of War Against the Southerners

Due to resentments and suspicions, tensions were beginning to rise high in the South, unfortunately at the time the country was about to gain independence. As such, there were occurrences of incidents whereby one incident would triggered to another, and the situation would gradually grew from bad to worse, leading into a total civil war that would last to this day. First there was an incident involving a dispute between, a Southern Liberal Party, Member of Parliament, Elia Kuze on one hand, and the local chiefs of Yambio supported by the Arabs administrators on the other hand. Kuze was finally sentenced to prison for charges that was bogus and in a court preceding that made a mockery out of the justice system. The illegal sentencing of Kuze resulted in riot, the result of it; eight Southerners shot dead by Arabs merchants and eleven more wounded. This incident would follow with another violent and tragic riot in Nzara, only 16 miles from Yambio, where Southern Sudanese workers, demanded for fair treatment, better working conditions, and reasonable payment for their hard labor. The result of the riot was also disastrous on the parts of the Southerners as four people laid dead and several more injured by the time damages were assessed. It was then that the Southerners concluded that the war was already declared on them by the

Northern Sudanese Arabs with whom they suppose to share the country.[284] To add to the already tense situation, an order purported to be from Sudanese Prime Minister Ismail al-Azhari was circulating around in Southern Sudanese towns where Southerners got hold of it. The order addressed to the Northern Sudanese administrators in the South Sudan reads in part:

> To all my administrators in the three southern proveniences: I have just signed a document for self-determination. Do not listen to the childish complaints of the Southerners…Treat them according to my orders. Any administrator who fails to comply with my orders will be liable to prosecution. In three months time all of you will come round and enjoy the work you have done.[285]

The circulation of this message was accompanied by information that Northerner troops were already being airlifted to Juba to take over the command of the South Sudan. With all these, it did not sound like a coincidence anymore because the unit of Equatoria Corp, Company number 2, which was stationed in Torit was ordered to report to Khartoum to participate in the ceremony of evacuation of the foreign troops, which was due to commence on January 1st, 1956. These soldiers defied the orders believing that it was a trap to lure them into North and have them arrested and eventually killed. By then a group of these soldiers were already detained in Juba. Among those detained in Juba, was a courageous and daring officer by the name Emideo Tafeng who was by then considered the best marksman in the entire Sudan, and a dangerous man at the same time, given his daring attitude. This group was lured into Juba and detained. As the standoff in Torit continued, an Arab commanding officer, a certain Saleh, begin to issue threats against the Equatoria Corp soldiers saying things like the Northern Sudanese Arab soldiers were being reinforced through the air in Juba and they were going to deal with the Southern Sudanese. As he realized that his commands were completely ignored and his verbal threats had no impact, he then committed a huge mistake by taking a gun, and shot one of the Equatoria Corp soldiers to death. He then promptly and cowardly jumped into his car, which he set ready for an escape, and sped off to Juba and all the way to Khartoum. This gave opportunity for the Equatoria Corp soldiers to act, and they acted in vengeance. The furious Equatoria Corp soldiers stormed the weapon storage and managed to take possession of all the weapons and ammunition in the storage to sustain their offense. They started killing any Arabs they could find. Those Arabs who were still alive took off running, and majority of whom where drowned in a small stream in Torit known as Kineti. That was when the Southern Sudanese confirmed that the Northern Sudanese Arabs could not swim. Perhaps the lack of thier swimming skills has to do with panic and fear. The lucky ones found refuge in a Catholic mission, where Father Saturnino Lohure protected them. But it wouldn't be long before these cunning Arabs would come back and turn against the very Catholics who protected them when they were at their own desperate moments. From Torit throughout the Southern Sudanese towns, the response to pursue the Arabs "spread like a forest fire throughout the length and breadth of Southern Sudan" as Deng D. Ruay puts it.[286] For more than two weeks, the rage continued in the entire the South. As a result, the Arabs were dislodged off the positions of power. They were set on the run. In some other parts of the South, they were ordered to pack and live. It was for the first time in the history of the Sudan since colonialism that the South was free, at least temporarily. This fact goes to defy the notion that the Southern Sudanese cannot free themselves. For those who are holding such notion, they don't need to be reminded time and again that in 1955, the Southern Sudanese actually managed to free themselves easily without encountering any difficulties. Even more interesting, the Southern Sudanese freed themselves without the help of any one, whether it is their neighbors or foreign power. This incident marked a significant era in Sudan's history—an era whereby the South Sudanese rose into arms in challenging an oppressed regime centered in Khartoum—the era that came to be known, the Torit Mutiny of 1955. Commenting on the symbolic significance of the Torit Mutiny of 1955, one author wrote:

> The mutiny became a symbol of 'Southern Solidarity'; a symbol of 'rejection of an alien rule' be it British, Egyptians or Northern Sudanese. It was also associated with remembrance of the 'beginning of the Southern cause' with all its legends of persecution, sacrifice and heroism. The August 18, 1955 became historic day in which Southerners remember the 'Torit martyrs'. The Flag of the Equatorial Corps was several times adopted by the Southern Liberation Movements as the "Southern National Flag". Despite the differences over the causes of the mutiny, its political, social and economic significance among Southern Sudanese seemed to have developed into a living legend.[287]

The symbolic significance of the Torit Mutiny of 1955, can never be undermined. The Anyanya, a Southern Sudanese first liberation movement could not find a suitable date to officially declare an arms struggle against the government in Khartoum other than the August 18th, 1963. Those Southerners who conspired to form what later to be become the Sudan People Liberation Movement/Army (PLM/A) couldn't look for another inspiring date than August 18th, but unfortunately in their case, their plan to launch a mutiny were betrayed through a leakage, which preempted them to mutiny earlier, on May 16th of 1983. In August 28 of 2007, the President of South Sudan while celebrating the opening of newly built school in the historic town of Torit declared that August 18th must be a national holiday for the South Sudan. For the Southerners, they are not short of supplies when it comes to being inspired. The inspirations are their in huge supplies set by those who bravely and courageously fought during the Torit Mutiny, therefore, no reason to lack inspirations. The motion for liberation was already set during the Torit Mutiny; therefore, they have no reasons to rest other than continue with the liberation struggle. The standard for Southern Sudan freedom was already set when the South was freed during the Torit Mutiny; therefore, they have no reasons to accept anything short of that total freedom and liberation.

The symbolism of Torit town has even a lasting impact to the Northern Sudanese Arabs and their successive governments in Khartoum. For example, the current President of Khartoum, Omer al-Basher is obsessed with Torit just as Northern Sudanese Arab generations before him were. He had to pull out of the peace negotiations in 2002, simply because the SPLM/A then drove his troops out from Torit town. Moreover, it was at a critical juncture when, they had just made headway in the negotiations by signing the Machakos Protocol, which paved the way for a comprehensive peace agreement between the South and North of Sudan. President Omer al-Bashir swore in the name of Allah that he could only return to negotiate when SPLM/A withdrew from Torit. If there is any important place for Sudanese Arabs that will evoke them to swear in the name of Allah, it is Torit. President Bashir was more determine than ever to recapture Torit, and he had to go out of his way to mobilize all sort of Jihadist he could find, the university students, street boys, the various militias, and even the foreign and notorious Lord Resistant Army (LRA) of Uganda, so as he could recapture Torit.

As for the Arabs of 1955, who were set on the run during the Torit Mutiny, they could not manage to contain the mutiny or recapture the South after the Southern Sudanese mutineers took charge of the South. Therefore, they had to beg for the intervention of imperial British, who then had to assure the Southern Sudanese mutineers that upon giving up their arms, they will be treated fairly and a thorough investigation will be carried out to determine the cause of the mutiny. Unfortunately, the British never kept their side of the bargain, but instead left the country in the safe control of the Northern Sudanese Arabs government. The event that followed was a reversed of the mutiny as the Arabs took the surrender of the mutineers as an opportunity for retributions. The investigation was done as to the causes of the mutiny and the grievances of the Southern Sudanese, but the recommendations of the investigation was not followed, and the findings of the investigation was kept hidden, only part of it was released as a political retaliation against the party of al-Azhari, the Nation Unionist Party (NUP) by the Umma Party when they gained power in 1956, shortly after declaring independence.

Those mutineers who surrendered or captured were summarily executed or imprisoned. Among prominent Southern Sudanese executed in the aftermath of Torit Mutiny was Second Lieutenant Renaldo Oleya who was the chief of the mutineers and signed the surrender agreement. As he was shackled on chains and thrown to jail in Juba prison, he met his colleague and a member of his ethnic group, Emedio Tafeng whom upon seeing him, shouted, *iyang yoi, onyo-iyang!* (my mother, the son of my mother!), a traditional way of expressing dareness in dealing with the unfolding situation. Another prominent individual who was also executed included Second Lieutenant Albino Tombe, who was actually the first officer to be executed in Torit. And then there were other prominent individuals including the police Inspector Placido Laboke, the Second Lieutenant of Prisons, Marcello Andal, the Second Lieutenant of Prisons, Alipio Lako, the school head master Samuel Kajiviro, and the Executive Officer Michael Wata. In all, most good men and prominent Southern Sudanese lost their lives in retaliation, but in what the Southern Sudanese would call the struggle for South Sudan.

And then those who survived the executions, thousands of them, were unfortunately imprisoned in the Northern Sudan labor prison camps. This would actually invoke some serious negative mummeries in some of those individuals that some of them ended up boycotting anything that had to do with Khartoum including refusal to eat a mere salt believed to have been produced in Khartoum. Others who remained in the bush continued to wage rather isolated raids on government of Khartoum posts. An example of those was a group led by Lance Corporal Latada Helir, a prison warden. The group sought sanctuary in Eastern Equatoria Mountains and when ever possible, they raid Khartoum government targets in Eastern Equatoria. One of this group's successful operations was when they forced a unit of the elite Haggana Camel Corps to retreat from Mountain Madok. Unfortunately, Lance Corporal Latada Helir was killed in a firefight in 1960. His death crippled the insurgency activities in Eastern Equatoria until 1963. The once proud and revered Equatoria Corps unit of South Sudan was completely disbanded. Khartoum armed forces personnel were increased steadily from 5,000 in 1956 to 12,000 strong in 1959, just in an effort to deal with insurgency in the South.[288]

By 1958, a military regime led by General Ibrahim Abboud took control of power in Khartoum with a precise purpose to crush Southern

Sudanese insurgencies. The Southern Sudanese hope of attaining federalism through a political process was abruptly dashed away with the military takeover and the abolishment of the democratically elected parliamentary government. Southerners once again felt betrayed by the Northern Sudanese Arabs who promised them federalism so as they vote for the declarations of independence. The Southern Sudanese politicians were harassed and threatened within their own country by the new military regime. One by one, most of them fled the country. Among the first to flee the country was Fr. Saturnino Lohure who was the president of Liberal Party and the head of the Southern Sudanese political parties Bloc in the parliamentary government of 1958. After learning of an imminent arrest, the Father escaped for Uganda in December of 1960, and later relocated into Congo. With his colleagues, the Father went on to found the first ever Southern Sudanese political party in exile, Sudan African Closed Districts National Union (SACDNU), which later changed its name to Sudan African National Union (SANU). The Father acted as the patron of this political movement and established his base in Congo at a Catholic mission in a place called Aru, which is closer to both Sudan and Ugandan borders. The Father continued on in organizing refugees in camps in preparation for military training to wage an armed resistance war against the Khartoum government. One example of the camps the Father modeled for training was the Adranga camp, which was strategically located inside Sudan but closer to both Uganda and Congo. The camp was disguised as a refugee camp but with intention of mobilizing Southern Sudanese who were ready for military training. The camp also helped provide basic services and materials for the Southern Sudanese who would otherwise suffer from lack of everything by lingering in Uganda and Congo. The product of that camp included individuals such as Captain Bernadino Mou, who was second in charge at the camp, and would later go on and lead a daring and deadly attempt to capture Wau in 1964.

Such model camps were strategically located throughout the Ugandan and Congo borders in Eastern, Central and Western Equatoria. Former Equatoria Corp soldiers made a nucleus of the recruits in these camps. More significantly, the regime of Abboud timely released as a good gesture over 800 Southerners who were detained as a result of the mutiny of 1955. There was no any amount of pardon or good gesture, which can make those Southerners trust the Arab government in Khartoum anymore, therefore, they swamped the training camps for preparation for war with the Arab government in Khartoum. They were later "followed by a steady trickle of literate trained police, NCOs, and police wardens who by 1963 had re-established the nucleus of a guerilla force" in those established training camps along the borders.[289]

The Southern Countered Offensive & Anyanya

By 1963, the Father already felt confident about the preparedness for the war. However, the problems were, most of those soldiers were ill trained and were barely equipped. The Father ignored the advice of Joseph Lagu on those soldiers lack of preparedness. Lagu who was a commission officer in the Khartoum armed forces, with a rank of a second lieutenant has just been lured to join the Southern Sudanese liberation movement, and the Father assigned him in charge of training the liberation movement soldiers given his military skills. For the Father, the time was of a great essence. They could not wait any longer to wage an armed liberation struggle against Khartoum government. He wanted to prompt the declaration of war against Khartoum government to coincide along with the anniversary of 1955 mutiny of Torit. As for his objectives, he wanted to alert the world that there were problems going on in Sudan. Moving ahead with military strike was the loudest one could speak on alerting the world on the problems affecting the Sudan. The Father had already published a book, written countless articles, and traveled the world, in an effort of educating the world of the problems in Sudan. Now the last resort is military strike to really prove that the problems were serious.

The second objective was to send a clear message to Khartoum that they could abolish a peacefully political process of resolving the issues of Southern Sudan, but the people of Southern Sudan were determined to continue through other means available including arms struggle. It was also to send a message to Khartoum that their military force which until now, was still being exercised against innocent Southern Sudanese civilians was not going to be tolerated. Instead, it was going to be countered vigorously with force. The African culture demands man-to-man faced off, and that was a lesson the Father expected the Arabs to learn as well. The ill-training and lack of military equipments were secondary concerns to the Father. One of the greatest generals the world ever produced, used to reassure his soldiers that "it's the unconquerable soul of man, not the nature of the weapon he uses, that insures victory." As long as the Father was confident of obtaining these objectives, he was ready to move on, and without delayed, he proposed the strike to commerce with the anniversary of Torit Mutiny of 1955.

From his base in Aru, the Father instructed Lagu with this proposal of a commencement of a first military strike against Khartoum government targets to be delivered to the SANU officials in Kampala. Lagu departed for Kampala and told, Joseph Oduho, the president of SANU about the proposal. Oduho in turn called on for a meeting. In that meeting held on August 18th, 1963, they deliberated among other things, to name their new rebel movement. The Father already suggested other names as the starting point. However, the SANU officials preferred a name with a local meaning and appeal. They came with the name Anyanya which is a Madi language for poison extracted from deadly sneak. The name was popularly used around Torit town by the locals at that period in time. Such appealing tone would capture the attention of the locals as they expected. They also set a fix date to carryout the attacks throughout Khartoum targets and installation in the South. They sent their emissaries to the deliver the resolutions to the Father as well as throughout the command centers to the military officers in charge. They came up with a resolution of war against the government of Khartoum, which declared:

> Our patience has now come to an end, and we are convinced the only use of force will bring a decision—from today onwards we shall take action for better or for worse—we do not want mercy and we are not prepared to give it...[290]

The Anyanya were operating regionally and in groupings. In the case of the Father, he directly commanded one of the groups with its headquarters in Tul, Eastern Equatoria. Besides having direct command over the soldiers, the Father's specialty in the military was blowing up the bridges. He learned the wiring and setting off bombs to blow bridges from the manual instructions in the books. The Father was detailed oriented and diligently practical in his approach. He also taught others such as Joseph Lagu in setting up bombs to blow bridges. During the course of tour of operation in the bushes of South Sudan, the Father managed to blow several bridges to hinder the mobility of the Khartoum military, which provided advantage to the Anyanya forces. The Anyanya operations were usually carried out during the rainy seasons. In the rainy seasons the Anyanya always inflicted great battle victories against the

Arab soldiers as they could carryout their raids and easily melt away in the green bushes. As for the Arab soldiers, they have difficulty moving with their equipments during the rainy seasons. Dry seasons is sort of holyday, even though the Anyanya did stay on alert and can only carry raids where they saw they have advantages over the enemy. It is also during the dry seasons that the Khartoum armed forces stepped up their operations, fixing up bridges and roads. In the dry season of late 1966, the Father took off from the battle field to go for abroad in getting more support for the movement as he usually did. On his way back from abroad, in trying to cross the Ugandan border, the Father was intercepted by the Ugandan troops who sealed the borders. The Father was killed by them Ugandan troops before he could cross into the Sudan and alert his soldiers of Ugandan plans in sealing off the borders.

The Death of Anyanya

The death of the Father would eventually lead to the death of the Anyanya forces. After the death of the Father, Joseph Lagu had to assume the command of the Anyanya soldiers. The Father left as his will for Lagu to take over the leadership in an event he was not around or dead. As such, Lagu then managed to bring all the different Anyanya units under his command. They were to still operate regionally though, so as to avoid the ethnic rivalry and conflicts among the Southern Sudanese different nationalities. Under the leadership of Lagu, the Anyanya also went on to secure non-stop supplies of weapons from the state of Israel. The Anyanya cleared dropping zone in Eastern Equatoria for weapons and ammunitions where Israeli cargo plane made large drops of weapons and ammunitions on a regular monthly basis. In addition, the Israeli reached an agreement with Ethiopia to establish training ground for Anyanya and they also made similar agreement with Uganda to use its territory in ferrying out military hardwire to the Anyanya, even though that agreement was to be reversed by the Ugandan government under the instruction of Libyan government of Maymar Gadafi. The Anyanya officers also went on to Israel to receive advance military training from Israel Defense Forces (IDF), which actually boosted their military capabilities. They were trained in "weapons and explosives as well as radio transmission, military management, and primary medical care."[291] The Israeli secret intelligent service, the Mossad, established its mission in South Sudan with its headquarters in Eastern Equatoria. Uri Lubrani, the Israeli Ambassador in Kampala was in charge of the mission.[292]

Besides the involvement of Israeli, there were also other foreign elements who were in one way or another involved with the Anyanya forces for one reason or another. For example, there are evidences suggesting that the United States of America (USA) were involved with Anyanya to some degree through the Central Intelligence Agency (CIA) and the American Peace Corps. Some of these information are suggesting that the Israeli operation in Sudan was supported in part through CIA funding. That from 1970 through 1971, twelve CIA operatives have passed through South Sudan.[293] The extent and level of the American involvement with the Anyanya may be buried in obscurity; however, their motives were very clear. The period was reaped for African liberation struggle and radical nationalist leaders were springing up throughout African continent with potentially serious threat to the Western interest, especially at the height of Cold War between the Western capitalists and the Eastern communists. By then the American CIA was actively involved in other numerous African countries. As such, South Sudan provided a vital ground to establish American based so as to infiltrate into Uganda where Milton Obote, another African radical nationalist was presiding as president, and so as to infiltrate into other neighboring countries.

Another foreign element that was actively involved in South Sudan was the British through its intelligent service. The likes of Alexander Gay and Blunden (pseudonym for another British secret operative) who all turned out to be secret British intelligence agents had established their permanent base in South Sudan at the time, and worked closely with the Anyanya. Ironically, the British did not care about the Southern Sudanese cause let alone whether they even sympathize with the Southern cause. The involvement of the British in South Sudan was to overthrow and assassinate the president of Uganda, Milton Obote and install Ida Amin as their puppet president. The British plan was to solicit the support of the Southern Sudanese who have closed ethnic affinity with Ida Amin to boast Amin militarily in his quest for power. It was not surprising that elements of Southern Sudanese made the core of Amin's soldiers during the Amin's coup and thereafter.[294]

It was not only the governments of various countries which descended into South Sudan for one reason or another, the Southern Sudan war of liberation at the time also attracted certain prominent soldiers of fortune or in other word, mercenaries who were willing to adventure into South Sudan in bolstering the Anyanya war. Among those notable soldiers of fortunes was a certain German by the name Rolf Steiner. Steiner started his military career earlier on as Nazi in Adolf Hitler's youth squad. After Hitler's defeat, Steiner joined the seminary, but becoming a priest was not a vocation of his calling. He instead turned into armed missionary. He literally escaped seminary and joined the French Foreign Legion. He was to go and saw actions in Korea, Indochina, the Middle East and Algeria. Not satisfy with these adventures, he went on in Nigeria and assisted the Igbo in the Biafra war for their quest of succession. From there, it seems he was attracted into the secessionist movements. He was then introduced into South Sudan by Caritas International, a confederation of

Catholic charity organization, where he immediately joined the Anyanya and proved to be very instrumental in training, strategizing, and lobbying for the Anyanya forces. Even though the Israeli warned the Anyanya of the fact that they did not appreciate working with a Nazi, Steiner luck only ran out when he was captured in Uganda by Milton Obote government on his way from South Sudan into Europe. He was extradited into Khartoum where in 1971, he was sentenced to death, but Nimayri commuted his sentence into twenty years imprisonment.[295] After the signing of the Addis Ababa Agreement in 1972, between the Anyanya and Khartoum government of Nimayri, he was released as a good will gesture. Steiner ended up in Europe and in 1978, he published a book, *The Last Adventurer*, detailing his adventurous journey throughout the world of soldier of fortune.[296]

As early as 1963, another German, a Hitler's Schutzstaffel (SS) by the name Henerick Rossi came to the assistance of the Anyanya. He helped train the Anyanya in various guerrilla warfare techniques including explosives, and Molotov Cocktails. There was a certain Frenchman who was also involved in Biafra war and came into helping the Anyanya's war of liberation as well. This man simply called himself Armo, but before much could be known about him, he mysteriously disappeared.[297] Despite the little but significant outside assistances the Anyanya received, their efforts were never translated into achieving their primary goal of independent South Sudan.

By early 1970s, Anyanya grew to be a strong military force numbering in the range of 10,000 to 20,000 strong. They sustained and fought bloody battles with the Khartoum soldiers until they signed a peace agreement in 1972—the peace agreement that came to be known the Addis Ababa Agreement. The Addis Ababa Agreement marked the ultimate death or the annihilation of the Anyanya soldiers. Per the terms of the agreement, they were absorbed into the Khartoum arms forces, police, and prisons as well as in other civilian occupations. The agreement established a Southern Command within the Khartoum armed forces, which was composed of 12,000 soldiers of which 6,000 must come from the South. This is not to factor the fact that the entire Anyanya force tripled the 6,000 marked, meaning that many Anyanya soldiers could not be integrated in the Khartoum armed forces. Matter of fact, some Anyanya soldiers ended up joining the Uganda military, given that the Khartoum system could not accommodate them and also, Idi Amin, the president of Uganda, preferred the Southern Sudanese more than some other groups in Uganda to serve under his military. The provision for the integrating Anyanya into Khartoum armed forces was so vague that it states, "these arrangements shall remain in force for a period of five years."[298] This was widely open to so many interpretations. The Northern Sudanese Arab politicians took great comfort in the interpretation of this language to mean the Addis Ababa Agreement would automatically be dissolved in five years time. As for those Northerners Sudanese Arabs in the military who resented seeing Southerners participating with them in the same armed forces, they view this integration as a temporary arrangement, which will end in five years. For them, those Southerners integrated in the armed forces would disappear in dismal, through transfers, retirements and resignations. All those views and analysis were to be proven to be quite correct.

By mid 1970s, some of the former Anyanya, predominantly from the Upper Nile and Behr al-Ghazel regions became discontented with the government in Khartoum. They rebelled by forming Anyanya II armed rebellion along the Sudan and Ethiopian borders with their training grounds in Ethiopia. And by 1983, fearful of a massive Southern rebellion, the Khartoum government made a forceful attempt to deploy the Southern Command units into the North of Sudan and tried to force early retirement on many of the Southern Sudanese in the military. However, the efforts backfired as some of the former Anyanya officers who by then rose into middle ranks in the Khartoum arms forces also rebelled to form the Sudan People Liberation Movement/Army (SPLM/A) under the leadership of Dr. John Garang who was then an Anyanya captain when he was absorbed into the Khartoum arms forces per the Addis Ababa Agreement. He was later to raise into a rank of colonel in the Khartoum arms forces by the time he rebelled. From 1983, the SPLA would go on to fight a successful war for more than two decades until January of 2005, when the Comprehensive Peace Agreement (CPA) was signed between the government in Khartoum and SPLM/A. Today, the SPLA represents the Southern Sudan armed forces. In Accordance with the Comprehensive Peace Agreement (CPA), the SPLA must have a full control of the South Sudan within the territorial of the Southern Sudan borders defined by the colonial British in 1956 while the Khartoum armed forces maintains the Northern Sudan under their control. In the essence, the SPLA is representing the Southern Sudanese armed forces. According to the agreement, the SPLA must also participate in the Joint Integrated Unit (JIU), which is made up of equal number of SPLA and the Khartoum armed forces. The JIU are to be strategically deployed throughout the Sudan and are sharing equal command structure between the SPLA and the Khartoum armed forces under Joint Defense Board (JDB). The unit is a symbol representing the national armed forces of the Sudan. In case the Southerners confirm unity of Sudan in referendum of 2011, the JIU would automatically become a national army, but in case, the South secedes in the referendum, the JIU would have to be dissolved.[299]

Chapter Endnotes

[270] Niccolo Machiavelli, *The Prince*, Penguin Books, Translated with Notes by George Bull & Introduction by Anthony Grafton

[271] John Garang, *The Call for Democracy in Sudan*, New York: Kegan Paul International, 1992. Edited & Introduced by Mansour Khalid.

[272] Joseph Lagu, Sudan: *Odyssey Through a State: From Ruin to Hope*, Omdurman: MOB Center for Sudanese Studies, Omdurman Ahlia University, 2006.

[273] Amir Idris, Conflict and Politics of Identity in Sudan, New York: Palgrave Macmillan, 2005.

[274] Petition to United Nations by Sudan African Closed Districts National Union (SACDNU), 1963.

[275] Fr. Neno Contran, *They Are A Target: 200 African Priests Killed*, Nairobi: Catholic Publishers in Africa, 1996.

[276] Carl Von Clausewitz, *On War*, London: N. Trübner, 1873. Translated by James John Graham.

[277] Marit Magelssen Vambheim "Making Peace While Waging War:—A Peacemaking Effort in the Sudanese Civil War, 1965-1966" MA thesis in history, University of Bergen, Spring 2007.

[278] Youssef Aboul-Enein, "The Sudanese Army: a historical analysis and discussion on religious politicization," *Infantry Magazine*, July-August, 2004.

279 Francis Deng, *War of Visions Conflict of Identities in the Sudan,* Washington, D.C.: Brookings Institution Press, 1995.

280 Douglas Hamilton Johnson, *The Root Causes of Sudan's Civil Wars,* Bloomington: Indiana University Press, 2003. p. 23.

281 Amir Idris, *Conflict and Politics of Identity in Sudan,* New York: Palgrave MaCmillan, 2005. Pg. 49.

_____ Francis Deng, *War of Visions Conflict of Identities in the Sudan,* Washington, D.C.: Brookings Institution Press, 1995.

282 Deng, Francis, *War of Visions Conflict of Identities in the Sudan,* Washington, D.C.: Brookings Institution Press, 1995.

283 Youssef Aboul-Enein, "The Sudanese Army: a historical analysis and discussion on religious politicization," Infantry Magazine, July-August, 2004.

284 Oliver Albino, *The Sudan: A Southern Viewpoint,* London: Oxford University Press, 1970.

_____ John G. Nyuot Yoh, "The historical origins of the Sudanese civil wars: The politics of gunboat diplomacy" A paper presented at a seminar entitled "Roll Back Xenophobia Campaign Media Seminar Series: The Conflict in Sudan" held at South Africa Human Rights Commission, Friday, 25 May 2001 Houghton, Parktown, Johannesburg.

285 Petition to United Nations by Sudan African Closed Districts National Union (SACDNU), 1963.

286 Deng D. Ruay, *The Politics of Two Sudans: The South and the North,* Uppsala: Nordiska Afrikainstitutet, 1994.

287 John G. Nyuot Yoh, "The historical origins of the Sudanese civil wars: The politics of gunboat diplomacy" A paper presented at a seminar entitled "Roll Back Xenophobia Campaign Media Seminar Series: The Conflict in Sudan" held at South Africa Human Rights Commission, Friday, 25 May 2001 Houghton, Parktown, Johannesburg.

288 Robert Collins, (forthcoming publication in 2007): "Chapter Five:

Parliamentary and Military Experiments in Government, 1956-1969" *The History of the Modern Sudan*, Hollywood: Tsehai Publ.

[289] Ibid

[290] John G. Nyuot Yoh, "The historical origins of the Sudanese civil wars: The politics of gunboat diplomacy" A paper presented at a seminar entitled "Roll Back Xenophobia Campaign Media Seminar Series: The Conflict in Sudan" held at South Africa Human Rights Commission, Friday, 25 May 2001 Houghton, Parktown, Johannesburg.

[291] Robert Collins, (forthcoming publication in 2007): Chapter Six: The Government of Ja'afar Numayri: The Heroic Years, 1969-1976" *The History of the Modern Sudan*, Hollywood: Tsehai Publ.

[292] Benjamin Beit-Hallahmi, *The Israeli Connection: Whom Israel Arms & Why*, New York: Pantheon, 1987. pp. 48.

[293] John Sorenson, Disaster and Development in the Horn of Africa, New York: St. Martin's Press, 1995.

[294] New Vision, "Uganda: The Making of Idi Amin," August 6, 2007.

[295] Time in partnership with CNN, "The Armed Missionary" Nov. 22, 1971.

[296] Rolf Steiner, *The Last Adventurer*, Boston: Little, Brown, 1978.

[297] Robert Collins, (forthcoming publication in 2007): Chapter Six: The Government of Ja'afar: The Heroic Years, 1969-1976" *The History of the Modern Sudan*, Hollywood: Tsehai Publ.

[298] The Addis Ababa Agreement: The Southern Provinces Regional Self-Government Act, 1972. Also see,

_____ Robert Collins, (forthcoming publication in 2007): Chapter Six: The Government of Ja'afar: The Heroic Years, 1969-1976" *The History of the Modern Sudan*, Hollywood: Tsehai Publ.

[299] The Comprehensive Peace Agreement between the Government of the Republic of the Sudan & the Sudan People Liberation Movement/ Army, Nairobi, Kenya, January 9th, 2005.

Chapter Six
Ideology and Strategy

"There are many roads to freedom. Ours seems to be the most difficult. Therefore, we must accept this reality and do only what we can" (Fr. Saturnino Lohure).

Religion

Fr. Saturnino Lohure life cannot be separated from his priesthood as he was an ordained Catholic priest who died as a priest due to his involvement in political activities including arms struggle. His life experience cannot also be separated from his Christian faith. He happened to lived in the era where the Catholic Church was faced with the controversy of "liberation theology," and at the same time in the country that oppressed its people. Liberation theology is a school of thought that views Jesus Christ not as just the Redeemer but a Liberator of the oppressed, therefore, liberation theology includes in its mission political activism to bring justice to the oppressed. The Catholic Church has in many occasions denounced liberation theology citing that some elements of it are not compatible with the Catholic teachings. Fr. Saturnino Lohure, though not officially designated by the Church as a liberation theologian, most of his activities in politics and military would certainly qualify him a liberation theologian, even though unique in his own category, given his activities, environment, and issues he was dealing with.

The liberation theology has its historical roots in Latin America and was very much tight to the ideological conflicts of the Cold War between capitalists on one hand and communists on the other. By 1950s and 1960s, nationalistic consciousness arose in Latin America as most of the Latin American countries developed industries, which largely benefited the minority in urban populations while neglecting the majority rural peasantries. Strong movement among the majority rural peasantries emerged demanding profound changes in the social and economic structures in governments and societies in the Latin American countries. In other words, they were demanding revolutionary changes among the Latin American countries. For those movements' inspirations, Cuba provided the model and the alternative. And for leadership, charismatic bishops and priests who often worked among the middle class and the poor began to encourage progressive changes. The Vatican II provided justification for those bishops and priests to liturgically interpret situations in the ways they saw fit. This in turn laid the foundation for liberation theology. More significantly, liberation theology became a drastic shift in theological history from theoretical approach which normally takes places within the seminaries and the within the doctrine of the church to practical approach among the parishioners who established their own liturgical forms of practices in dealing with issues at hand, mainly, social, economic, and political.

This bottom up approach is a threat not only to the doctrine of the

Church but to the much centralized system in the Catholic Church hierarchy. It was Pope John Paul II and Cardinal Joseph Ratzinger (currently Pope Benedict XVI), who vigorously countered the liberation theology with reconciliation theology. Through the Congregation for the Doctrine of the Faith (CDF) led by Cardinal Ratzinger, the Catholic Church condemned the elements of liberation theology that support Marxism and violence on two occasions in 1984 and again in 1986. Edward A. Lynch says the elements of Marxism and violence supported by liberation theologians, set them apart from the orthodox Catholics on the issue of unity. As for their differences, Lynch explains, "for the liberationists, unity will come when economic and social divisions are eliminated, and they are willing to use violence to achieve this end. For their opponents, the unity that matters is cultural, spiritual, and far removed from economics."[300] Cardinal Ratzinger on his part, attacks the whole notion of class struggle, which is also a communist element. The Cardinal wrote, "the class struggle as a road toward a classless society is a myth which slows reform and aggravates poverty and injustice. Those who allow themselves to be caught up in fascination with this myth should reflect on the bitter examples history has to offer about where it leads."[301] The Cardinal went on to add, "they would then understand that we are not talking here about abandoning an effective means of struggle on behalf of the poor for an ideal which has no practical effects. On the contrary, we are talking about freeing oneself from a delusion in order to base oneself squarely on the Gospel and its power of realization."[302]

On the violence aspect of liberation theology, Cardinal Ratzinger, wrote:

> The truth of mankind requires that this battle be fought in ways consistent with human dignity. That is why the

systematic and deliberate recourse to blind violence, no matter, from which side it comes, must be condemned. To put one's trust in violent means in the hope of restoring more justice is to become the victim of a fatal illusion: violence begets violence and degrades man. It mocks the dignity of man in the person of the victims and it debases that same dignity among those who practice it.[303]

The biggest threat of liberation theology seems to stem from its elements of communism and the revolutionary zeal, which is its driving force. Cardinal Ratzinger made this very clear when he wrote:

By the same token, the overthrow by means of revolutionary violence of structures which generate violence is not ipso facto the beginning of a just regime. A major fact of our time ought to evoke the reflection of all those who would sincerely work for the true liberation of their brothers: millions of our own contemporaries legitimately yearn to recover those basic freedoms of which they were deprived by totalitarian and atheistic regimes which came to power by violent and revolutionary means, precisely in the name of the liberation of the people. This shame of our time cannot be ignored: while claiming to bring them freedom, these regimes keep whole nations in conditions of servitude which are unworthy of mankind. Those who, perhaps inadvertently, make themselves accomplices of similar enslavements betray the very poor they mean to help.[304]

For Fr. Saturnino Lohure, he seems to hold a unique theology of his own within the Catholic Church, when it comes to question of liberation, arms struggle, and the fight for freedom and justice. First, of all, he was born at a time and place when and where Catholicism was only just one year old by the time he was born. The Catholic missionaries arrived and established the Torit mission in 1920, a year before, the Father was born. Of course, Pope John Paul II was born at the same time when the Catholic mission was established in Torit, however, in a different place called Wadowice, Poland where Catholicism already established stronger root.[305] And the current Pope, Benedict XVI was born six years after the Father, and also in a place where Catholicism has strong presence.[306] These contrasting differences are the beginning of the circumstances that separate the Father on one hand and the two Popes on the other as far as their theological understandings are concern within the Catholic Church in the issue of liberation. For example, Cardinal Wojty³a (Pope John Paul II) is remembered in his participation in Vatican II for contribution in drafting the Constitution Gaudium and for participation in all the assemblies of the Synod of Bishops while his successor Cardinal Ratzinger (Pope Benedict XVI) is remembered as an expert in theology and theological advisor for Cardinal Joseph Frings, Archbishop of Cologne. They are both remembered for the things which were directly related to the proceedings of the Vatican Council meetings. However, Fr. Saturnino Lohure, was present at the Vatican Council meetings to make the cause of South Sudan be known, a sharp contrast to the objectives and proceedings of that council and to these two Popes.

To begin with his theological journey, the Father made his mission to seek Christ redemption very clear. He challenged a missionary bishop who pursued reconciliation theology (in line with Pope John Paul II and Cardinal Ratzinger) in dealing with the Arabs of Sudan by writing:

...admit with me that the peace tactics followed up to now by the Church in Sudan did not bear good results; but rather the opposite: the Arabs became more daring. They reached their objectives: the systematic destruction of the Church with the new anti-missionary law.[307]

The Father went on to stress, "what is the use of baptizing babies, if in the future, it would become impossible to instruct them? Or if to get a job or employment they must become Muslims."[308] The environment in which the Father was in, presented him with a dilemma if he was to seek the redemption of Jesus Christ. Through the anti Christian laws enacted by the Khartoum Northern Islamic Arab government, the activities of Christians were restricted. Given the reality of the situation, following the teaching of Christ was not the first option; leave alone whether it was even an option. Instead there were only two options; one was to become a Muslim and two to resist Islam. The former is the easiest option as it requires submission to Allah, the God of the Muslims. The situation was such that the Muslims of Sudan were forcing the non Muslims to submit to Allah. They insist that, after all, a total submission to Allah was not only necessary but the easiest thing one could ever do. It is as easy as reciting, "there is no divinity but God, and Muhammad is His Prophet."[309] One expert insists that the process is very easy to the point where, "no other test is necessary, and it would not matter if he (a convert) had never heard of Mecca or even the Koran."[310] However, if one does not meet such basic requirements, or in other words, if one does not profess the faith of Islam, they should be dealt with. According to their book, known as the Holy Koran, it states, "...fight and slay the Pagans wherever ye find them, and seize them, beleaguer them, and lie in wait for them in every stratagem (of war)..."[311] Another passage from this same Holy Book says, "fight those who believe not in Allah nor the Last Day, nor hold that forbidden which hath been forbidden by Allah and His Messenger, nor acknowledge the religion of Truth, (even if they are) of the People of the Book..."[312] It was those provoking verses in the Koran, which justify the Muslims of the Sudan to wage a Jihad or a holy war to the none Muslims of the South Sudan. For example, one of the Northern political party in its politic statement, declared:

> It is our top priority to speed up the spread of the Arabic language throughout the South and in the Nuba Mountains. In this era of modern national identities the importance of language as a means of consolidating the Arab and Islamic culture is obvious. We regard the spread of Arabic in these areas as part of Jihad (wholly war) for the sake of Allah and Arab nationalism. Our policies toward the South thus outlined must be followed very soon by similar ones towards the Nuba Mountains and Darfur.[313]

In the context of Sudan, Arabic language and Arabic culture was synonymous with Islamic religion. The forced Arabization was equal to the forced Islamization as evidenced in schools in the South where students before joining elementary schools must first master the Koran as a means of learning Arabic. In other words, becoming a Muslim was a prerequisite of learning Arabic. Commenting on the Muslims of Sudan, Amir Idris, argued, "...those groups that didn't speak Arabic as their first language nevertheless regarded Arabic as the language of 'civilization' and religion."[314] Another individual, Abd al-Rahman al-Bashir argued that in order to be considered authentic Arab in Sudan; one must "speak Arabic, the good language of the Koran."[315] For the Northern Sudanese

Arabs, Sudan could only be identified with Arabic and Islamic culture as Sadiq al-Mahdi argued, "…this nation will not have its entity identified and its prestige and pride preserved except under an Islamic revival."[316]

Given this situation, the Father opted for the second option, which is of resisting Islam, of course at a serious risk. Resistance in this sense was not an end but a means of achieving an end. In the case of the Father, it was a means by which Christianity could flourish or to put it in a more christianly way, it was a means of seeking redemption of Jesus Christ. Resistance in political context means to fight, which often culminate into formation of a political grouping or movement. Currently, there are several resistance movements in the word including in Sudan, which are waging arms struggled against what they perceived as aggression or oppression. The term resistance has a political overtone that it competes with similar terms like freedom, liberation, emancipation, etc. One of its effective elements is the use of force to realize its objectives. It is against this background that the Father became a liberator within the Catholic teaching. He had made it abundantly clear that Christianity could only be practiced in a free society. According to the Father, "religion is a matter of individual consciousness," that can be practiced freely without being coerced or imposed on others.[317] That is why for the Father, professing the faith of Christianity was as much important as liberating the oppressed. Therefore, the Father was as much a spiritual leader who preached Christian faith just as he was a political leader for the society who preached liberation struggle with objective aim of achieving freedom.

Political

The Father used the quotation, "exclusion from the government of one's country is exclusion from all the benefits that accrue from such government" as a foundation to lay out his political ideology and thoughts. Applying this to the situation of Sudan, the Father deplored the undemocratic rule practiced in Sudan, especially the military rule. Sudan has a long history of military rule from the time it had independent to present. The years of military rule outnumbered civilian rule in ratio of thirty-nine to only twelve (39: 12) years of civilian rule. Every time a civil government took power it never been allowed to last more than five years. The most despicable thing the Father opposed about the military regimes was that they suppressed all sort of freedom such as press, association, or religion. An element of military rule that the Father opposed is the power to decree. This provided the military ruler or rulers absolute power to arbitrary confiscate peoples' properties, arrest individuals, or even execute them at will. During General Abrahim Abboud rule in 1960s, the number of Southern prisoners was estimated at 10,000 who were imprisoned for mere political reasons. Prominent among those were Fr. Paulino Dogale who was sentenced to twelve years for allegedly lending his type writer to one of the students who involved in a demonstration. Others such as Dominic Mourwel and Ezibon Mandiri were sentenced to ten years each. And there were many more others who were rounded up and imprisoned, putting the total for those imprisoned into thousands. The executions of innocent civilians were rampant, moreover done in public, just as to demonstrate the ruthlessness of the regime.[318] According to the Father, the solution to this dictatorial rule was a free election in all level of governments through secret ballots.

When it comes to the political situation in the South, the Father was convinced that all the Northern governments whether civilian or military, elected or otherwise, agreed on oppressing the people of the South Sudan. In the volume of his book, *The Problem of Southern Sudan*, which best represents, the political thought of the Father, he argues:

The case of the South is not political in the usual meaning of the term, as it is for one of the Satellite States of the Communist world. It is something greater: actually it is the question of life or death, of racial slavery....From the present Northern Sudanese attitude and the policies applied to the South, we are irresistibly led to the conclusion that their aim is to destroy the African personality and identity in the Sudan and to replace it with an Arabized and Islamized South, thus driving a wedge of the Arab world deep into the continent.[319]

He challenged the successive governments in Khartoum to come out clearly and institute a racial government such as the apartheid regime in South Africa so as the liberal Arabs would side with the African Sudanese in challenging the government. But without coming out clearly, the Father said, successive governments in Khartoum were deceiving the Northern Arabs whom they claimed to be representing. According to him, the solution for the Southern Problems is for the South to have a federal system where Southerners would have more saying in their affairs, and if that is not achievable then the South must opt for complete independence through the free will of the Southerners in a plebiscite. And if a plebiscite for the Southerners is not allowed to take place so as they determine for themselves, then they must pursue independence for South Sudan through arms struggle. This was actually the stage the Father reached, carrying out arms struggle for a complete independence of South Sudan. His experience and the attitude demonstrated by the Northern Sudanese convinced him that the last option was to carryout arms struggle for a complete independence of the South Sudan. He was convinced that arms struggle would yield a better result. Judging from the

Torit Mutiny of 1955, were Southerners rose in arms and freed themselves temporarily, the Father wrote, "Southerners nearly freed themselves using the very force" Arabs use against the Southerners.[320] The Father would reassure himself and others who were equally determined in following this process by saying, "there are many roads to find freedom. Ours seems to be the most difficult. Therefore we must accept this reality and do only what we can" including "…die fighting rather than to serve the Arabs of the Sudan or the international policy."[321] As for any political negotiation or arrangement with the Northerners, the Father was very pessimistic about it. He showed such pessimism in a piece written to the East African Standard newspaper, by arguing, "if the political parties of the North do not take to heart in a more realistic manner the Southern Problems, the perspectives of reaching a positive final solution in a democratic way are extremely remote, if not impossible."[322] The Father doubted very much the Northern Arabs positive political maneuverings, viewing them as a means of luring Southerners so as they could be oppressed even more. He remained consistently pessimistic in any prospective of reaching a solution for Southern Problems through a peaceful means. Just before he was killed, the Father would frustratingly conclude, "we are now crossing a decisive moment. We don't want to give up. The Arabs also don't want to give up. But we don't want to lose heart. Our capital sin: we are not united. Soldiers and politicians (from the South), they don't have the same vision… Never the Arabs will accept the idea of a federation!" Indeed it was a decisive moment not just for the South Sudan in general but for him in particular as he was eventually killed by the Uganda soldiers in the border as he attempted to crossed back to the South to rally the soldiers and inform them of Ugandan plan in intercepting the Anyanya soldiers within the borders. As for the Southerners, they were lured in through the

Addis Ababa Agreement, just as the Father predicted. The same Northern government, which signed the Addis Ababa Agreement, was the very government which finally abrogated it, confirming the Father's attitudes of having doubts in the intentions and political maneuverings of the Northern Sudanese Arabs governments.

In 2005, the government in Khartoum under the presidency of Omer Hassan al-Basher and his Islamic party, the National Congress Party (NCP) signed an agreement with a southern rebel movement the Sudan People Liberation Movement/Army (SPLM/A). However, three years later into the agreement, there is already pessimism on whether the agreement will hold. This agreement known as the Comprehensive Peace Agreement (CPA) was brokered under internationally supervised body, but today there is profound fear that the international body is paying less attention to the implementation of the CPA, risking its collapsed. International Crisis Group in its report warned, "the overwhelming international concentration on Darfur has come at the expense of the broader quest for peace in the country."[323] Another report referring to the crisis in Darfur states that it "basically just sucks all the oxygen out of the air."[324] As the world diverts all its attention to Darfur, the situation in the South is deteriorating from bad into worse.

The most critical provisions of the CPA are only implemented in papers. The CPA calls on implementation to go in the order of demarcation of South-North borders, a national census, a free general election, and finally referendum to take place in 2011. Midway through the interim period, none of these happened yet. In another report, it indicates, "the anticipated disputes over borders, national resources, and the census could assume violent proportions and set the stage for a descent into war."[325] Such view is confirmed by the Southern Sudanese president, Salva Kiir Mayardit. In his address to the Southern Sudan

Legislative Assembly, President Mayardit feared by saying, "I'm worried Mr. Speaker that it is likely that Sudan will reverse again to war."[326] Currently, the Northern troops are not only withdrawing from the Southern region as stipulated on the CPA, but deploying on the Southern oil rich region. There is an estimated 16,600 Northern soldiers in Upper Nile. 687 Northern soldiers are still in Malakal town. The Northern soldiers who withdrew from Rubkona are reported to have returned with civilian clothing. Another report indicated that special unit recruited from Khartoum presidential guards has infiltrated the oil rich southern town of Bentiu. A military general from the southern region is quoted to have been convinced, "the politics have failed... The border will be established through the force of arms..."[327] In the overall assessment, there is a consensus among observers and analysts that the Northern Arab government will not relinquish the southern oil fields without putting a fight. As time progressed, much is to be witnessed.

Economic

When it comes to the economics, the Father did not separate it with politics. He argues that both economics and politics go hand in hand. To him, the fact that the South was lagging behind economically was because it lacked political powers to decide on matters related to its economy or the economic political decisions being made on the South were detrimental to its economic prosperity. During the colonial rule, the British were the ones deciding and most of the economic programs they had for the South Sudan never materialized because some of them were later transferred north during the independence or were simply forgotten. The economic disparity between the South and North is one of the contributing factors to the war—the war which actually devastated the South even more. Examples of such economic projects designed for the

South were the rice production, paper industry, coffee production, tobacco manufacturing, sorghum production, sugar production, tea growing, fruit canning, cattle trade, fisheries, logging industry, and wildlife industry. Out of these projects, the tobacco and logging schemes were only developed into a limited scale which only met the demands of the Northern Sudan. The other schemes such as the Nzara cotton factory, Malakal cotton pump, Malakal fish-canning, and Mongalla sugar refinery were transferred to the Northern Sudan. Vocational institutions which used to train Southerners in the filed of clerical work, bookkeeping, medical and in agricultural fields were closed down and some of their buildings were turned into military barracks. The qualified Southerners in those fields of works were not required anymore as the prerequisite for those jobs was to know Arabic language very well. By 1960s, majority of government workers in the South were overwhelmingly Northerners. There were disproportionally fourteen Southerners in scale of 'G' and upwards compared to 138 Northerners. The scale 'J' and upwards had 217 Southerners compared to 335 Northerners. And this is not to count the military which was almost Northerners.[328]

The government in Khartoum made economic decisions, which made South Sudan dependence on the North economically. The South was deliberated excluded from the share of national budget. The Northern Arabs were dominating businesses in the South creating unfavorable competition with the locals who aspired to conduct businesses. The profits for their businesses were taken for the development of the North. Worse yet, the government set very difficult conditions for the Southerners to obtain licenses in conducting businesses. If the British could take pride for their contribution to Sudan by linking the South and North through accident of the River Nile then the Arabs must equally take pride in their contribution by linking the South and North through the a single and short railway line. As for the Southerners, they have to yet reap the benefit of both contributions. It was a British high official Cromer, who even had a title of the 'Lord,' after politically securing the Nile waters, he boasted, "the waters of the Nile, from the lakes to the sea, are brought fully under control, it would be possible to boast that man— in this case, the Englishman—has turned the gifts of nature to the best possible advantage."[329] It still remains to be explained on how the Southern Sudanese could benefit from the pride of Englishman who boasted around about the waters that he never created and is not even in his land. As for the railway which the Northerners boasted about, the benefit of it to the Southerners was and is still disastrous because the aim of the railway is primarily to transport the troops to south in a massive number who in turn ending up massacring the Southerners. The secondary aim of this railway was and is still to transport animals from the South to the North, which Southerners cannot afford as it is very expensive almost the cost of the animal. What the South Sudan needs is not a short and single railroad that ended in Wau and its aims are destructive to the Southerners, but a crisscross network of both railways and roads throughout the South, which can link the South not just with the North but with its other African neighboring countries. It is still baffling today that in South Sudan land communication is a major problem. For example, today, traveling from Juba, the capital of the South to Kaju-Keji is inaccessible by land. One had to go through entering Uganda back and forth. In essence, neither the British nor the Arabs contributed to the economic wellbeing of the South Sudan, even though they boasted about their contributions which are, by the way, more negative than positive.

The Father dismissed the argument that the South of Sudan was poor. This was at a time when oil was not discovered in South Sudan and most of the major discoveries and surveys were not undertaken yet. However, the Father used expert studies conducted at the time to drive home his point that the South was actually more richer than the North, given economic potentials the South had. One of such examples the Father cited was a study from Germany, which pointed to the "Southern Sudan potential in paper production is so immense that if carried out the Southern Sudan could rank among the leading countries in the production of this commodity. The possibility of hydro-electric power from Nimule would make the development of a paper industry possible."[330] The other report was from the Chinese study, which argued, "if the vast plains of Aweil in the Bahr el-Ghazal and the plains south of Malakal were put into rice farming, the South could have enough rice to feed the 700 million Chinese."[331] In addition to this, a recent report published in 2005, estimated fishing "contributes on average between 10 and 20% of annual food baskets in the region." This is despite the lack of marketing for the commodity. Another report the Father cited was that the chairman of the Jonglei Investigation Team, who was a British, stated, "given the money, the technical know-how and the experts, the Southern Sudan could easily become one of the riches countries in Africa."[332] The Father went on to point that another expert report from Canada concluded, "North East Equatoria has ideal conditions for cattle ranching, that if developed could become a big meat producing area in this part of Africa."[333] Today there is a talk of the same area being richly invested with minerals. A news report on August of 2007, indicated that the government of South Sudan issued exploration licenses to two companies from Britain and South Africa to explore the possibilities of gold and uranium in the area.[334] This is a follow up from the survey conducted in 1970s, which "estimated that about 300,000 km2 of the South is underlain by igneous and metamorphic rocks; and 200,000 km2 is covered by sediments which includes alluvium and swamp deposits."[335] The follow-up exploration to this discovery "confirmed existence of gold, iron, copper, uranium, chromium, zinc, tungsten, diamond, mica, magnetite, salt, manganese, gemstones, petroleum, and other metallic, industrial, and chemical minerals." To further argue his point, the Father cited yet another report by a Northern Sudanese Arab, which stated, "the papyrus in the South could produce all types of paper which will not only satisfy the home market and be the saving of millions of pounds, but will become an important export product, especially the paper pulp and cellulose. Other possible uses of papyrus are the production of fuel briquettes, alcohol, acetone, building board, pig and poultry food, and plasters."[336] Even though the Father argued that Sudan was home for wild animals with greatest potential for tourism, at the time, he did not have a conclusive studies and surveys to back up his argument. However, the later studies and surveys have proven the argument of the Father to be right. A survey taken in early 1980s indicated a reliably good numbers of wild animals in the South. During the long years of bloody war, from 1983 through 2005, almost everyone concluded that population of wild animals in the South must have been wiped out, but instead, they thrived in thousands and even millions. The recent aerial surveys carried out in 2007, stunningly revealed spectacular video footage of wild animals streaming in thousands in an area that covers 1,600 kilometers in Boma National Park, Southern National Park, and the Jonglei region. J. Michael Fay, a Wildlife Conservation Society (WCS) biologist and National Geographic explorer-in-residence who helped lead the survey was very astonished with the results of the finding. In astonishment, all he was left with was to say, "seeing thousands upon thousands upon thousands of white-eared kob streaming under the aircraft, day after day, was like I had died and was having the most unbelievable dream you could ever have."[337] That to him was a tipping point for his career as he concluded, "all my life I have been watching wildlife, and when I saw the kob in Sudan I said to myself, You can die now, Fay, you finally saw what you could have never imagined you would ever see on this planet."[338] The movement of wild animals in South Sudan today is consider among the largest land migration in the world rivaling that one of wildebeest exodus across the Serengeti Park.[339]

Given these reports, analyses, surveys, and conclusions of Southern Sudan potential for economic growth, the Father was more than convinced that the South needed better economic policies, capital, and technical know-how to exploit those economic potentials in turning the South into a rich nation. Unfortunately, to this day, none of those economic potentials are undertaken seriously, especially with the flow of oil, the rest of economic potentials are ignored completely by both the Khartoum government and the Southern Sudan government. Today, the only source of income for South Sudan government is a fifty percent share of oil revenue extracted from the Southern region, which is hardly enough for building a region devastated by decades of war and suffered through negligence from the successive central governments in Khartoum. The oil, a euphemism for the "curse" came with negative impact of its own with devastating toll to the people of South Sudan. First, the discovery of oil in the south resulted in the local population being forced militarily from their ancestral homes, which led to lost of lives properties, and whatever dignity that was left on the population. The revenue of the oil does not benefit the people of the South in any meaningful way. The little the South gets as a result of the peace dividend is barely enough, and that is not to mention on how it is being mismanaged, corrupted, and looted by some officials in the government of South Sudan. The former South Sudan financial secretary, Arthur

Akuien Chol, not surprisingly enough, is among the people implicated in a ring of corruption in South Sudan. Under South Sudan President, Salva Kiir declaration of zero-tolerance on corruption, Arthur Akuien Chol is detained awaiting corruption investigation. On positive development, there are attempts being made to revive and expand the Aweil Irrigation Rehabilitation Project (AIRP) for the production of rice.[340] However, challenges still remains for the success of the project including the commitment from the government of South Sudan and the partners involved.

Social

On the social front, the Father views the relationship between the Arabs and African of Sudan as: survive

> ...one of the born masters for the Arabs and of slaves for the Southerners and descendents of ex-slaves who live in the North, some of whom have accepted their inferior position as inevitable. This is the position the Arabs want to create in the South, one of inferiority.[341]

At the time, the Father suspected that slavery was still on going in Sudan where the slaves were sold to Saudi Arabia, across the read sea from the Sudan. As for evidence he cited an August 1962 report, which appeared in London on *News of the World* by a French traveler, Francois d'Harcourt. The report in part, reads:

> Arabia is still wrapped in the slumber of the dark ages. Bin Rashid (an Arab guide) explained the working of the trade. He told how entire cargoes of human merchandise arrive

from Eritrea, the Sudan, the Somaliland Coast, Afghanistan, the Indies and even the Far East. Some land at Djeddah, others on the coasts of Oman. On arrival groups are separated into two lots; the slaves for the kitchen (Djaria el Mebach) and the slaves for the bed (Djaria el Sirrir). Bin Rashid estimates there are more than one million slaves in Saudi Arabia. At Mecca they can be seen tethered in groups or seven or eight. And should any slave try to escape and get recapture there is only one punishment—death by beheading.[342]

One of the most sensitive issues that carried with it a huge stigma was the issue of slavery which basically set apart the Arabs and the Black African of Sudan. An economic disparity was also another factor that contributed into a social stigma between the Arabs and Black Africans of the Sudan. Black Africans were considered low class and not worthy of any dignity. A good example of that was in marriages where Black African men could not marry Arab women, but the Arab men could use Black African women as concubines or sex slaves. Dr. L.A. Fabunmi, a Nigerian, wrote that he was "reliably informed by a Northerner Sudanese friend that it is practically impossible for a Southerner to marry a Northern woman, but that a northern male can easily marry a Southern beauty."[343] The government seized on this opportunity as a means of assimilation or rather coercive unity. The Northerners who worked in the South were given huge allowances so as they could marry as many Black Beauties on the temporary bases and also be able to support their real wives in the North. For Muslims are polygamies by nature and law. Even worse, the Arabs introduced into Southern Sudan homosexuality, a phenomenon alien to the Southern cultures. Southerners were often shocked of rampant cases of rapes of young boys by Arabs. Those Arabs carrying out these horrible rapes were often let go free without being charged by the law—the law which is controlled by the Arabs. In earlier 1960s, two cases of rape in Rumbek and Tonj, involving senior government officials were reported, and in all those cases, evidences were destroyed. There was only one case in Yei, in 1960 where a Northern Arab by the name Mohammed Hassan was sentenced to seven years in prison for raping a twelve year-old boy. In this case, the evidence was overwhelming because the perpetrator was caught on the act; therefore, they could not find ways to destroy the evidence.[344]

The Father was a firm believer in competition between private organizations and the government in providing social services. It is through competition that the best service would prevail. However, that was not the case in South Sudan. The missionaries, who were responsible for providing social services, were instead kicked out of the Sudan through the Missionary Act, enacted by dictator general Abboud. The Southerners were left to scramble for themselves as the government could not provide the services, which the missionaries used to provide. While in the North, they allow private organizations to compete with the government in providing services.

Education

With the coming of independence, education in South Sudan degraded both in quantity and quality. Prior to independence most of the functional schools in the South were of the missionaries. So, instead of adding more schools to the already existing ones, or at least maintained those ones who are already running, the government closed them down. They schools, which were closer to the missions, were transferred far away for the fear of Christian influence. Other schools were transferred north, were Southerners could not go. Statistics of 1960 indicated a disproportional number of Southern Sudanese students enrolled in higher education. Out of 1,216 students in the University of Khartoum, only sixty of them were Southerners. In Khartoum technical school, there were 1,000 students and only thirty of them were Southerners.[345]

At the elementary level, it was even worse as the Southern students were deprived of real learning. During the colonial period, the foundation for education in the South was well grounded. In the beginning, the students started learning vernacular and later on transform into English at a higher level. The system used to produce quality education. However, with the new system after the independence, the beginners started with the teaching of Koran, moreover, not in regular schools, but the Islamic schools called *Khalaws*. The system left Christian children with no option but to join Islamic schools, meaning registering as Muslims to learn Koran as a means of learning Arabic so that they become competitive in elementary schools. They also have no option of learning Christianity until they turn eighteen by which they have to obtain license to first by baptize and then learn Christianity. The law restricted Christian activities through its licensing policies, and any Christian activities required license which most of the times could not be obtained. As such, Christian securlar education which was once superior was dead.

The Blueprint

The book, *The Problem of Southern Sudan*, published in May 1963, by the Institute of Race Relations (London, Oxford University Press), and attributed to the authorships of Joseph Oduho and William Deng, is perhaps not only represents, Fr. Saturnino Lohure political thoughts but is also a blueprint for Southern Sudan. It is the first book of a kind about South Sudan and written by a South Sudanese. Since it is written by someone who directly participated in the Southern Sudanese struggle, it is written with such passion and authoritative tone. The books goes into much details in explaining the subjection of the South Sudanese people in politics, economic, religion, social and in education. The book is a major source for the history of Southern Sudan struggle, given the historical accounts and sources it employs. Interestingly, only few people are aware of the fact that this masterpiece was the work of the Father. In fact, it was the Father who had written the book but because of his position as a priest, he avoided any implication by attributing the authorship of this book to two of his prominent colleagues, Joseph Oduho and William Deng. Of course, all the Southern Sudanese politicians in exile including Joseph Oduho and William Deng subscribed to the analysis and diagnosis of Southern Problems as outlined in that book. They did not do so out of respect for the Father but because of the truthfulness contained in the book. Otherwise, Oduho and Deng would not have accepted the authorship to be attributed to them, had they held different views. It was not the only time the Father attributed authorship of his work to others. Actually, most of his articles he used to write about the plight of South Sudan for the newspapers were signed under the pseudo name, Pedro Pro, a Mexican Jesuit Priest who was martyred by the Mexican government for defying anti-Catholic policies.[346]

History of Deliberate Exclusion of Southern Sudanese from Decision-Making

The book lays out the political problems of South Sudan in a systematical historical manner. It stresses of the fact that the relationship between the South and North was of a bitter and bloody one due to the Arabs involvement in slave-trades where they raided and terrorized the African population. The stigma of that relationship contributes to the present predicament. The book goes on to explain the systemic and deliberate exclusion of the Southern Sudanese from decision making process since the Anglo-Egyptian took power in Sudan in 1899 through the time the book was published in1963. This period covered the Anglo-Egyptian rule as well as the Sudanese Arabs rule. After chasing the Mahdists and taking control, the British signed an agreement with Egypt to set up Anglo-Egyptian condominium rule in Sudan. In doing so, Southern Sudanese were neither consulted nor represented. The British became the sole ruler of the Sudan and in instituting a Closed District Ordinance; the British literally closed the Southern Sudanese not only from the outside world but from progressing political, economically, educationally, and even socially. That was going to be the same policy successive regimes in Khartoum would follow in dealing with South Sudan after the British left.

By 1944, in preparing Sudan for self-government, the British assisted the Northern Sudanese Arabs to establish Advisory Council, which deal with issues related to the government. Again, South Sudan was ignored and where not even informed of the existence of Advisory Council or its role. In 1946, the British Governor-General of Sudan, Sir Hubert Huddleston convened a conference in Khartoum with the Northerner Sudanese Arabs and decided among other things to unite the South and North of Sudan in the event of independence of Sudan. Here again, the Southern Sudanese were deliberately excluded on the ground that "Southerners had not reached a standard of education which would enable them to represent their compatriots in such a Council."[347] In the first ever Sudan Legislative Assembly, which opened its session in 1948, only thirteen Southerners were represented in the Assembly. Those thirteen Southerners were all handpicked by the British government as oppose to getting elected. When the Constitution Amendment

Commission was formed under the British supervision, South Sudan was represented by only one member. That one member was overwhelmed with the majority Northern Sudanese Arabs where in frustration he walked out, forfeiting his membership and that of South Sudan from participation in the Constitution Amendment Commission. In the Cairo Agreement of 1953, signed between the British and Egyptian, which paved way for the independence of Sudan, the Southern Sudanese were intentionally kept out of the deal. In 1954, a Sudanization Committee was appointed of five-member, none of them was a Southerner. Prior to the independence, when 8,00 servant positions were to be filled by the Sudanese, only four junior positions were awarded to the Southern Sudanese. Even in the first and second parliamentary elections of Sudanese Assembly, Southerners were deprived of their share of representatives given their population, which was thirty percent of the general population of Sudan. Southerners were also deliberately excluded from the arms forces. The only Southern battalion in the military was disbanded after the Torit Mutiny of 1955. Sudanese army was increased steadily in number without reflection of Southern participation as Southerners were considered rebels.

The list is long, and the pattern of deliberate exclusion of Southerners from decision-making is continuing to the present day Sudan. Currently, per the Comprehensive Peace Agreement (CPA) signed in 2005, between the Southern rebel movement, the Sudan People Liberation Movement (SPLM) and Khartoum government, the Southern share in the ministerial post in the central government is denied to them in a deliberate and dare act. In this supposedly power sharing government, the Northern Sudanese Arabs maintain the powerful ministries of energy and mining, defense, interior, finance and justice. The SPLM tried in vain to get either the financial ministry or the ministry for energy and mining. Such daring move let even some Arabs such as Hafiz Mohamed, Sudan program director for the London-based advocacy group Justice Africa to conclude, "it is clearer than ever that the South will go for independence."[348] This is echoing the Southern Sudanese sentiment which doubt very much the idea of unity between the South and North come referendum day in 2011 for Southern Sudanese to vote on self-determination. Matter of fact, by the time this book went on production, the SPLM suspended its activities from the Government of National Unity, demanding that the CPA must be implemented fully.

The book makes a detail account of the declaration of war the Northern Arabs made to the Southern Sudanese people starting with the massacre that took place in Yambio in the aftermath of the illegal and unjust sentencing of a Southern Member of Parliament, Elia Kuze and it goes on detailing the Nzara riot massacre and the massacre of the aftermath of Torit Mutiny of 1955. However, those are not the only massacred carried against the Southerners as similar massacres followed later after the book was published. The most famous ones were the massacres in big towns of Juba and Wau and their surrounding areas which took place simultaneously in 1965. The dead in those massacres numbered in thousands.[349] In 1987, another serious massacre was inflicted to the people of South Sudan in El-Diem where thousands of innocent Southern Sudanese lost their lives.[350] This massacre and the one of 1965, took place under a civilian elected governments, showing that all the successive government in Khartoum, either civilian or military, elected or otherwise are as just brutal when dealing with the Southerners. And then there was the al-Jebelien Massacre of 1989 and Juba massacre of 1992, which both claimed the lives of the innocent Southern Sudanese. A report by one of the International advocacy group puts it better, when it emphasizes:

There are several other present government officials alleged to have been involved in numerous massacres that should be held accountable for crimes of genocide, crimes against humanity, and/or other war crimes. Some particularly noted massacres that should be investigated specifically for alleged individual accountability under the principle of command responsibility are the 1965 Wau Massacre, the 1987 Al Dhaein Massacre, the 1989 Al Jebelien Massacre, the 1992 Juba Massacre, as well as many other more recent massacres and other war crimes committed throughout the southern provinces and the Nuba Mountains that 'shock the conscience of mankind.'[351]

With such atrocities, which no one is always held accountable to, it presents a challenge for the international community at large and African Union (AU) in particular. In his book, which was published prior to the formation of any of the African continental organization, like a prophet, the Father posts such challenging question for the future leaders of Organization of Africa Unity (OAU) and its successor the African Union (AU), by questioning:

The principle of 'divide and rule' has wrought havoc among once-subjected peoples: can it be said that Pan-Africanism or African solidarity form part of this principle? The interpretation given to the two terms is the only determining factor; if the terms convey the idea of a continental union between the oppressed and the oppressors each retaining the status quo, then they are destructive and not constructive; but if they mean a union of the once oppressed Africans, some of whom today are free, some under subjection, then here is another challenge to the Pan-Africanism in which sides must be taken—either with the oppressed or the oppressor.[352]

Would these continental organizations rise to the challenge? Perhaps not! Evidence thus far shows they are not and they will not likely do so in the nearest future. It is up to those oppressed to free themselves with whatever means possible.

Chapter Endnotes

[300] Edward A. Lynch "The Retreat of Liberation Theology." This appeared in the February 1994 issue of *The Homiletic & Pastoral Review*.

[301] Cardinal Joseph Ratzinger, "Instruction on Certain Aspects of Theology of Liberation:" *Sacred Congregation for the Doctrine of the Faith*, August 6, 1984.

[302] Ibid

[303] Ibid

[304] Ibid

[305] His Holiness John Paul II Short Biography, Holy See Press Office [online] http://www.vatican.va/news_services/press/documentazione/documents/santopadre_biografie/giovanni_paolo_ii_biografia_breve_en.html

[306] Biography of His Holiness, Pope Benedict XVI, Libreria Editrice Vaticana [online] http://www.vatican.va/holy_father/benedict_xvi/biography/documents/hf_ben-xvi_bio_20050419_short-biography_en.html

[307] Fr. Neno Contran, *They Are A Target: 200 African Priests Killed*, Nairobi: Catholic Publishers in Africa, 1996. pg. 144.

[308] Ibid. p. 143.

[309] Francis Deng, "Sudan—Civil War and Genocide: Disappearing Christians of the Middle East," *Middle East Quarterly*, Winter 2001.

[310] Ibid

[311] From Qur'an 9:5 cited on BBC "Religion & Ethics: Islam"[online] http://www.bbc.co.uk/religion/religions/islam/history/earlyrise_1.shtml

[312] From Qur'an 9:29 on BBC "Religion & Ethics: Islam"[online] http://www.bbc.co.uk/religion/religions/islam/history/earlyrise_1.shtml

[313] Marit Magelssen Vambheim "Making Peace While Waging War:—A Peacemaking Effort in the Sudanese Civil War, 1965-1966" MA thesis in history, University of Bergen, Spring 2007.

[314] Amir H. Idris, *Sudan's Civil War: Slavery, Race and Formational Identities*, Lewiston, New York: The Edwin Mellon Press, 2001.

[315] Francis Deng, "Green is the Color of the Masters: The Legacy of Slavery and the Crisis of National Identity in Modern Sudan" Yale University. [online] http://www.yale.edu/glc/events/cbss/Deng.pdf

[316] Marit Magelssen Vambheim "Making Peace While Waging War:—A Peacemaking Effort in the Sudanese Civil War, 1965-1966" MA thesis in history, University of Bergen, Spring 2007.

[317] Petition to United Nations by Sudan African Closed Districts National Union (SACDNU), 1963.

[318] Ibid

[319] Joseph Oduho and William Deng, *The Problem of Southern Sudan*, London: Oxford University Press, 1963.

[320] Petition to United Nations by Sudan African Closed Districts National Union (SACDNU), 1963.

[321] Fr. Neno Contran, *They Are A Target: 200 African Priests Killed*, Nairobi: Catholic Publishers in Africa, 1996

[322] Ibid

[323] International Crisis Group "A Stratergy for Comprehensive Peace in Sudan" Africa Report N°130—26 July 2007.

[324] Dan Morrison "Sudan has Bigger Crisis than Darfur: '05 Peace Pact Falling Apart" San Francisco Chronicle, Sunday, August 12, 2007. P. A15

[325] Ibid

[326] Salva Kiir Mayardit, First Vice President of the Republic, and President of the Government of Southern Sudan, at the opening of the second session of the Southern Sudan Legislative Assembly, juba, September 10, 2007.

[327] Ibid

[328] Petition to United Nations by Sudan African Closed Districts National Union (SACDNU), 1963.

[329] Terje Tvedt, *The River Nile in the Age of British: Political Ecology and the Quest for Economic Power*, London: I B Tauris & Co Ltd, 2004.

[330] Petition to United Nations by Sudan African Closed Districts National Union (SACDNU), 1963.

[331] Ibid

[332] Ibid

[333] Ibid

[334] Skye Wheeler "International companies to begin exploration for gold and uranium" *Gurtong*, August 10, 2007.

[335] Benaiah Yongo, "Sudan Economy Research Group Discussion Papers: Peace Dividend and the Millennium Development Goals in Southern Sudan," University of Bremen, Germany, Aug. 2005.

[336] Petition to United Nations by Sudan African Closed Districts National Union (SACDNU), 1963.

[337] Nick Wadhams, "Massive Animal Herds Flourishing Despite Sudan War, Survey Reveals" *National Geographic News*, June 12, 2007. This is accompanied by a video titled "Massive Antelope Herds Seen From the Air in Sudan."

[338] Ibid

[339] Ibid

[340] Aweil Irrigation Rehabilitation Project, September, 2005.

[341] Petition to United Nations by Sudan African Closed Districts National Union (SACDNU), 1963.

[342] Ibid

[343] Ibid

_____ L. A. Fabunmi, *The Sudan in Anglo-Egyptian Relations: A Case Study in Power Politics*, 1800-1956, London : Longmans, 1960. p 364.

[344] Petition to United Nations by Sudan African Closed Districts National Union (SACDNU), 1963.

[345] Ibid

[346] Fr. Neno Contran, *They Are A Target: 200 African Priests Killed*, Nairobi: Catholic Publishers in Africa, 1996.

[347] Juba Conference "Proceeding of the Juba Conference on the Political Development of the
    Southern Sudan" June, 1947.

[348] IRIN "Sudan: Political Developments Raise Concern, Analysts Say," November 15th, 2005.

[349] Fr. Neno Contran, *They Are A Target: 200 African Priests Killed*, Nairobi: Catholic Publishers in Africa, 1996. p. 133.

[350] Mahgoub El-Tigani, "Solving The Crisis Of Sudan: The Right Of Self-Determination Versus State Torture," *Arab Studies Quarterly* (ASQ), Spring, 2001.

[351] Survivors' Rights International, "Special Alert Report: Eradication of Terrorism Forestalled by Khartoum's Genocidal Policies & Oppressive Rule, October-November 2001. Prepared following the terrorist attacks on America of September 11, 2001. Released November 12, 2001.

[352] Joseph Oduho and William Deng, The Problem of Southern Sudan, London: Oxford University Press, 1963.

Chapter Seven
Posthumous Fr. Saturnino Lohure & South Sudan

"Far away from home, far off in the cold surrounding of the little village of Lokung, one day in January 1967, lay the body of Rev. Saturnino Luhore, riddle with bullets. His wish was to come and minister to the parishioners in one small village in South, which will be his parish and home" (The Vigilant).

The Father Resting Place

It is very sad indeed that Fr. Saturnino Lohure's wish to "come and minister to the parishioners in one small village in South" never comes true. But even more sadder is that decades after his death, his body is still laying miles away from home in a foreign land. So, it is not only the live Father who never made it home on that tragic January 22, 1967, but it is also the deceased Father who never made it home. He might have thought that his body was laying in a foreign land only temporarily just as he was living in a foreign land temporarily; but apparently it has been decades since his body was laid to rest and coming home for him is not in sight yet. It could not be more tragic than this for the soul of a great human being like the Father to not have reached home while he was alive and worse never even reach home in his death and in his spirit.

To add to the sadness, there is no any recollection, memory, discussion, or even conversation to bring to live, the Lotuko, the hunter, the dancer, the singer, the farmer, the Catholic, the priest, the intellectual, the orator, the parliamentarian, the rebel, the refugee, the Father and the patron of South Sudan movement, the Rev. Fr. Saturnino Lohure. Not even his picture exist on the public domain, which leaves one to wonder on whether he had ever taken a picture in his life or the pictures are simply ignored either intentionally or unintentionally. It seems that most intimate things about him have died along with him and perhaps died with some of the people who were intimately involved with him. Some of the things about him are apparently lost in some people's memories. Few things about him are printed here. Other things about him are buried on pages of few books one can be lucky to find around. Others are in archive of some antiquities some places like Italy or at that famous library in Durham University. And other things about him are in spirit lingering around, perhaps on the Ugandan side of the border. The only thing existing in South Sudan bearing Fr. Saturnino Lohure's name is a non-for-profit organization in Eastern Equatoria affiliated with Pax Christi. One can only hope that that organization lives up to Fr. Saturnino Lohure's ideal. But in all, Fr. Saturnino Lohure is like dead and then after his death, he was killed again and again just as the Arabs wished that he should have been devoured by that "beast of the forest" which would have completely consumed him to the oblivious. The least one can do is pray that God Almighty rest his soul in peace and fulfill some of his dreams about South Sudan!

The Leadership Qualities of the Father

Despite the tragedy and the little information we know about the Father, one can be able to assess, though not with precise accuracy on how he would have fared up in his posthumous South Sudan. There is no doubt that the Father was an outstanding leader such that others argue he was born ahead of his time.[353] For some reasons, those who devote their time studying leadership could not come to consensus when it comes to defining leadership. It is actually said that "there are as many definitions of leadership as there are number of the researchers in the field."[354] However, in their studies, Robert House and Philip Podsakoff, (two of the most renowned names in the field of leadership studies), made an attempt to find a common threads among different definitions of leadership. In their findings, common to all definitions of leadership is the concept that leadership involves "individuals that, by their actions, facilitate the movement of a group of people toward a common or shared goal or objective."[355] The implication is that leadership is the consequence of "interaction between individuals organized around some commonly agreed-upon mission or purpose."[356] The studies go on to identify some of the most common threads as effective style of outstanding leadership. That good leadership style must involve a vision that promised better future and the vision that is deeply held by the followers and passionately valued by the leader. The leader must self-sacrifice for the interest of the vission and must have confidence, determination, and persistence to attain the objectives of that vision.

The Father did not only possess but demonstrate those common traits found in effective leadership style as defined above. He might have impressed the Catholic Church with his intelligence and devotion for Christianity given that he just finished his primary school in two years as oppose to the normal four years. From thereon, he sailed faster through the seminary. Just out of seminary into priesthood, the Catholic Church requested him to represent the South Sudan and the Church on 1947, Juba Conference, but since he was a fresh priest, barely two years old, he declined the request and asked that Fr. Guido Akou, a senior to him, go and represent the Church and the South at the conference.[357] In 1956, the Father was chosen Vicar Delegate of the Rumbek, a position, second to the bishop of Rumbek. The Catholic Church had never forgotten him, because later on, the Catholic Church elected him to represent the interest of the Christians in the Sudanese constituent draft committee after Sudan's independence. And again, he was later on identified with a fellow priest, Fr. Paulino Daggole to represent the interest of the Church and that of the South in the parliament of the newly independent Sudan. As a result, he ran for election representing Torit and he overwhelming won, guaranteeing him a seat in Constituent Assembly of 1958.[358]

After the parliament was dissolved due to the takeover of the government by the military regime, the Church once again approached him with a proposal in ordaining him a bishop of the new Vicariate of Juba. He declined the offer knowing that by becoming a bishop, it will restrict his activities of freeing the South Sudanese people. For him, the interest of the Church can be safeguarded in a free South Sudan, therefore, the fight for freedom comes first, and becoming a bishop second. He was absolutely right to assert that the Church cannot serve its interest without freedom, because few years later he was proven right as all the Christian missionaries were kicked out of Sudan. Only 31 Catholic priests including him were left in Sudan. Those who remained were referred to as the "dogs of the church" and they were either killed or imprisoned or harassed so as that they abandon the Church activities. For example, Fr. Ali Archangel was killed by soldiers who raided his compound and looted everything from his compound. A fellow priest,

Fr. Joreme Bidai was sent running into exile by flying bullets that by grace of God barely missed him, "the cruel bullets of the soldiers which had not missed Fr. Archangel," as he would later described it. Another fellow priest, Fr. Deng Barnaba was captured by these same murderous soldiers and killed on spot where he was captured. Fr. Anywar Leopoldo was killed while trying to cross from Uganda to Sudan to deliver some assistance to the South Sudanese people. The Father himself died for the same reason as his fellow priests before and after him.[359] The destruction of the Church in Sudan never stopped as it continues to this day because of the oppressive Northern Sudanese successive governments.

The interest of the Church was as much at stake as that of South Sudanese people; therefore, the Church required leadership to steer them out of these destructions, and the Father seemed to be the ideal answer at the time. He could safeguard the interest of both the Church and that of the people of South Sudan through the struggle for freedom, justice and equality. Despite his political activities including leading an arms rebellion movement, the Catholic Church with its strict disciplinary rules never bothered to reprimand or excommunicate him, but instead supported him. He also had opportunity to quit priesthood, but he never did. Others may argue that the reason he never quit was because he was using the Church to build himself as a political leader. As valid as this argument may sound, it will be difficult to prove. He had made in no vague terms his interest of serving the Church and the people at the same time. He complemented those duties very well throughout his life. There is no indication whatsoever that he was going to leave the Church for some personal self satisfactory endeavor. A devoted priest, wherever he went, he would always like to preach to the Christians whether they are Sudanese, Ugandans, Congolese, or even Italians.[360] An editor of an Italian magazine, Nigrizia, wrote:

With the passing away of Fr. Saturnino, the people of Southern Sudan have lost one of their most brilliant and noble son: a man of integrity. In life and spirit, he incarnated in himself the sufferings of his oppressed people. In some countries, e.g. Latin America, or even in Africa, many priests who opted to fight for the human rights of their people usually abandoned the priestly ministry. Fr. Saturnino did not. He remained a humble and faithful priest of the church. As an MP and human rights activist he always behaved with wisdom proper of people of his caliber.[361]

That can hardly be a person with an interest to leave the Church for something else that he could gain personally from. He never indulged in any activities that would be considered morally wrong or any activity that could compromise his moral integrity as a priest. The independent Sudanese newspaper, Al-Ayaam of October 25th, 1966, filed this report from Kampala from its correspondent in Uganda:

Where does help go? It is said that it is placed in the hands of the "Father," the unknown and temporary Saturnino. It is said that the priest is not so much unknown when the matter is about funds donated. The donors do not hand over the funds to other than the Father. The Father does not appear here in the clubs and cafes as the others do, notwithstanding that he comes to Kampala, and from here he proceeds to the guerillas from South Sudan. Then he goes back to Nairobi, Kinshasa and Rome. He is always on the move. He does not remain in the same locality. He is always active. Only few intimates know the program of his activities.[362]

On his death, *The Vigilant* newspaper added by writing, "he was incorruptible man."[363] These testimonies are enough prove to show that the Father was serving the interest of the people other than his personal interest. The Father took a covenant with God swearing an oath to fulfill the Sacrament of priesthood where he became a priest and died as a priest. Luckily, he also received a priestly burial, with cassock placed on his deformed body and a coffin nailed with crucifix. This is despite the fact that the requiem mass for the repose of his soul was prevented from taking place in Khartoum by the authorities on the pretext that he was a rebel who tried to divide the country, the very country that this regime in Khartoum devastated with their policies of oppression. The news of his death may not have received wide publicity like that of his martyred idol, Padre Pro, but like Padre Pro, he bravely faced his enemies who executed him by firing at him at a point blank. He might not be beautified as a saint, but once a priest, a priest forever, he was. Indeed, his wish was, "to minister to the parishioners in one small village in South" when the South becomes free but not to become the president of the South Sudan.[364] After all, his idols whom he emulated were not John F. Kennedy, Nikita S. Khrushchev, or Mao Zedong, but saints of the Catholic Church who sacrifice their lives for a cause, faith and principles. The Father used to always remark that for the South Sudan, the "Lamp of sacrifice are the best of his sons."[365] The Father is among those sacrificial "best of sons" whom their sacrifices are required to save the South Sudan. They may die but their legacy can live forever. No expression can describe this better than his eulogy which states:

> For the Father we shed no tears, for it is not the custom among us Africans to weep for someone killed in cold blood. The Father has died, but his soul lives. What he stood for has

not died with him; neither can it be buried as his body is now buried[366]

While in the assembly, the Father demonstrated tremendous leadership in not only leading the Liberal Party but leading the entire Southern Sudanese. Through his leadership, he created a South Sudan bloc in the parliament in which he became their leader and spokesperson where he effectively represented the interest of the South Sudan. While some South Sudanese parliamentarians where being corrupted, the Father helped steer some of them out of the corruption and refocus them toward the interest and goals of the South. Throughout the years of struggle, the Father remained extremely instrumental in providing leadership and patronage as well as providing spiritual support and materialistic assistance to the Southern Sudan movement. His role did not exclude carrying out combat operations in the battle fields.

The Father took his leadership seriously that he was almost flawless. To his enemy, the impact of his performance was immensely devastating. With the outside honest observers, he was showered with praises and admirations. Among his people, he enjoyed less criticism but earned the respect of almost all. In the Father's posthumous, an attempt to belittle him surprisingly came from the most unusual and unsuspected source, in the name of Joseph Lagu. To say that the struggle for liberation movement was imposed on Lagu perhaps would not be the right characterization. However, it is important to note that Lagu never joined the movement for struggle willingly, but instead, he was persuaded by those who started the struggle. While in the movement, the Father did not only groomed Lagu for leadership but strongly pushed Lagu for leadership by urging as his will for the Anyanya soldiers to follow Lagu in the event of his absence or death. Most of those soldiers wished to get rid of Lagu in a heartbeat. Majority of whom were from the Lotuko ethnic group like the Father and were not happy that Lagu from Madi ethnic group would be their leader while there were few Madis in the army. But because of the Father's will and wish they were able to maintain Lagu all the way. They were even willing to suppress their own Lotuko ethnic members who were challenging Lagu's leadership.[367] There is no evidence anywhere in the history of the South Sudan struggle that a leader affirms the succession of his subordinate, leave alone whether there is any evidence of a leader who left a will on that effect. Nonetheless, the Father did it, and Lagu acknowledges that but yet after the death of the Father, in his autobiographical book, *Sudan Odyssey Through a State From Ruin to Hope*, Lagu tries to embellish his own image at the expenses of the Father and some of his colleagues in the liberation struggle who unfortunately are all dead. It is also imperative to note that the Father and his deceased colleagues had opportunities to write their autobiographies and describing their adventurous journeys in the liberation struggle, but instead, they utilized their writing skills to write books, pamphlets, articles, and letters pleading the cause of South Sudan. They never made any attempt to indulge themselves in self-praises through their writings. Speaking about the Father, Fr. Hilary Boma put it succinctly when he said, "Saints didn't create themselves. They were not born so. But the citizens who saw them born, lived, worked and died in what they believed in, are the witnesses."[368] It was through this tradition that the Father was born, lived, worked, and died.

Lagu's Attempt of Badmouthing Colleagues

In his attempt to portray a negative image of the Father, Lagu accused the Father of being responsible in the power struggle that plagued the SANU in Kampala. However he offers no evidence in that regard, because he knows too well that the Father never contested in any of the positions in the SANU executives. The Father was the National Patron for the liberation movement, a position that was uncontested and unchallenged until the Father's death. It beats logic to claim that in such a position the Father would involve in a power struggle, unless the Father was involved in the power struggle by himself and within himself, but then again, Lagu may need to explain how that happened and even then provide the evidence.

The other equally bogus charge Lagu levels against the Father is that since the Father came from the same ethnic group as Joseph Oduho, the Father was actually struggling for power through Oduho. This is speculative at best as Lagu could not provide evidence to back his claim. Secondly, this is an attack not on the Father but on Joseph Oduho by trying to portray him as a stooge of the Father. But the fact is, Oduho was a leader on his own right, perhaps of a high quality than Lagu. There are ample of evidence to prove this including the fact that it was Oduho who persuaded Lagu by appealing to him to join the Southern Sudan liberation movement while Lagu was serving as a military officer for the enemy. Lagu without knowing how contradicting his bogus accusation is even acknowledged the fact that the Father and Oduho were not getting along given their different personalities. Now the question is where is the logic in the argument that the Father was using Oduho to get to power because Oduho is form the Father's ethnic group? Perhaps there is no logic, and Lagu has a lot of explaining to do that is if he is capable in explaining without contradicting the facts.

The most devastating accusation of all is when Lagu tries to portray both the Father and Aggrey Jaden as power hungry individuals. In that, Lagu narrated a story of an alleged encounter between the Father and Jaden in Leopoldville (Kinshasa) where both the Father and Jaden displayed their darker human sides. Interestingly, the story itself does not seem credible and if some of it is true it cannot be verifiable. Therefore the story does not only put a burden of prove on Lagu but put his own reputation and credibility on the line. First, it is worthy of remembering that Lagu had a fall out with Jaden when Jaden demoted him from a position of commander in chief of the Anyanya and promoting Emedio Tafeng instead. It was an honest attempt by Jaden to reflect broader representation of all of the Southern Sudanese nationalities in his administration. It is historian, Robert Collins who wrote that Jaden's appointment of Tafeng into the position of commander-in-chief of Anyanya "sealed Lagu's contempt for the southern politicians."[369] Now, one would hope that Lagu is still a Christian and may forgive Jaden for demoting him as it is required of Christians to forgive.

Anyway, in this alleged encounter between the Father and Jaden, Lagu claims that they were on delegation trip to Leopoldville (Kinshasa) with Jaden, and they ran into the Father while in town. By then Jaden was just elected president of SANU replacing Joseph Oduho. Lagu writes that Jaden informed him on the intention of the Father trying to replace him from the presidency and putting Oduho. He claims that he was hesitant to believe Jaden partly because the Father visited them regularly in their hotel and they talked and joked as normal. But before long, Lagu claims he began to confirm the worse from both the Father and Jaden. The first incident, Lagu describes as follows:

> On another occasion at a family to which the Father took us, a child ran to me and jumped into my arms. I responded lifting it up above my chest our traditional way of acknowledging a child's welcome. Mr. Jaden quietly took note and later in the hotel, he said: "Did you notice? Even the

happy little child could not move the Father. He showed no interest in the child. Children are like angels. They can read the hearts and minds of the people. You must have a good heart. That was why the child selected you and jumped into your arms.[370]

It is hard to believe that a leader of a national character such as Jaden would degenerate that low in embracing superstition, no matter how much he feared of the Father's intentions, he would not have gone that low. Even if the story is true, Lagu who claims to be the only sane person (who could move children) would have allayed Jaden's fear by assuring him that there was no bad intention from the Father's side because the child also was not moved by Jaden, which did not in any way meant that Jaden was evil. Anyways, the story sound fabricated and it is not worthy to put more credence to it even though it is good to clarify.

Another incident that Lagu claims happened was when Jaden fell of the toilet, breaking the toilet top and injuring himself in the process. And then he claims that the Father in a gossiping way confided to him that what kind of savage head of state Jaden would be if he is going around breaking toilet seats? He adds that the Father urged him to leave Jaden and instead joined him because they are both from Eastern Equatoria. He said Jaden on the other hand told him he was worried that the Father was going to make a big deal out of the incident, and may called him a savage. In other words, the portrayal of the bitter encounter between the Father and Jaden is to win over Lagu, or at least that is what Lagu wants everyone to believe. To begin with, this is the least convincing of all these seemingly fabricated stories. First of all, Aggrey Jaden lived and worked in Nairobi, arguably the most developed and technological advanced city in comparison to Leopoldville. So, Jaden could not have fallen off the toilet seat like a savage as Lagu may want people to believe. The story of someone falling from using the toilet can only apply to someone who comes from a village and not familiar with the toilet setup systems in the cities. That can hardly be Jaden who worked and lived in one of the Africans most developed and advanced cities. Secondly, Jaden should not have worried about the Father gossiping about his alleged savagery. Apparently it is Lagu who tells the whole world of this embarrassing savagery incident in his book. If at all the story is true, then, Jaden should have worried more about Lagu being a gossiper that he should have worried about the Father. Now who is the true friend of Jaden? After all, the world never heard this story from the Father, but they read it from Lagu's book. This story seems as if it is intentionally manufactured to embarrass Jadden and demonize the Father while elevate Lagu.

What Others Say About the Father

If people like Lagu cannot appreciate a person that they used to call "Father," it would not stop others from showing their appreciation to the Father. The real Father is described in the Sudanese Catholic Clergy as an "excellent priest, leader, disinterested, prudent and courageous."[371] A priest who knew the Father very well describes the Father as being, "delicate in his feelings, uncompromising in his principles, constant, he got deeply involved and open to the problems, respectful of all, a bit inclined to pessimism. He willingly jokes without falling into irony. He was esteemed by all."[372] Another person who got to know the Father very well, Sr. Michaelangela Operto had this to say about the Father:

I knew him since 1936 at Okaru when he was in the 4th year of Intermediate. I had another chance of seeing him in Lirya with Fr. Guido, as well as in Juba. I remember him as a serene, kind and respectful man who was loved by all. He was also a very humble man. One day, when I saw him on the lorry with children, I asked him to get into the cabin. He jokingly answered me that standing among the children on the top of the lorry was like standing in the Parliament. I remember he sent me one day a Christmas card in which he was asking me to pray for him and his work. Really, he was an exemplary priest who loved his people for whom he prayed, worked and suffered, giving up his life for the people. Even now, I can still see him very serene, full of sympathy and kindness...[373]

The Father humility is well acknowledged as it is remarkable. His nurturing behavior, especially with children, left permanent memories on many. For example, some of the South Sudanese children who were growing up in town of Gulu in Uganda remember a jovial Father who always passed them sweets and biscuits on their encounters. Interestingly, some of these children did not equate him to the prominent politicians or leaders of the time as his appearance portrayed an image of a simple person, a student wearing uniform like clothing and carrying book bag. Sometimes he drove in the car, sometimes he rode on bicycle, and in most cases he was walking on foot. This is hardly the Father whom Joseph Lagu is trying to portray. In addition to this, the Father attributed authorship of his book, *The Problem of the Southern Sudan*, to two of his colleagues, Joseph Oduho and William Deng. Given these facts, it is difficult to prove the assertion that the Father was selfish and after his personal interest if in fact he could sacrifice, even his live for that matter. In Congo, the Father had in his company a group that included people from his tribe such as Guido

Lohuyoro, but yet, he selected Oliver Albino who is not from his tribe to head the entire group.[374]

The Weakness of the Father

The Father's leadership weakness which Lagu failed to discuss was his secretiveness and lack of complete trust and confidence toward others, especially his colleagues. The South Sudanese historian, Robert Collins, said he had met the Father on several occasions, but the Father "was always very secretive and not very forthcoming."[375] Collins goes as far to identify the Father as "enigmatic" figure throughout his book, *The Modern History of Sudan*.[376] The *Al-Ayam* newspaper called the Father, "the unknown and temporary Saturnino...only few intimates know the program of his activities."[377] The problem was that some of those people who intimately involved with the Father were for the most part, very young Southern Sudanese nationalists to carryon with the activities of the liberation struggle in the absence of the Father. This is despite their abilities and competence. Matter of fact, that was one of the reasons he was occasionally accused by the Southern Sudanese politicians of his age for trying to build puppet leaders through those young people. However, his secretive actions can also be explained and justified such that the secrecy was for security purposes. The lack of trust among his colleagues could be due to the fact that he has no confidence in them. Among his contemporaries, the Father was very educated, intelligent, well exposed to the global world, and full of confidence in himself. These might have contributed to him looking down to his colleagues or setting him apart from them in terms of ability, vision, level of confidence etc. At one point, evoking his profession of Christian faith, the Father acknowledged lack of unity and vision among the Southern politicians and soldiers by referring to it as "a capital sin."[378] This is a harsh assessment coming from a priest toward his colleagues. Interestingly, it was none other than the very Joseph Lagu who was able to gain the trust and confidence of the Father. Two incidents can best highlight the reasons on why Lagu gained the confidence of the Father. The first one was when the Father sent Lagu to Nairobi to purchase military uniforms for the Anyanya soldiers. After transactions, Lagu accounted for all the funds on his possessions. The Father was impressed with such responsible behavior. The Father was known for being a "thrifty management and could not tolerate all the non-strategic excesses" when it comes to spending for the movement.[379] The second highlighted incident was when Lagu proved his military competence in the presences of the Father in the bushes of South Sudan while fighting the Arabs. The Father believed in military struggle as a solution, hence admiration for Lagu's military capability. These plus other things left the Father to lean more toward Lagu and have trust and confidence in him as a potential leader. Lagu admitted that the Father and him became to closed.[380] But even so, the Father never revealed too much to Lagu, especially with his contacts from abroad. After his death, the only contact that Lagu was able to connect with was with the Father's Catholic contacts in Moroto, Uganda, particularly Bishop Sisto Mazaldo and few others who were willing to assist Lagu on a limited basis but advised him to the reach to the Israel Embassy in Kampala for more support. In his part, Lagu admitted that the Anyanya Israel connection was something that had already been established. Lagu had confirmed this fact by saying that Joseph Oduho introduced him to the Israel embassy in Kampala when he first joined the Southern Sudan movement in 1963.[381] Another historian wrote, "in 1965 the southern intellectual, Oliver Albino, had met with an Israeli consular official in Nairobi where he was introduced to General Moshe Dayan, then the Israeli minister of agriculture," and again, "in 1966 Joseph Oduho renewed the movement's contacts with

Israel, and under Aggrey Jaden's SSPG Sarafino Wani Swaka, had followed-up Oduho's initiative."[382] In his book, *The Israeli Connection*, Benjamin Beit-Hallahmi reveals, "Israeli involvement in Southern Sudan was in evidence as early as 1963, through contacts with Israeli embassies in Uganda, Ethiopia, the Congo, and Chad."[383] It seems this contact came as a result of Father's connection. One author confirms this as he wrote, "…the Verona Fathers in particular, were no doubt aware what use Lohure—a Catholic priest—was making of their cash…and the Verona Fathers might have been instrumental in introducing the Southerners to the Israelis."[384] If anything, all that Lagu did was to follow up an already established relationship between the Israeli and the Southern Sudanese resistant movement. Because the Israeli involvement was very much shrouded in secrecy, the extent in which the early contacts were made and with whom the contacts were made, would continue to remain mystery to the general public.

Besides Lagu, another potential individual who would have gained the Father's trust and confidence to lead, would have been Fr. Anywar Leopaldo. Fr. Leopaldo was a simple humble priest who has no any other interest other than serving the poor. One priest remembered him as being, "like Fr. Saturnino, he carried out his mission wholeheartedly."[385] He was also a courageous and hard working individual. Like Fr. Saturnino Lohure, he used to travel in unfamiliar and treacherous terrains to serve the poor. At one point, his team of volunteers crossing to Sudan fell into Ugandan ambush some of them got killed, but for Fr. Leopoldo, he escaped getting lost in the forest and after days he made his way to safety. It was already concluded that he was already dead, but when he showed up, people say he would not risk his live again, and they were wrong, because he would continue to risk his live until he died. Among his courageous missions was to risk his live serving the Congolese people amidst turmoil and conflict in the region. Fr. Leopaldo refused to actively participate in politics with the Father as he concentrated more on spiritual activities and in the priestly ministry. But after the death of the Father, Fr. Leopaldo started to perform exactly some of the activities of the Father until he was tragically killed just like the Father while trying to cross from Uganda to Sudan bringing along with him material supports for the Anyanya soldiers.

Eventually, Father Saturnino Lohure ended up dying like the others before and after him leaving behind a huge vacuum of no strong foundation that can be built on what is already being built by him. His death left a myth behind in his own village of Loronyo where it is believed that in his dying moments the Father cursed the people of Loronyo not to produce any leader of a national prominence because his two companions who were escorting him during his death were all from Loronyo and were alleged to have abandoned him to be savagely killed by the Ugandan soldiers. Now in Loronyo, the death of any of their emerging leaders such as Edward Otome, Alfred Amanya, Osman Asai, just to mention a few is a confirmation of this mythical belief of a curse by the Father. If the myth is true, then, is such a curse also applicable to the entire South, especially the fact that the South Sudanese leader, the first who to have genuinely became vice president of the Sudan, Dr. John Garang died mysteriously along the same border where the Father died—and to this day the South is still longing for real leadership. Anyway, whatever one believes, whether a myth or a curse, it is important to acknowledge that the Father also bore witness in the name of God Almighty when he testified, "the whole world may be against the South," but he was very "sure that God is with the people of the South and through God" the South must win.[386] Hopefully, this powerfully testimony in the name of God can overshadow any negative curse the

Father might have cast to the people of South Sudan if at all there was any. Despite all these, there were those who still wondered on who really Fr. Saturnino Lohure was. Others suggested that he was born ahead of his time, but yet others were wondering on whether he was dropped among the Southern Sudanese from somewhere else, or perhaps a gift from God. There were those close to him who permanently went to the state of insanity on hearing the death of Fr. Saturnino Lohure. These all add to the mystery of the man, Fr. Saturnino Lohure. The Catholic would say there are things beyond the knowledge of humankind and those things will remain unknown to human, given "how limited are the resources of the human intellect."[387]

The Khartoum Regime

The Father died at the time when Sadiq al-Mahdi was in power. Sadiq al-Mahdi the great grandson of Islamic revolutionary, Muhammad Ahmad al-Mahdi was educated at a Catholic Comboni College school. He went on to study in Khartoum University and continued with advance studies in the Great Britain. By far, he is considered a moderate compare to the other Northern Sudanese Arab leaders and politicians. Unfortunately, his short period in power is infamously noted for brutal period in South Sudan history, given the scale of atrocities, which were committed by the Khartoum armed forces under his leadership. Soon after assuming power, al-Mahdi visited a Southern town of Bor. While in town, he was reported to have visited a burial site for Northern Sudanese soldiers killed in the battle by the Anyanya forces. Standing on top of one of the grave of a young Northern Sudanese Arab officer recently killed, the thirty-year-old, al-Mahdi shed tears profusely, like a little child. It is said, "no sooner had al-Sadiq left the town than the army, electrified by the Prime Minister's tears, went on a rampage. Twenty four Dinka chiefs, including some who were detained under custody by the police, were slaughtered."[388] Such atrocities among the innocent Southern Sudanese civilians were to follow with similar atrocities throughout Southern Sudan until al-Mahdi relinquished power. Today, al-Mahdi is still hanging around with determination, but little propability of regaining power in Khartoum. He lost his political power base, which he used to count on in Western Sudan and in other rural areas among the most disfranchised Northern Sudanese. From within his own party of Umma, which is more of a family monopoly and fiefdom, he is experiencing desertion, including from his cousins who deserted him.

The most notorious of all the characters and the more determining factor in the death of the Father was Muhammad Ahmad Mahgoub whom al-Mahdi briefly took power from. In the observation of one author, Mahgoub "had been at the center of power more frequently than perhaps any other Sudanese politician."[389] Mahgoub was actually lucky to capitalize on the situation as a result of Anyanya intensifying their military offensive, which led to the fall of General Abboud who could not managed the situation and eventually to the rise of Mahgoub as the Northern Sudanese Arabs were looking for new civilian leadership and he suited the characteristics of that leadership. Mahgoub who careless about Southern Sudanese came to power vowing to crush the Southern Sudan resistant movement as the Southern Problems was what led him into power. He declared that the "only language Southerners understand is force."[390] Indeed he did used force, but unfortunately against innocent Southern Sudanese who were massacred in thousands during his reign.[391] Mahgoub then was temporarily forced out of power from 1966 through 1967, and he reemerged again. He had done more harm to the Southerners by going as far as pressuring the neighboring countries in an attempt to crush the Southern Sudan resistant movement. He was successful to some degree in his foreign policies. From his Arab allies, he managed to secure arms, ammunition and funds for the purpose of crushing the Southern Sudan resistant movement. He also managed in persuading countries like Uganda to deal away with the Anyanya. Historian Robert Collins wrote that when Mahgoub returned to Khartoum from his trip in Uganda he was "convinced that Milton Obote, president of Uganda, would intercept arms shipments north to the Anyanya."[392] The Khartoum soldiers and their counterparts, the Ugandan soldiers were crisscrossing each others borders in an effort to quell the Anyanya like no other before. A middle ranking army officer from Khartoum was later to confess on his particular role he played along the Ugandan-Sudanese border, especially of his desire to capture and kill Joseph Lagu.[393] The cold blooded murder of the Father by the Ugandan troops was a direct result of Khartoum collaborative effort and pressure on the Ugandan government of Milton Obote in dealing away with the Southern Sudan resistant movement. *The Vigilant* newspaper reported that on hearing of the news of the assassination of the Father, the Khartoum government was jubilant and sent to Uganda a congratulatory message for their collaborations in carrying out the assassination of the Father.[394] Good enough, few days later, the same newspaper carried a message warning Khartoum government on how assassinations of leaders would not resolve any political problem.[395]

The warning was right because the death of the Father did not stop the struggle for the freedom of the South Sudanese people. The Father may die and so are other South Sudanese leaders, irrespective of how they meet their death, but what they stood for and what the people of South Sudanese stand for will continue to survive as long as there are Southern Sudanese people alive. Maghoub himself did not enjoy that many successes after the death of the Father. His successes did not last as long as he might have wanted. By late 1968, he suffered a serious stroke where he had to be rushed out of the county to a foreign nation to recuperate for months before he could come back to the country. Upon his return to the country, the ailing Mahgoub was rendered politically useless and dispensable. By April of 1969, he was forced to resign from power. Few days later, in May 15th, 1968, before Mahgoub could even lament on disposition of his power, Colonel Muhammad Ja'afar Numayri and his Free Officers took control of the government in a military coup d'état. And then, Magoub was incapacitated by another serious stroke, this time removing him permanently from political scene where by 1976, the hour eventually caught up with him and he had to capitulate to nature as the nature finally took its heavy toll on him in a due course.

Like his predecessors, Numayri was equally determined to crush the Anyanya rebellion by use of force. The regime thought that by equipping its army better and boosting their mobility, they can crush the Anyanya. However, by the time Numayri took control, the Anyanya were already well equipped with the newly acquired weapons from Israel. They were armed with much newer functional automatic rifles, antitank, landmines, grenade launches, artilleries such as the 82 millimeters, and an open route of weapon supplies as promised by Israelis. They controlled much of the countryside and were capable of mining major roads, destroying armored vehicles, and even downing planes. Anyanya also swelled in numbers, and by 1971, they were estimated at 13,000 strong fighting force. It was also united with command and control structure where their actions were better coordinated and managed throughout the South. The Anyanya offensive grew more deadly and spreading to the towns. By the 1970s, Anyanya mined all the major roads in Equatoria, confining the Arabs in major towns. They also began to shell Juba with artillery, something they never done before.

Numayri responded by ordering all out offensive in the South. He sent in Soviet Union military advisors with helicopters, MIG 17s, and Egyptian commandoes to support his almost demoralized soldiers who recently have been plagued by all sort of logistical problems and incompetent commanding officers. For their victory, they were able to capture Owiny-ki-Bul, the headquarters of Joseph Lagu, the leader of Anyanya. The airplanes carried out indiscriminate bombings of towns and villages, unfortunately killing civilians and cattle, and in most cases, burning villages down. None of those sorties were effective against the actual Anyanya soldiers who melted away easily as they control the countryside. More peace villages were created for the civilians so as to deprive the Anyanya of their supports. Unfortunately, the civilians on those peace villages were the ones to suffer, given the horrible conditions imposed on them.

But none of these so-called victories stopped the Anyanya versatility. The Anyanya fought back fiercely shooting down several helicopters. More specifically, in Western Equatoria, Anyanya overran a major military garrison at Naupo. With their new antitank, they were able to destroy the armored vehicles sending fear through to the enemy whom their line of defense was more reliant on the armored vehicles. In Malakal, the greatest victory came when the Anyanya overran several posts leading to their capture of Pachala. In those attacks, the Anyanya killed many enemy soldiers. Prior to that, they carried out ambushes on military conveys, which resulted into huge loses for the Khartoum soldiers. They also managed to sink a steamer at Sobat River. In Wau, the Anyanya successful disrupt the railway. In the end, even though the Anyanya did not capture the South, they were able to prove that they were the military force to be reckoned with.

Feeling the heat but not willing to concede on the Anyanya ferocity, the government in Khartoum turned into their usual tactic of propaganda so as to undermine the Anyanya's effort. They portrayed the Anyanya as renegades, bandits, terrorist who were disorganized, poorly equipped, and ruthless beings. However, one incident that took place on December 6, 1971, would change the image of the Anyanya for better. At the time, a routine Sudanese Airways flight from Khartoum to Malakal en route lost its way, ending up crash-landing into the Anyanya territory after it ran out of fuel. In their part, the Anyanya took in all the survivors treated the wounded and fed them. Few weeks later the Anyanya escorted the survivors to the nearby Khartoum military post in Mundri, setting them free. The Anyanya good gesture received wide publicity with the survivors parading themselves in the media to testify on how humane the Anyanya were in treating them. The Khartoum cannot anymore portray the Anyanua in any bad way due to these overwhelming testimonies by the survivors and wide media publicity. Now with military stalemate and failed propaganda from Khartoum's side, it was just a good excuse for both sides to negotiate a peaceful political settlement. It was then that they did initiate negotiation with intention of signing a peaceful agreement.

The situation was somewhat reaped, the stakes were very high, and the issues were overly sensitive as both parties, the Anyanya and the Khartoum government of Numayri agreed on negotiable settlement. The Anyanya moved faster, but carefully in selecting its delegation for the negotiation. Ezbon Mondiri was chosen as the head of the delegation. A vibrant politician, a tough negotiator, and an article politician, Ezbon Mondiri just seemed like the right choice. He has been active in the Southern Sudanese resistant movement, as Minister of Defense for the Anyanya forces. His effort to centralize the Anyanya command and control structure was impressive to say the least. A hard working and humble individual, Mondiri covered the jungle and rugged terrains of South Sudan walking on foot. Prior to that he was an active member of the Southern Sudanese party in Khartoum, the Southern Front, where he went on to serve in Khartoum as Minister of Communications and Transportation in the Transitional Government of 1964-1965 before he could join the people of the bush. But before that, he was among the first tough Southern Sudanese Members of Parliament. Dr. Lawrence Wol Wol, a Southern Sudanese hardliner and an Anyanya representative in Paris was designated secretary of the delegation. Mading De Garang, also a Southern hardliner, was an Anyanya representative in London and the editor of the, *Grass Curtain,* an Anyanya publication, acted as the spokesperson for the delegation. Colonel Frederick Brian Maggot was Special Military Representative of the team. Angelo Voga, a personal secretary to Joseph Lagu was among the members of the delegation. And then there was a vocal, Oliver Batali Albino, Rev. Paul Puot, and Job Adier de Jok who were also members of the delegation.

As for the Khartoum government, the selections of its delegation were also carefully vetted out. They involved individuals whom their knowledge of South Sudan is marred with ignorance, long history of stereotyping and even those who did not favor negotiations but rather a military solution as a resolve for the Southern Problems. Abel Alier, the Vice President and Minister of State for Southern Affairs in Khartoum and the only Southern Sudanese in the delegation, was ceremoniously offered with the courtesy to lead the delegation even though with no real negotiating powers. Alier would actual found himself isolated in the caucus discussions by both Anyanya and Khartoum delegations since in a real sense, he did not belong to either of the group. Dr. Mansour Khalid was Numayri's designated Minister of Foreign Affairs. He was a bit sympathetic to the Southern cause, even though with little powers to sway the others. Jaafar Mohammed Ali Bakheit, Minister for Local Government could only grant the Southern region limited autonomy, but would like to see Anyanya soldiers dismantled. Major General Mohammed El Baghir Ahmed, the Minister of interior had been commanding Khartoum armed forces in the Southern Sudan and had little regards for the Anyanya and the Southern Sudanese people. Abdel Rahman Abdalla, Minister of Public Service and Administrative Reform in Numayri's government and who had also been chairman of the Twelve Man Committee on the Round Table Conference of 1965, had a twisted view of South Sudan, because he had also served as director of the Academy of Public administration, which trained Northern Sudanese administrators to serve in South Sudan. Brigadier Mirghani Suleiman and Colonel Kamal Abashar who had been classmates of Joseph Lagu and Colonel Frederick Brian Maggot respectively at the Khartoum Military College had little sympathy for Southern Sudanese.

Despite all these contrasting differences among the delegations, the negotiations moved on, starting officially on February 16, 1972, at Hilton Hotel in Addis Ababa. Emperor Haile Selassie of Ethiopia offered his blessings and the actual talks were opened by the Ethiopian Foreign Minister with Nabiyelul Kifle acting as the Representative of His Imperial Majesty, the emperor of Ethiopia. Burgess Carr, the General Secretary of All Africa Conference of Churches was to moderate the talks on the condition that since he was a foreigner, he should have no decision on issues. On evening of March 27, 1972, His Majesty, Emperor Haile Selassie presided over the signing ceremony for the agreement and Joseph Lagu and Mansour Khalid officially ratified the agreement known as the Addis Ababa Agreement of 1972.

Reasons on Why the Father Would Reject the Addis Ababa Agreement

As evident by these events, since the death of the Father, so many things had happened among the major things to have happened was the signing of Addis Ababa Agreement, something that the Father never envisioned let alone whether he would have supported it. In one of his last recorded interviews to an Italian Magazine conducted in Entebbe, the Father said:

> I am coming from Gulu. We are now crossing a decisive moment. We don't want to give up. The Arabs also don't want to give up. But we don't want to lose heart. Our capital sin: we are not united. Soldiers and politicians (from the South), they don't have the same vision... Never the Arabs will accept the idea of a federation.[396]

This was not the first time the Father expressed his determination and willingness to fight until the end. It was not also the first time he expressed skepticism in negotiating a peaceful settlement with the Arabs. The Father has been consistently demonstrating his resolve for the arms struggle as the solution and showing suspicion on Arabs intentions of trying to lure Southerners through a political settlement so as to oppress the Southerners even more. The Father has been touring around stressing to the whole world that no any other obstacle would hinder the Southerners as they would "prefer to die fighting rather than to serve the Arabs of the Sudan or the international policy."[397] The Father understood very well the situation at hand as he said, "major responsibility for the emancipation of the Southern Sudan lies" with the South Sudanese.[398] He also accepted the reality and difficulties of the struggle when he said, "there are many roads to find freedom. Ours seems to be the most difficult. Therefore, we must accept this reality and do only what we can."[399] When new emerging regimes in Khartoum were busy exchanging powers and calling for a political negotiations with the Southerners, the Father was quick to dismiss them by calling them as "nothing other than the North's changing of tactics in order to stay in the South."[400] The Father said as long as the "political parties of the North do not take into heart in a more realistic manner the Southern Problems, the perspectives of reaching a positive final solution in a democratic way are extremely remote, if not impossible."[401] The Father even went as far as condemning the Southerners who were cooperating with the Arabs in a political process when he said, "the Southerners who are weak and thinking only about themselves, are tempted to surrender" to the Arabs.[402] In other words, the Father is implying that any political negotiation with the Arabs without a genuine prospect of resolving the Southern problems is tantamount to surrendering to the whim of the Arabs.

Given these facts and evidences, there emerge at least three major possible reasons on why the Father would not have agreed in accepting an Agreement such as the Addis Ababa Agreement or anything that looked similar to it. The first possible major reason why the Father would not have involved in the Addis Ababa Agreement would be because of the personalities of the people involved in initiating that agreement. The first attempt for negotiation was initiated by the Sudanese Ambassador in London, Abdin Isma'il who confided to Mading de Garang, the representative of Southern Sudan Liberation Movement (SSLM), and editor of its magazine, the *Grass Curtain*, that he would be able to convinced the Khartoum government of Numayri to negotiate with SSLM a peaceful settlement. For some strange reasons, Lagu is said to have authorized Mading de Garang to go ahead and write Ambassador Ismai'l expressing the willingness of SSLM to negotiate on the basis of united Sudan. That initiative never went anywhere as it was killed by a council of ministers in Khartoum some of whom included Southerners as members. The Southern communist, Joseph Garang, who was Minister for Southern Affairs, dismissed Mading de Garang referring to him as "imperial stooge," therefore, must not be taken seriously.[403]

On the other hand, Abel Alier, who was also a minister in Numayri's government, took the issue of peaceful negotiation with Anyanya as his personal mission. According to Alier, he accepted a ministerial post in the Numayri's government on the condition that the government made a clear statement as a commitment to a peaceful solution to the problems of South Sudan, based on regional autonomy. He managed to finally convinced Numayri to accept negotiation with SSLM with his 11-point proposal as a basis for negotiation. The Father would probably have fewer problems with Mading de Garang personality as he was with the SSLM, however, he would have dismissed the Mading De Garang-Sudanese Ambassador's initiative on the ground that the basis of the negotiation was unity. As for Abel Alier, the Father would have dismissed him outright. Alier is among the people, the Father referred to as Southerners who are tempted to surrender because they "are weak and thinking only about themselves."[404] Alier was not only on the inside but was activity participating in the governments of Khartoum throughout the 1960s, and by then he was already in the higher position in the government. One wonders how much trust and confidence the Father might have accorded Alier. The idea that a Southerner would negotiate with a Southerner on the issues, which are clearly perpetuated by the Northern Arabs would have stunned the Father. Perhaps the Father would have preferred committing suicide than negotiating with a Southerner on a such occasion. To make it worse, the Father was not a person who could easily trust people, especially when he suspected the motives to involve personal gains. As for the case of Alier, the Father might have most likely concluded that his motives were purely personal greed, even though he understood that Alier also had the South in heart, but the question is which one comes first, the South or the personal gain? That no one would know but all can speculate and make conclusion base on speculations.

The other personalities or actors, which actively involved in the Addis Ababa Agreement, were the councils of churches such as the Sudan Council of Churches, the World Council of Churches, and the All-African Council of Churches (AACC). However, they were not the initiators of that negotiation to start with; therefore, they would have less sway on the Father to accept the initiative. Matter of fact, those councils of churches hooked up with Numayri's regime in the most obscure circumstances that would not have been possible had the Father been around. In 1971, United Nations High Commissioner for Refugees (UNHCR) had launched a worldwide campaign to raise funds for the refugees as the year was designated "Year of Refugees." By then, the Southern Sudanese refugees in the neighboring countries were numbering over half a million. Numayri, not willing to pass on the opportunity, launched his publicized fundraising campaign with Abel Alier his representative. It was through these fundraising campaigns that they were able to connect with these councils of churches which were also campaigning on behalf of the refugees.

However, had the Father been alive, these churches would not have even come close to the Numayri's regime, because the Father was more credible and stood a better chance to pull them away from a dictatorial military regime like the one of Numayri. First of all, the Father was not only associated with the refugees but he was a refugee himself who plighted with the refugees throughout their suffering. Those half a million plus refugees including the Father became refugees as a direct result of the policies in Khartoum where Numayri was presiding over. For all these years of refugees suffering, the Father was there lobbying for their cause. But there was no Numayri or the government in Khartoum. If they involved at all, they did it in a negative way by instigating the host governments of those refugees to mistreat the refugees even killing them as in the case of the Father and others. Not only that, the Father was a priest who is well connected with the churches to be able to convince these churches not to involve Khartoum in any of their humanitarian work. In short, the churches would not have involved in the Addis Ababa agreement, and the Alier initiative would have not gone anywhere.

Even if this initiative proceeded through, the second possible reason why the Father would have objected to it is the basis in which this agreement was negotiated. The basis for the Addis Ababa Agreement was regional autonomy within a united Sudan. Among the major issues the Addis Ababa resolved is that the South shall be one region as defined by the boundaries at independence of January 1st, 1956. The People's Regional Assembly and a High Executive Council (HEC) would constitute a governing body in the Southern region. The People's Regional Assembly shall be elected while sadly enough the president of the High Executive Council shall be appointed by the president of the Republic of the Sudan. The regional government should have authority over local governments, education, public health, natural resources, and police. Meanwhile, the national government control defense, foreign affairs, currency, inter-regional communications, and national economic, social, and educational planning.[405]

The proposal of a two states solution by the two Southern hardliners Mading de Garang and Lawrence Wol Wol was considered to be out of line and thrown out of the discussion. The proposal for the South to maintain its own army was also considered out of line and thrown out as well. It is reported that the discussion on security "was so sensitive that Abel Alier, the southern leader of the government delegation, was excluded from the discussions" by his Arab colleagues who supposed to be his subordinates.[406] One wonders how Alier felt about his exclusion from a discussion of a team that he was supposed to be the head. In responsed Alier wrote, "this is how I wished it to be." When Joseph Lagu joined the negotiation with new delegations to resolve some of these pressing issues, the Southerners continued to insist that the South maintains its own independent army and conduct its own foreign trade independently. The negotiation continued, but abruptly, for mysterious reasons only known to Lagu, he had a changed of a mind, and signed the Addis Ababa Agreement without resolving those pressing issues. Others like John Garang who was a low ranking officer during the Anyanya and went on to lead the next phase of the movement for liberation struggle said that the reason Lagu signed the Addis Ababa Agreement because their were job offers. On signing the agreement, Lagu was rewarded with the most senior ceremonial rank in the Khartoum armed forces of a Major-General. It was a rank of a general without a command or army, something every military officer despises, but Lagu was happy to accept it all the same. As part of that alleged job offer, Lagu was inducted into a Politburo of Numayri's ruling party, the Sudan Socialist Union (SSU). His Anyanya soldiers were integrated into the Khartoum armed forces and he was awarded with the responsible for overseeing their integration. Numayri also never forgot Abel Alier, who started it all. For his part, he was rewarded with the honor of presidency of the Interim High Executive Council.[407] This left many to wonder on how Alier who was on the wrong side of the negotiation would personally reaped the benefit from the opposing side? No one was more bitter on this than Lagu.

Besides this view of job offerings, historian Robert Collins argues that Lagu might have actually had few options when he was presented with opportunity to sign the Addis Ababa Agreement. Collins weighs on those possible options and explains them as follows:

> He could not ignore the joyous celebrations by the southern peoples aroused by the expectations of peace, nor could he snub the demands by the powerful southern political leaders in Khartoum and exile in London for him to sign the agreement. Although Israel had promised increased assistance if Lagu refused to ratify the agreement, the Sudan and Uganda governments had already agreed to expel "elements hostile to the other state" that included the Israelis. Moreover, in March 1972 Muammar Qadhafi had persuaded Idi Amin to sever diplomatic relations with Israel and expel all Israeli military advisers from Uganda, terminate the Israeli conduit for arms to Lagu, and deprive him of a safe-haven to reorganize if hard-pressed by the Sudan army which had already captured Owiny-ki-Bul.[408]

In his own defense, Lagu insisted that he was arguably contended with the terms and conditions of the Addis Ababa Agreement. He went to argued that the only concern he had was the security arrangement, which states, "Southern Command, composed of 12,000 officers and men, of whom 6,000 shall be citizens from that region and the other 6,000 from outside the Region."[409] For Lagu, he wanted the 6,000 to be solely from his Anyanya force, and once he was assured that the 6,000 have to be from Anyanya, he signed off on the terms and conditions of the agreement. For the accusation that he signed the agreement because of jobs, Lagu simply dismisses this notion by saying had he wanted to be a general in Khartoum armed forces, he would not have defected in the first place but remain in the Khartoum armed forces and gradually obtain the rank of the general. However, what Lagu did not answer is that upon signing the agreement, he was awarded a rank of a Major-General, making him two ranks ahead of his batch and colleagues. As to the argument that the Addis Ababa Agreement was not perfect, Lagu admitted this fact by saying he knew he did not provide the Southerners with the best agreement the Southern Sudanese deserved because he knew then that next time around the Southern Sudanese will get something better such as the Comprehensive Peace Agreement (CPA) signed in 2005, between the Sudan People Liberation Movement/Army (SPLM/A) and the Khartoum government. But the question still lingers on how Lagu could have possibly known that a better peace agreement would be signed in years to come so as for him to come to that conclusion. The reason is because Lagu neither participated nor supported or even anticipated the emergence of the SPLM/A, which brought the CPA for him to make such a claim in advance. With respect to the SPLM/A, even though it was made up of Lagu's junior Anyanya officers, Lagu did not anticipate them to wage a liberation struggle, citing that he personally did not expect another war at the time SPLA emerge as an arms struggle movement. Ironically, it is the very war that Lagu did not anticipate and support, which brought about the CPA. Worse yet, Lagu rather portrayed the SPLM/A as reactionary movement which resulted from Numayri's foul attempt to transfer the Southern Command to the north by use of force.[410] Such portrayal undermines SPLM/A underground efforts to organize and execute a liberation movement as if there were no enough political, economic, and social reasons other than mere forceful transfer of the Southern Command to the north, which compellingly warrant the rebellion of SPLM/A.

At any rate, any of those views could have been true in influencing Lagu's decision in signing the Addis Ababa Agreement regardless of the fact that the agreement lacked basic safeguards for the South Sudanese. However, none of those factors would have possibly affected the Father or would have possibly influenced him had he been in the same position as Lagu was. On the job offers, the Father would be the last person to take one. He had declined even the most prestigious job of becoming the first bishop of Juba at the time when the future for him was not even certain. And he would not have sacrificed the Anyanya soldiers for the sake of jobs in the Khartoum armed forces if the Anyanya could be independent soldiers in their own country of the South Sudan. It was true that the Southern Sudanese were longing for peace, but struggle for real peace could never be sacrificed with hysterical joyous celebration for a false peace. Perhaps an old adage which states, "war is better than a bad peace" could have prevailed. Thirdly, there would not have been any powerful Southern Sudanese whether in Khartoum or London who could intimidate the Father in signing an agreement as they might have done for Lagu. The Father has no use for those Southerners in Khartoum and the ones in London were certainly no powerful than the Father was by any stretch of imagination. Actually, the death of the Father created a leadership vacuum and an opportunity for many leaders to emerge, sadly, including the ones in Khartoum. Fourthly, the Father and the group, including Lagu, started the struggle from scratch where there was no Israeli support and a military headquarters. Cutting off support from Israeli and losing a military headquarters would have for sure dealt a blow to the Anyanya forces and morale, but not destroy the Father's will and determination to press forward with the arms struggle. Fifthly, Uganda had acted with utmost hostilities toward the Father and his group since the time they landed in Uganda and that the hostilities continued throughout. So, Uganda could not have been more hostile than killing the Father, killing some of his colleagues and mistreating the refugees in the manners they did.

Beside these reasons, the Father was the champion of self-determination in which he believed through federation would eventually lead into freedom for South Sudanese. He advocated for the "principle of free self-determination, which reason and democracy grant to a free people."[411] The underlining principle of his argument is "free self-determination" where citizens of the South will decide for themselves as free people. However, the Father even grew more impatient as he realized that the Arabs would not accept federation, therefore, calling for a total separation to be achieved through arms struggle. In this scenario of Addis Ababa, where it grants autonomy for the South, the Father, an ardent separatist, would not have agreed on anything less than a federation that guaranteed self-determination for the Southerners. The guarantees would have empowered the South Sudan to retain its own arms forces, conduct its foreign affairs, conduct international trade, and running its own education system. For the Father, his ultimate goal is an independent South Sudan. And he warned the Arabs about that as earlier as 1958, when he stated, "the South will at any moment separate from the North if and when the North so decides, directly or indirectly, through political, social and economic subjection of the South."[412] For the Father, the Southerners can only live in a united Sudan whereby they have greater saying in their own affairs but if that is not possible, then the ultimate alternative is a total independence. He had already concluded that the idea of federation was impossible, therefore, independence was the option, and it can be achieved through arms struggle or a plebiscite, something that the Addis Ababa never offered. Writing on behalf of the Southern Sudanese people to the United Nations, the Father argued:

> ...beyond doubt that the people of the South want nothing short of complete independence within the framework of Black African unity. If there is any doubt about this intention on the part of the North, then we are calling on them to put aside the arms and to conduct a plebiscite under the supervision of the United Nations to enable the people of the South to decide whether they would like to have any link with the North or to be completely independence. This right of self-determination was given to the people of the North to decide whether they would like to have any relations with Egypt or to be completely independent and they chose to be independent, although the differences between the North and Egypt are not as acute as those between North and South Sudan. We do not see why the South should not be given the same right.[413]

The Addis Ababa actually offered the opposite of what the Father refers to as the principle of "free self-determination, according to reason and democracy, which may lead to the status of a free people."[414] Even though the agreement guarantees autonomy for the South, the people of the South where not free per se as they were under a dictatorial regime of Numayri and his Sudan Socialist Union (SSU) party. The first mishap was for the Southern leaders including Lagu to be absorbed in the SSU and then for the whole Addis Ababa Agreement to be buried under the SSU constitution. Adopting SSU as a sole legal political party was not only the most undemocratic practice, but confused system ever. The system was so blur that there was no distinction between SSU and the government as both duplicated each others duties. According to one observer, "to the Sudanese the SSU simply represented another agency of the government, not an independent dynamic political organization."[415] Transfer such confused system to the South, the result of which was disastrous. For example, Joseph Lagu used his seniority of SSU to unseat the government of Abel Alier from the autonomous regional government in Juba. In retaliation, given that Numayri was the ultimate power, all he needed was a little bit of convincing for him to issue a decree, and indeed he was convinced in decreeing to dissolve the government of Lagu. A combination of a confused system of SSU plus a dictatorial president with ultimate power for decrees was not what the Southerners deserved and surely not what the Father would accept.

Then, there is this prevailing argument being floated around as a substitute for truth, which is used as a justification to explain the obstacles that prevented the demand for separation of the South by the Southerners. Convincing this argument may sound with all its flaws, it is centered around the spirits and overwhelming feelings of the members of the Organization of Africa Unity (OAU), which emphasized for the unity of African states on the principle of maintaining the borders inherited from colonial rule (whatever that means). This argument even goes as far as alleging that the demand for separation of the South was not only unacceptable but impossible given that African states feared similar dissent would lead to secessions in their own countries. This argument is baffling to intelligent minds, even with the benefit of the hindsight; it is still dominating the intellectual discourse in assessing the possibilities of separatist movement of the South Sudan.

It was true that African leaders and the leaders of most other countries didn't accept the concept of separation. It is even still true today.

However, what was not true is that the demand for separation for the South was not that impossible as many people claim that it was impossible. For example, the Addis Ababa Agreement was negotiated in Ethiopia, and Ethiopia is among those countries alleged to have opposed to the concept of separation, therefore, making it impossible for the South to demand for separation. What people need to differentiate is that when something is not acceptable it does not mean it is also impossible. In the case of Ethiopia, today with the benefit of hindsight, we know with a hundred percent certainty that Eritrea separated from Ethiopia. This goes to say if Ethiopia could not stop Eritrea from separation, how could it made the South Sudan demand's for separation impossible? When the Southerners went to negotiate in Addis Ababa in 1972, they were not negotiating what were acceptable to the Ethiopians or OAU but negotiating the demands of the South Sudanese people—the demands that they can achieve with or without Ethiopia or OAU. Even then, Emperor Haile Selassie could not have dictated to the Southerners when in fact he could not have dictated to the Eritrean who were already struggling and with their zeal, determination, perseverance and vision, now we know they won themselves independence. The same zeal, determination, perseverance and vision are also applicable to the Southerners, and "nothing on earth would have prevented the demand for separation" by the Southerners, as the Father noted as earlier as in 1958.[416]

To look into this Ethiopia versus Eritrea from a more realistic angle, it would lead into the question that if the Khartoum government which was a member of OAU could directly support the Eritrean separatist movement, why would Ethiopia not support the Southern separatist movement in return? Another question along the same line, did Khartoum hesitate to support Eritrean separatist movement for the fear that separation of Eritrea from Ethiopia would encourage the separation of the South from the North of Sudan? Whatever the answer is, what we do know is that the Khartoum government's support for Eritrea resulted into the separation of Eritrea. Speaking of using wrong example, this is a classic one, which people often use without putting much thought into the whole factors involved. The reality of politics is not what is acceptable or unacceptable and who accept it or who does not; it is what one is capable of doing. In the case of Khartoum, with the separatist movement in the South, it continued to support other separatist movements in the neighboring countries of Eritrea, Central African Republic and Congo. In the words of one historian, Sudan employed a contradicting policy by "eagerly supporting radical pan-African agenda, on the one hand, while killing African Southern Sudanese, on the other."[417] Nigeria with its separatist movement was sympathetic to the Southern cause. Actually when the activities of the Father were restricted in East Africa, he opted for Nigeria. Even though, the Father never proceed to reside in Nigeria he maintained close contact with them.[418] Congo with its raging separatist movement war was able to assist the Anyanya to some degree.[419]

The argument which alleged that the demand for the separation of the South was impossible because of growing fear among African states that similar situation may unravel in their own countries is simply based on a false premises and analogy. This phenomenon has already been proven to have no basis as in the cases mentioned above. What is needed to be made clearer is that Sudan is unique in its own way and it is ought to be treated as such. The evidences of Sudan being unique are there in abundant. Gabriel Warburg, a historian and an Islamic expert argues that the imposition from outside of a nation-state to Sudan which let to the "assumption that nation-states are suitable forms of government for multiethnic and multi-religious societies, such as the Sudan, is mistaken."

Another, historian Robert Collins describes Sudan "neither African nor Arab, a hybrid orphan suspended between the Middle East and Africa."[420] Gordon Mortat at the discussion of the Round Table Conference of 1965 blamed the British for uniting the South and North Sudan as it was the British tendency and legacy to "impose unity where it is not wanted and divide where unity is demanded." In the British colonial reported submitted in 1947, by Fabian Colonial Bureau, the Southern Sudan is describes as "in human terms, it belongs to the African South of it" not to north as it stands today.[421]

Uniting the South and North of Sudan was not a well thought out move by the British. After administering the South and North of Sudan separately throughout their colonial period, on their departure, the British suddenly decided that the South and North now can unite on flimsy commonality. What a hasty and tragic move. The so-called civilized British, ignored all the factors that hinder unity between the South and North, but only one factor which unite the South and North caught their attention, and that one factor was the River Nile. The British officials who decided on the unity of South and North Sudan justified their position that since Southern Sudan "by accidents of geography, river transport and so on, must turn more to the North rather than to Uganda or the Congo."[422] If it is "by accident of geography," that the South should unite with the North then it is up to the British to explain how this accident occurred. But what is known as facts in geography, the South and the North of Sudan are diametrical oppose to each other as far as their physical characteristics are concern. The South is part of African tropical forest with rainfall for most part of the year while the North is a dry desert land. As for the "river transport, and so on," those British officials actually forgot the fact that the River Nile has its source in East Africa and it goes through Uganda and passes beyond Sudan with some tributaries flowing in from other places. So, if the fate of the Southern Sudanese can be tight to the River Nile, and then why not to joined all the East African Countries, Sudan, Ethiopia, and Egypt altogether as a one Nile nation since all share the Nile at one point or another? If the British are among the so-called civilized and logical, in this case, they failed to demonstrate such characters of being civilized and logical people. Even though the British were genuine in their effort in uniting the South and the North for the interest of both, the question is, how many Southern Sudanese live along the river, and how many benefited from it for their fate to tragically be decided on the river? But anyway, it is not surprising that the people of the same descent as that of John H. Speke, the man who supposedly claimed to have discovered the source of River Nile would tragically twist the fate of the entire South Sudanese people on the river irrespective of its consequences. It might have been true that the British came to Sudan partly because of the river. That is, all right. However, the people of South Sudan don't worship the river like that. So, given these overwhelming evidences, it is not the separation of South Sudan which is impossible but instead the unity of Sudan. The fact that the war between the South and North started right in time of uniting Sudan and continued to this day is another overwhelming piece of evidence against the unity of Sudan. The experiment of unity of Sudan is a colossal failure, which requires immediate reversal. In some of the Northern Sudanese Arabs words, the independence that Sudan claims to obtain in 1956, was actually a fraud as one of its authored admitted that it was, "a fraudulent document" which came about "through false pretenses," because the Northern Sudanese had to lie to the Southerners by "pledging that the Constituent Assembly would give full consideration to the claims of Southern Sudanese members of Parliament for a federal system."[423] They latter on reneged on that promise.

To put all these into historical prospective and in a more contextual manner, before there was OAU and before these African countries came to existence, there were the Southern Sudanese people struggling for their freedom. As earlier as most African countries could not even dreamed or imagined of independence, the Father declared unequivocally in the Sudanese parliament that "the South will at any moment separate from the North if and when the North so decides, directly or indirectly, through political, social and economic subjection of the South."[424] Therefore, it would be hard to argue that such a sincere determination, will, and vision held by some Southern Sudanese leaders like the Father would suddenly be oblivious with emergence of weak continental organizations such as OAU or it would go dead with the emergences of African countries, which are, by the way, more preoccupied in their own backyards with their own problems. When the organization of OAU was founded in 1963, the Father had an opportunity to present a petition to the African head of states who attended the meeting. The Father demanded that the South Sudan to be declared an independent state. Following from that event, the Father rendered that organization of a little use as far as the struggle for the South Sudan is concern. The Father even went as far as accusing that organization of only "considering the more clamorous cases of South Africa, Angola, Mozambique and Rhodesia."[425] Even prior to the OAU formation, the Father seriously challenged its core principles. The Father's challenge was as much valid then, in 1963, as it is still today. In challenging the core principles of such organizations as the OAU, the Father wrote the following:

The principle of 'divide and rule' has wrought havoc among once-subjected peoples: can it be said that Pan-Africanism or African solidarity form part of this principle? The interpretation given to the two terms is the only determining factor; if the terms convey the idea of a continental union between the oppressed and the oppressors each retaining the status quo, then they are destructive and not constructive; but if they mean a union of the once oppressed Africans, some of whom today are free, some under subjection, then here is another challenge to the Pan-Africanism in which sides must be taken—either with the oppressed or the oppressor.[426]

If the OAU failed then in resolving the cases of the oppressed and marginalized like the ones of Sudan and its successor the AU failed in similar cases, it is because the organization either chose to maintain the status quo or the organization based their solidarity with the oppressors just as the Father stated. It is not a new phenomenon that this organization tend to side with the oppressors when presented with two choices given the fact that two years in the row (2006 & 2007) the AU offered its chairmanship position to Omer Hassan al-Bahshir, the President of Sudan which his government is committing genocide in Darfur, western region of Sudan. Thanks to the Americans, in both cases, they exerted much effort and pressure to other African countries to deny dictator al-Bashir such privilege of chairing a continental organization and at the same time presiding over genocidal regime in Khartoum.[427] Now the idea of United States of Africa (USA) is being advanced as a possible unification of Africa as a federated sovereign entity. However, the monumental challenges remain, especially with the fact that if the present existing continental organizations cannot resolved issues such as the ones in Sudan, how would they resolved African issues as a whole. One even wonders more when issues such as ones in Sudan are considered internal affairs of by the same organization, and how would these issues be called under a federated sovereign African entity? For this effort to progressed remains to be seen, but with the current trend it is doomed to failure.

The truth is, someone of the Father's principle and determination could never have compromised to the whim of AOU or some other African countries at the expense of Southern Sudanese interest. The Father could not make it more clearer than when he stated that the Southerners rather die fighting "than to serve the international policy."[428] Despite the feelings of OAU or what was acceptable or not acceptable to the dictators like Haile Selassie and any other African nation, the South Sudan cannot just simply abandon its interest of independence, especially when it is blessed with people who are determined to sacrifice for the cause of the South. It is illogical that the interest of other nations would be an obstacle to the aspiration of South Sudanese people for independence. The Father knew very well that the South Sudan was not lucky that the whole world may not sympathize with it, but he was very sure that God was with the people of South Sudan when he said, "the whole world may be against the South, but I am sure that God is with the people of the South and through God we shall win."[429] Such powerful testimony to God delivered by a spiritual figure on behalf of the South Sudanese people carries immense spiritual value. The Father was also convinced that the solution for the South lies in the interior of the South Sudan and with the South Sudanese people and not anywhere else.[430] Unfortunately, the people of South Sudan are reminded time and again by these idealistic proponents of Organization of African Unity (OAU), African Union (AU), United States of Africa (USA), African states, Pan-Africanists, or what have you that the fate of South Sudan can be decided by what is accepted or not unaccepted by the non-South Sudanese.

The third possible major reason on why the Father would have objected to the Addis Ababa Agreement would have been the Father's lack of trust for the Arabs to implement the agreement if there was any. The Arabs are infamously known for being "cunning, crafty, dishonest, untrustworthy, and racially as well as culturally arrogant."[431] To put those behaviors into practice, one author wrote, "within the space of less than a year the agreement, which had been enshrined in the 1973 Sudanese Constitution, was in a shred."[432] Treating the autonomous Southern Government like his lot, Numayri ignored the Addis Ababa provision which states that the Regional Assembly shall elect the President of the High Executive Council (HEC) to be appointed by the president of the republic, but instead Numayri nominated, non other than the author of *South Sudan: Too Many Agreement Dishonored,* Abel Alier, as the sole candidate for president of the HEC angering the Regional Assembly members. Numayri would continue to appoint or dismiss the head of HEC as his wished. As the oil was been discovered in the Southern region, Numayri pretended as if it is not in the South, instead places like Bentiu suddenly came to be known as "the southern part of western Sudan" or rather "450 miles south of Khartoum."[433] When it was discovered that this was actually Bentiu that Numayri was referring to, then Numayri had no choice but to extend the northern borders southward so that the oil fields must be in the north. totally ignoring the agreement on the south-norht border. The list of the violation of the agreement is long, the result of which was the ultimate abrogation of the Addis Ababa agreement with the introduction of the Sharia Law in Sudan including the South as a nail in the coffin.

Gabriel Warburg wrote, "it was therefore no wonder that Alier regarded the abrogation of that treaty (Addis Ababa Agreement), on 5 June 1983, as a disaster for the Sudan and a personal tragedy for himself."[434] It took Abel Alier that rough ride for him to acknowledge in his book, *South Sudan: Too Many Agreements Dishonored,* how vicious these people in the north could be. Alexis Heraclides commenting on Numayri's ability in dismantling the Addis Ababa Agreement wrote:

> It is in a way ironic that Numayri, whose single greatest achievement was to help reconcile Northerners and Southerners, will enter the annals of history as having undone his accomplishment, thus forfeiting his main claim to perpetuity. The series of measures he took are so confounding that outsiders not familiar with Numayri—a man of limited caliber, plagued by insecurity, who largely survived by constantly switching allies and pitting them against each—would wonder how it was ever possible to reach a miracle of the Addis Ababa Agreement in the first place.

Indeed, Numayri was an individual of a limited intellect and talent such that another historian notes that Numayri's "talents on the football field were more conspicuous than his performance in the classroom and barely sufficient to obtain an appointment to the Sudan Military College."[435] Perhaps Numayri, a man of such limited caliber, did not deserve to even negotiate with the Anyanya to begin with, or would not deserve opportunity to trample over the South. Numayri's survival which was based on the character of switching alliances and pitting them against each other is a well documented fact even before the Addis Ababa Agreement. The Southern Sudanese leaders would have taken note of such character before they could even embark in negotiation with such a character or before they could start wooing favoritism from him.

Numayri's act of betrayal started right from the time when he dismissed from Revolutionary Command Council (RCC), his colleagues, Babikr al-Nur Sawar al Dahab, Faruq 'Uthman Hamdallah, and Hashim al-'Ata. After that, Numayri then went on legitimizing his power by embracing the Sudanese Communist Party (SCP) whom he needed their support rather for temporary survival. Soon he exploited the rift between the two factions of the SCP, and eventually crushed the SCP. He maintained Joseph Garang in his cabinet because he needed a Southerner then, until he rendered him expandable and killed him when the right time came. In fact, it is said that when Numayri and his gang took up power, they "simply did not know what to do with the Southern Sudan," besides trying to use force in crushing the resistant movement. Therefore, conveniently maintaining Southerners like Joseph Garang in the cabinet.[436] On the foreign affairs front, Numayri equally didn't know what to do; he had to juggle between the Communist East and the Capitalist West. Luckily, Numayri couldn't continue with such opportunistic maneuvers, because eventually, it was the Islamist who fooled him, leading to his demise. So, it wasn't any wonder that he ended up leading a low level refugee life in a foreign country and only to return to Sudan as useless old man. In reality, Numayri was an opportunist who survived by sheer luck. One author wrote that Numaryri's "unpopularity can best be measured by nine plots to overthrow him uncovered by his security forces" prior to signing of the Addis Ababa Agreement.[437]

One still wonders, how the Southern leaders hooked up with such dubious and dump character and could even go to the extent of wooing him for favors. The abrogation of the Addis Ababa Agreement would never have come as surprises for someone of the Father's mental state. In his classic work, *The Art of War*, Sun Tzu wrote "if you know the enemy and know yourself, you need not fear the result of a hundred battles."[438]

Going through the Father's speeches and writings one would notice that he knew as much about what was happening in Khartoum as he knew what was happening within the South Sudan liberation movement. For example, the Father was among the first people who predicted the fall of Abrahim Abboud as earlier as in the beginning of 1963, as he then wrote, "in fact another counter revolution which will be dangerous to the general (Abboud) is reported to be cooking. Abboud and his wing therefore believe that they can only unite all the Muslims by declaring a holy war to promote Islam in Southern Sudan."[439] A year later, General Abboud was overthrown by a civilian demonstration as he could not resolve the Southern Problems. Not only that the Father also warned that a military takeover of the government would not only affect the Southern Sudanese negative but the Sudan as a whole, the harsh reality that some of the Northern Sudanese politicians could only learn through the hard way. In the case of Numayri's regime, the Father would have thoroughly analyzed that regime *modus operandi* as well as its prospects for survival. His decision in dealing with such regime would have been an informed one through a thorough analysis. Not only that, the Father learned through experience and history not to trust the Arabs to begin with. After the Arabs promised amnesty for those who revolted in Torit Mutiny of 1955, they then turned around, and began to execute and imprison those Southerners. While the Arabs asked favor from the Southerners to vote for the declaration of independence and in return they would agree on federation for the South, they ended up reneging on their own promise to the Southerners. And it was the Father who passionately fought them over the issue of federation in the parliament of 1958, the very federation they promised the Southerners as a condition to vote for the declaration of independence. These personal experiences plus historical facts taught the Father to be skeptical about the intentions of the Arabs. The Father is being known for his skepticism in dealing with the Arabs. One of the Father's fellow priest described him as "a bit inclined to pessimism" when it comes to the issue of Arabs of the Sudan.[440] When several civilian governments where exchanging hands in Khartoum in 1960s, the Father called it "introduction into Sudan of a false appearance of democracy."[441] It was during those civilian governments that the Arabs intensified their violence and terroristic actions against the people of South Sudan.[442] When those governments began to invite the Southerners to participate in the government in Khartoum, the Father was the first to be skeptical of their motives viewing them as just "changing of tactics."[443] Given the Father's thorough analytical insights and distrust for the Arabs, he would not have accepted the Addis Ababa Agreement, especially with Numayri as the President and Abel Alier, a Southerner as Numayri's negotiator. And we would not know what would have happened, but given that nothing good happened with Addis Ababa, with exception of a relative lull of no war, another option would have probably be better.

South Sudan and the Future

By 1983, as the Addis Ababa Agreement was officially abrogated with the introduction of Sharia law in Sudan, the period that proceed was once again characterized by another long war between the South and North, the war that would last more than two decades. At the time the war began, Numyari was in charge in Khartoum, but he was losing power and popularity in a more faster pace. In the bush, Dr. John Garang was commanding the rebel, the Sudan People Liberation Army (SPLA). Even though SPLA is a Southern homegrown movement, it had a different objective than its predecessor, the Anyanya movement. While the Anyanya was fighting for the independence of South Sudan, the SPLA claimed to be fighting for "united Sudan under a socialist system that affords democratic and human rights to all nationalities and guarantees freedom to all religions, beliefs and outlooks."[444] For more than two decades, SPLA waged a bloody war against the successive governments in Khartoum. As a result of the war, over two millions Sudanese, mostly South Sudanese estimated to have been killed, several millions fled the country, and many more are displaced from their homes. However, fortunately, by 2005, the Sudan People Liberation Movement (SPLM), the political wing of SPLA signed a peace deal with the Khartoum government. According, to the terms of the peace agreement it sets an interim period of six years from the signing of the Agreement whereby the Southerners would have to vote on a referendum on whether to be united with the north or to separate. During the interim period, Sudan must be a one country with two systems of governments where the South has its own government independent of Khartoum. The South also has its own armed forces, the police, prison guards and other security forces. The South must share from the oil revenue by drawing fifty percent of the revenue from the oil extracted from the South. In short, the South runs almost a parallel government to that of Khartoum. Come referendum time in 2011, the South must vote either for unity or separation.[445] The question then is, will that confirm the Father's prophesy about the South?

The year was 1958 and the place was the parliament in Khartoum. Fr. Saturnino Lohure stood up as a head of the Liberal Party and the head of an umbrella group for South Sudanese political parties, and on behalf of the South Sudanese, he spoke eloquently and succinctly:

> Sir, the South has no ill-intentions whatsoever towards the North; the South simply claims to run its local affairs in a united Sudan. The South has no intention of separating from the North, for had that been the case nothing on earth would

have prevented the demand for separation. The South claims to federate with the North, a right that the South undoubtedly possesses as a consequence of the principle of free self-determination, which reason and democracy grant to a free people. The South will at any moment separate from the North if and when the North so decides, directly or indirectly, through political, social and economic subjection of the South.[446]

Two points must be highlighted for emphasis and implications. The first one is, "the South has no intention of separating from the North, for had that been the case nothing on earth would have prevented the demand for separation." The second one is, "the South will at any moment separate from the North…" These highlighted points are valid and will continue to be valid as long as the South is not separated. So, if the South failed to separate in the upcoming referendum of 2011, these highlighted points would serve an inspiration to the next warrior generations of South Sudan who will pick up with the struggle and carryon with the next war for independent South Sudan.

Chapter Endnotes

[353] Rogato Ohide "Otuho Leadership in the Context of Modern Sudan Governance: The State of Its Sabotaged and Undermined Credentials" A paper presented at Otuho Speaking Community of North America Historic Conference, December 24-25, 2005, Erie, Pennsylvania, USA.

[354] Robert J. House & Phillip M. Podsakof, *Leadership effectiveness: Past perspectives and future directions for research in Organizational Behaviour. The State of Science,* Hillsdale, NJ: Lawrence Erlbaum Associates, 1994. Edited by Jerald Greenberg.

[355] Ibid

[356] Ibid

[357] Fr. Hilary Boma, "Fr. Guido Akou and Fr. Saturnino Lohure" *Email,* Dec. 19, 2006. "One day my father told me that the 1955 Torit Mutiny did not begin in Torit but in Loronyo, and by a young brilliant priest called Saturnino Lohure. My father, Mr. Tafeng and Rinaldo Lolia were all N.5 Company, and my father said these officers talked a lot about Fr. Lohure.Some years after the Addis Ababa Accord, my old teacher(in Kapoeta, Mr. Adelio Lodongi, told me also that, when the 1947 Juba conference took place, Fr. Saturnino was the one chosen to represent the Catholic Church. But because he was just a year old as a priest, and

because in front of him was Fr. Akou, he asked that this later go for that Conference."

[358] Fr. Neno Contran, *They Are A Target: 200 African Priests Killed*, Nairobi: Catholic Publishers in Africa, 1996.

[359] Ibid

[360] Ibid

[361] Bonfanti, Adriano, "Padre Saturnino ha Compiuto la Sua Missione" *Nigrizia*, Aprile, 1967 Translate by Fr. Hilary Boma

[362] Al Ayaam, October 25, 1966 quoted in Fr. Neno, *They Are A Target: 200 African Priests Killed*, Nairobi: Catholic Publishers in Africa, 1996. pg. 148.

[363] "Fr Saturnino is Dead but His Soul Liveth" *The Vigilant*, February 7th, 1967.

[364] Ibid

[365] Joseph Lagu, *Sudan: Odyssey Through a State: From Ruin to Hope*, Omdurman : MOB Center for Sudanese Studies, Omdurman Ahlia University, 2006.

[366] Ibid

[367] Ibid

[368] Fr. Hilary Boma "The Patron and Martyr" *Email*, September 5, 2007.

[369] Robert Collins, (forthcoming publication in 2007): Chapter Six: The Government of Ja'afar Numayri: The Heroic Years, 1969-1976" *The History of the Modern Sudan*, Hollywood: Tsehai Publ.

[370] Joseph Lagu, *Sudan: Odyssey Through a State: From Ruin to Hope*, Omdurman : MOB Center for Sudanese Studies, Omdurman Ahlia University, 2006.

[371] Fr. Neno Contran, *They Are A Target: 200 African Priests Killed*, Nairobi: Catholic Publishers in Africa, 1996.

[372] Ibid

[373] Adriano Bonfanti, "Padre Saturnino ha Compiuto la Sua Missione" *Nigrizia*, Aprile, 1967 Translate by Fr. Hilary Boma

374 Oliver Albino "Fr. Saturnino Question" *Email,* August 3rd, 2007.

375 Robert Collins, "Request for Information" *Email,* Jun 13, 2007.

376 Robert Collins, (forthcoming publication in 2007): "Chapter Five: Parliamentary and Military Experiments in Government, 1956-1969" *The History of the Modern Sudan,* Hollywood: Tsehai Publ.

377 Al Ayaam, October 25, 1966. Cited in Fr. Neno Contran, *They Are A Target: 200 African Priests Killed,* Nairobi: Catholic Publishers in Africa, 1996.

378 In an interview with Fr. Neno Contran, the Editor of Comboni Italian magazine, *Nigrizia.* Entebbe, July, 1966.

379 Luka Monoja, "SPLM-Diaspora@yahoogroups.com," Email, Aug. 11, 2006.

380 Steve Paterno "Phone Conversation with Lagu" August 11th, 2007.

381 Joseph Lagu, *Sudan: Odyssey Through a State: From Ruin to Hope,* Omdurman : MOB Center for Sudanese Studies, Omdurman Ahlia University 2006.

_____ Steve Paterno "Phone Conversation with Lagu" August 11th, 2007.

382 Robert Collins, (forthcoming publication in 2007): Chapter Six: The Government of Ja'afar Numayri: The Heroic Years, 1969-1976" *The History of the Modern Sudan,* Hollywood: Tsehai Publ.

383 Benjamin Beit-Hallahmi, *The Israeli Connection: Whom Israel Arms & Why,* New York: Pantheon, 1987. p. 48.

384 Alexis Heraclides, *The Self-determination of Minorities in International Politics,* London: Routledge, 1991. p. 125.

385 Fr. Neno Contran, *They Are A Target: 200 African Priests Killed,* Nairobi: Catholic Publishers in Africa, 1996. p. 155.

386 Ibid

387 J.A. McHugh *The Catholic Encyclopedia,* Volume X., New York: Robert Appleton Company. Transcribed by Douglas J. Potter [online] http:// www.newadvent.org/cathen/10662a.htm

[388] Mansour Khalid, *The Government They Deserve: The Role of the Elite in Sudan's Political Evolution*, London: Kegan Paul International, 1990. p. 228.

[389] Cecil Eprile, *War and Peace in the Sudan*, Newton Abbot: David & Charles, 1974.

[390] Amir Idris, *Conflict and Politics of Identity in Sudan*, New York: Pagrave Macmillan, 2005. p. 52.

[391] Fr. Neno Contran, *They Are A Target: 200 African Priests Killed*, Nairobi: Catholic Publishers in Africa, 1996. p. 126.

[392] Robert Collins, (forthcoming publication in 2007): Chapter Six: The Government of Ja'afar Numayri: The Heroic Years, 1969-1976" *The History of the Modern Sudan*, Hollywood: Tsehai Publ.

[393] Joseph Lagu, *Sudan: Odyssey Through a State: From Ruin to Hope*, Omdurman : MOB Center for Sudanese Studies, Omdurman Ahlia University 2006.

[394] Fr. Neno Contran, *They Are A Target: 200 African Priests Killed*, Nairobi: Catholic Publishers in Africa, 1996.

[395] Ibid

[396] In an interview with Fr. Neno Contran, the Editor of Comboni Italian magazine, *Nigrizia*. Entebbe, July 1966.

[397] Fr. Neno Contran, *They Are A Target: 200 African Priests Killed*, Nairobi: Catholic Publishers in Africa, 1996.

[398] Ibid

[399] Ibid

[400] Ibid

[401] Ibid

[402] Ibid

[403] Robert Collins, (forthcoming publication in 2007): Chapter Six: The Government of Ja'afar Numayri: The Heroic Years, 1969-1976" *The History of the Modern Sudan*, Hollywood: Tsehai Publ.

[404] Fr. Neno Contran, *They Are A Target: 200 African Priests Killed,* Nairobi: Catholic Publishers in Africa, 1996.

[405] The Addis Ababa Agreement: The Southern Provinces Regional Self-Government Act, 1972.

_____ Robert Collins, (forthcoming publication in 2007): Chapter Six: The Government of Ja'afar Numayri: The Heroic Years, 1969-1976" *The History of the Modern Sudan,* Hollywood: Tsehai Publ.

[406] Collins, Robert (forthcoming publication in 2007): Chapter Six: The Government of Ja'afar Numayri: The Heroic Years, 1969-1976" The History of the Modern Sudan. California: Tsehai Publ.

[407] Madut Arop "Interview John Garang" *Heritage,* Khartoum, Monday, Nov. 2, 1987. p. 4.

[408] Robert Collins, (forthcoming publication in 2007): Chapter Six: The Government of Ja'afar Numayri: The Heroic Years, 1969-1976" *The History of the Modern Sudan,* Hollywood: Tsehai Publ.

[409] The Addis Ababa Agreement: The Southern Provinces Regional Self-Government Act, 1972.

[410] Joseph Lagu, *Sudan: Odyssey Through a State: From Ruin to Hope,* Omdurman : MOB Center for Sudanese Studies, Omdurman Ahlia University 2006.

_____ Steve Paterno "Phone Conversation with Lagu" August 11th, 2007.

[411] Joseph Oduho and William Deng, The Problem of Southern Sudan, London: Oxford University Press, 1963.

[412] Ibid

[413] Petition to United Nations by Sudan African Closed Districts National Union (SACDNU), 1963.

[414] Joseph Oduho and William Deng, *The Problem of Southern Sudan,* London: Oxford University Press, 1963.

[415] Robert Collins (forthcoming publication in 2007): Chapter Six: The

Government of Ja'afar Numayri: The Heroic Years, 1969-1976" *The History of the Modern Sudan*, Hollywood: Tsehai Publ.

[416] Rev. Fr. Saturnino Lohure "Speech: Second Sudan Parliament" Khartoum, 1958. Cited in Joseph Oduho and William Deng, *The Problem of Southern Sudan*, London: Oxford University Press, 1963.

[417] Robert Collins (forthcoming publication in 2007): Chapter Six: The Government of Ja'afar Numayri: The Heroic Years, 1969-1976" *The History of the Modern Sudan*, Hollywood: Tsehai Publ.

[418] Fr. Neno Contran, *They Are A Target: 200 African Priests Killed*, Nairobi: Catholic Publishers in Africa, 1996.

[419] Joseph Lagu, *Sudan: Odyssey Through a State: From Ruin to Hope*, Omdurman : MOB Center for Sudanese Studies, Omdurman Ahlia University 2006.

[420] Robert Collins, (forthcoming publication in 2007): Chapter Six: The Government of Ja'afar Numayri: The Heroic Years, 1969-1976" *The History of the Modern Sudan*, Hollywood: Tsehai Publ.

[421] Petition to United Nations by Sudan African Closed Districts National Union (SACDNU), 1963.

[422] Juba Conference "Proceeding of the Juba Conference on the Political Development of the Southern Sudan" June, 1947.

[423] Mansour Khalid, *The Government They Deserve: The Role of the Elite in Sudan's Political Evolution*, London: Kegan Paul, 1990. p. 231.

_____ Muhòammad Ahòmad Mahòju‾b, *Democracy on Trial: Reflections on Arab and African Politics*, London: Deutsch, 1974. p. 57.

[424] Joseph Oduho and William Deng, *The Problem of Southern Sudan*, London: Oxford University Press, 1963.

[425] Fr. Neno Contran, *They Are A Target: 200 African Priests Killed*, Nairobi: Catholic Publishers in Africa, 1996.

[426] Joseph Oduho and William Deng, *The Problem of Southern Sudan*, London: Oxford University Press, 1963.

[427] Alfred de Montesquuiou, "Sudan Pressing to Lead African Union" *Associated Press*, January 29, 2007.

[428] Fr. Neno Contran, *They Are A Target: 200 African Priests Killed*, Nairobi: Catholic Publishers in Africa, 1996.

[429] Ibid

[430] Ibid

[431] Amir Idris, *Conflict and Politics of Identity in Sudan*, New York: Palgrave Macmillan, 2005. p. 46.

[432] Alexis Heraclides "Janus or Sisyphus? The Southern Problem of the Sudan" *The Journal of Modern African Studies*, 1987. p. 218.

[433] Gabriel R. Warburg "Sudan: 1898-1989, The Unstable State. (book reviews)" *Middle Eastern Studies*, January 4th, 1993.

[434] Ibid

[435] Robert Collins, (forthcoming publication in 2007): Chapter Six: The Government of Ja'afar Numayri: The Heroic Years, 1969-1976" *The History of the Modern Sudan*, Hollywood: Tsehai Publ.

[436] Ibid

[437] Ibid

[438] Sun Tzu, *The Art of War*, edited & forwarded by James Clavell

[439] Petition to United Nations by Sudan African Closed Districts National Union (SACDNU), 1963.

[440] Fr. Neno Contran, *They Are A Target: 200 African Priests Killed*, Nairobi: Catholic Publishers in Africa, 1996.

[441] Ibid

[442] Amir Idris, Conflict and Politics of Identity in Sudan, New York: Palgrave Macmillan, 2005. p. 52

[443] Fr. Neno Contran, *They Are A Target: 200 African Priests Killed*, Nairobi: Catholic Publishers in Africa, 1996.

[444] John Garang, *The Call for Democracy in Sudan*, New York: Kegan Paul International, 1992, Edited & Introduced by Mansour Khalid.

[445] The Comprehensive Peace Agreement between the Government of the Republic of the Sudan & the Sudan People Liberation Movement/ Army, Nairobi, Kenya, January 9th, 2005.

[446] Fr. Saturnino Lohure "Speech: Second Sudan Parliament" Khartoum, June 1958 cited in Joseph Oduho and William Deng, The Problem of Southern Sudan, London: Oxford University Press, 1963.

Bibliography

Organizational Sources

The Addis Ababa Agreement: The Southern Provinces Regional Self-Government Act, 1972.

Aweil Irrigation Rehabilitation Project, September, 2005.

Biography of His Holiness, Pope Benedict XVI, Libreria Editrice Vaticana [online]
http://www.vatican.va/holy_father/benedict_xvi/biography/documents/hf_ben-xvi_bio_20050419_short-biography_en.html

The Central Intelligence Agency, World Fact Book [online]
https://www.cia.gov/library/publications/the-world-factbook/geos/in.html

Church Missionary Society Archive, Africa Missions: Sudan, Adam Matthew Publications Ltd. [online] http://www.ampltd.co.uk/collections_az/cms-4-07/description.aspx

Comprehensive Peace Agreement (CPA), signed between Sudan People Liberation Movement (SPM) and National Congress Party (NCP), January 9th, 2005.

Daniel Comboni, 1831-1881, Roman Catholic, Sudan [online] http://www.dacb.org/stories/sudan/comboni1_daniel.html

Daniel Comboni 1831-1881, Vatican, [online] http://www.vatican.va/news_services/liturgy/saints/ ns_lit_doc_20031005_comboni_en.html

Eastern Equatoria-Sudan. Map Printed by CDE, University of Berne, Switzerland for the Federal Department of Foreign Affairs.

Gentges, Mary E. "Father Pro of Mexico" Angelus [online] angelusonline.org

His Holiness John Paul II Short Biography, Holy See Press Office [online] http://www.vatican.va/news_services/press/documentazione/ documents/santopadre_biografie/ giovanni_paolo_ii_biografia_breve_en.html

Homily of John Paul II, "Canonization of the Three Blesseds" Sunday, October 5th, 2003. [online] http://www.vatican.va/holy_father/ john_paul_ii/homilies/2003/documents/hf_jp- ii_hom_20031005_canonizations_en.html

Human Rights Watch, "Slavery and Slave Redemption in the Sudan" March 2002 [online] www.hrw.org

John F. Kennedy, Inaugural address, January 20, 1961.

Juba Conference "Proceeding of the Juba Conference on the Political Development of the Southern Sudan" June, 1947.

Mayardit, Salva Kiir, First Vice President of the Republic, and President of the Government of Southern Sudan, at the opening of the second session of the Southern Sudan Legislative Assembly, juba, September 10, 2007.

The memorandum presented by the Sudan African National Union to the Commission of the Organisation of African Unity for Refugees, Kampala-Uganda, November 1964.

Ohide, Rogato, "Otuho Leadership in the Context of Modern Sudan Governance: The State of Its Sabotaged and Undermined Credentials" A paper presented at Otuho Speaking Community of North America Historic Conference, December 24-25, 2005, Erie, Pennsylvania, USA.

Petition to United Nations by Sudan African Closed Districts National Union (SACDNU), 1963.

Simonse, Simon, "Conficts and Peace Initiatives in East Bank Equatoria, South Sudan: 1992-199" Report, Pax Christi, Netherlands, November 12th, 2000.

Survivors' Rights International, "Special Alert Report: Eradication of Terrorism Forestalled by Khartoum's Genocidal Policies & Oppressive Rule, October-November 2001. Prepared following the terrorist attacks on America of September 11, 2001. Released November 12, 2001.

United States Commission on International Religious Freedom "Policy Focus: Sudan" Winter 2006 also visit www.uscirf.gov

University of Belgrade "The Beograd Student Center" A Student Residence Hall named under Patrice Lumumba's name. [online] http://www.sc.org.yu or www.vodickrozbu.com/standard_en/st_centar_bg.htm -19k

Unpublished Sources

Albino, Oliver, "Fr. Saturnino Question" Email, August 3rd, 2007.

Boma, Fr. Hilary, "Fr. Guido Akou and Fr. Saturnino Lohure" Email, Dec. 19, 2006.

_____Boma, Fr. Hilary, "Fr. Lohure questions" email, June 26, 2007.

_____ Boma, Fr. Hilary, "Humility of the Patron and Martyr of the South Freedom Movement," September 6, 2007.

_____ Boma, Fr. Hilary "The Patron and Martyr" Email, September 5, 2007.

Collins, Robert, "Request for Information" Email, Jun 13, 2007.

"Definition of Culture" [online] http://fog.ccsf.cc.ca.us/~aforsber/ccsf/culture_defined.html

Deng, Francis, "Green is the Color of the Masters: The Legacy of Slavery and the Crisis of National Identity in Modern Sudan" Yale University. [online] http://www.yale.edu/glc/events/cbss/Deng.pdf

Elia, Fr. Vitale Otililing, "Saturnino Ohure: Rev. Fr., Rebel and a Leader," May 23, 2006.

In an interview with Fr. Neno Contran, the Editor of Comboni Italian magazine, Nigrizia: Entebbe, July 1966.

Monoja, Luka, "SPLM-Diaspora@yahoogroups.com," Email, Aug. 11, 2006.

Mukhtar, Al-Baqir al-Afifi, "The Crisis of Identity in the Northern

Sudan: A Dilemma of a Black People with a White Culture," a paper presented at the CODESRIA African Humanities Institute tenured by the Program of African Studies at Northwestern University.

Paterno, Steve, "Phone Conversation with Lagu" August 11th, 2007.

Prah, Kwesi Kwaa, Race, Discrimination, Slavery, Nationalism and Citizenship in Afro-Arab Dorderlands with Particular Reference to Sudan. Paper prepared for United Nations Research Instituted for Social Development (UNRISD) Conference on Racism and Public Policy, September, 2001, Durban, South Africa.

Sconyers, David, "British Policy and Mission Education in Southern Sudan—1928-1946" Unpublished Dissertation, University of Pennsylvania, 1978.

Stereotype inevitability, From Wikipedia, the free encyclopedia [online] http://en.wikipedia.org/wiki/Stereotype_inevitability

Vambheim, Marit Magelssen, "Making Peace While Waging War:—A Peacemaking Effort in the Sudanese Civil War, 1965-1966" MA thesis in history, University of Bergen, Spring 2007.

Yoh, John G. Nyuot, "The historical origins of the Sudanese civil wars: The politics of gunboat diplomacy" A paper presented at a seminar entitled "Roll Back Xenophobia Campaign Media Seminar Series: The Conflict in Sudan" held at South Africa Human Rights Commission, Friday, 25 May 2001 Houghton, Parktown, Johannesburg.

Yongo, Benaiah, "Sudan Economy Research Group Discussion Papers: Peace Dividend and the Millennium Development Goals in Southern Sudan," University of Bremen, Germany, Aug. 2005.

Articles & Books

Aboul-Enein, Youssef, "The Sudanese Army: a historical analysis and discussion on religious politicization," *Infantry Magazine*, July-August, 2004.

Albino, Oliver, *The Sudan: A Southern Viewpoint*, London: Oxford University Press, 1970.

Aldo, Gilli MCCJ "Daniel Comboni: Africa Or Death" New People, March-April, 1996.

Alier, Abel, *South Sudan: Too Many Agreement Dishonoured*, London: Ithaca Press, 1992.

Alzobier, Ahmed, "The Intellectual Degeneration in Sudan" Sudan Tribune, April 3rd, 2007 [online] http://www.sudantribune.com/ spip.php?article21140&var_recherche=higher%20education

Arop, Madut, "Interview John Garang" Heritage, Khartoum, Monday, Nov. 2, 1987.

Atiyah, Edward, *An Arab Tells His Story: A Study in Loyalties*, London: John Murray, 1946.

The Black Book of the Sudan on the Expulsion of the Missionaries from the South Sudan: An Answer, Milano: Istituto Artigianelli, 1964.

BBC, "Country profile: India," [online] http://news.bbc.co.uk/2/hi/south_asia/country_profiles/ 1154019.stm

_____BBC News "Garang's death is blamed on pilot" April 18th, 2006. [online] http://news.bbc.co.uk/2/hi/africa/4920322.stm

_____BBC News "Kabila party' formed in DR Congo" April 2, 2002. [online]
http://news.bbc.co.uk/2/hi/africa/1907252.stm

_____ BBC News "More killings in Algeria" February 6, 1998. [online]
http://news.bbc.co.uk/1/hi/world/africa/54067.stm

_____ BBC News "Naming children for a head start in Africa" December 15, 2003.
[online] http://news.bbc.co.uk/1/hi/world/africa/3321575.stm

_____BBC News "Sudan crash cause is 'not clear'" August 5th, 2005. [online]
http://news.bbc.co.uk/2/hi/africa/4748061.stm

Beit-Hallahmi, Benjamin, *The Israeli Connection: Whom Israel Arms & Why*, New York: Pantheon, 1987.

Beshir, Mohammed Omer, *The Southern Sudan*, Khartoum: Govt. Print. Press, 1970.

_____ Beshir, Mohamed Omer, *The Southern Sudan: background to conflict*, London: C. Hurst & Co., 1968.

Bonfanti, Adriano, "Padre Saturnino ha Compiuto la Sua Missione" Nigrizia, Aprile, 1967. Translate by Fr. Hilary Boma.

Catholic News Agency, "Blessed Miguel Pro Juarex, Priest and Martyr" [online]
http://www.catholicnewsagency.com/saint.php?n=397

Clausewitz, Carl Von, *On War*, London: N. Trübner, 1873. Translated by James John Graham.

Collins, Robert O., (forthcoming publication in 2007): *The History of the Modern Sudan*, Hollywood: Tsehai Publ.

_____Collins, Robert O., *The southern Sudan in historical perspective*, New Brunswick, NJ: Transaction, 2006.

Contran, Fr. Neno, *They Are A Target: 200 African Priests Killed*, Nairobi: Catholic Publishers in Africa, 1996.

Dellagiacoma, Fr. Vittorino, "Sudanese Catholic Clergy" Provincial Comboni House, Khartoum, Sudan. [online] http://www.dacb.org/ stories/sudan/ohure_saturnino.html

Deng, Francis Mading, *Dinka Cosmology*, London: Ithaca Press, 1980.

_____ Deng, Francis, "Sudan—Civil War and Genocide: Disappearing Christians of the Middle East," *Middle East Quarterly*, Winter 2001.

_____Deng, Francis, *War of Visions Conflict of Identities in the Sudan*, Washington, D.C.: Brookings Institution Press, 1995.

De Montesquuiou, Alfred, "Sudan Pressing to Lead African Union" Associated Press, January 29, 2007.

De Witte, Ludo, *The Assassination of Lumumba*, Trans. by Ann Wright and Renée Fenby, London: Verso, 2001.

El-Affendi, Abdelwahab, "Discovering the South: Sudanese Dilemmas for Islam in Africa" (written in 1990). [online] http:// www.islamfortoday.com/sudan.htm

El-Tigani, Mahgoub, "Solving The Crisis Of Sudan: The Right Of Self-Determination Versus State Torture," Arab Studies Quarterly (ASQ), Spring, 2001.

Emerson, Ralph Waldo, *A collection of 20 Essays by Emerson including Self-Reliance, The OverSoul, Experience, and Nature*, New York: Houghton Mifflin Company, 1883.

Eprile, Cecil, *War and Peace in the Sudan*, Newton Abbot: David & Charles, 1974.

Fabunmi, L. A., *The Sudan in Anglo-Egyptian Relations: A Case Study in Power Politics, 1800-1956*, London : Longmans, 1960.

Ga'le, Severino, *Shaping a Free Southern Sudan: Memoirs of our Struggle*, Nairobi: Paulines Publications Africa, 2002.

Garang, John, *The Call for Democracy in Sudan*, New York: Kegan Paul International, 1992. Edited & Introduced by Mansour Khalid.

Gibbon, Edward, *The History of the Decline and Fall of the Roman Empire: Chapter LI: Conquests By The Arabs*. Part VIII.

Henderson, K. D. D., *Sudan Republic*, New York: F. A. Praeger, 1965.

Heraclides, Alexis, "Janus or Sisyphus? The Southern Problem of the Sudan" *The Journal of Modern African Studies*, 1987.

_____Heraclides, Alexis, The Self-determination of Minorities in International Politics, London: Routledge, 1991.

The Holy Bible, Old Testament: Isaiah 18:6-7:

House, Robert J., & Phillip M. Podsakof, *Leadership effectiveness: Past perspectives and future directions for research in Organizational Behaviour: The State of Science*, Hillsdale, NJ: Lawrence Erlbaum Associates, 1994. Edited by Jerald Greenberg.

Idris, Amir, *Conflict and Politics if Identity in Sudan*, New York: Palgrave Macmillan, 2005.

_____Idris, Amir H., *Sudan's Civil War: Slavery, Race and Formational Identities*, Lewiston, New York: The Edwin Mellon Press, 2001.

IRIN "Sudan: Political Developments Raise Concern, Analysts Say," November 15th, 2005.

International Crisis Group "A Stratergy for Comprehensive Peace in Sudan" Africa Report N°130—26 July 2007.

Johnson, Douglas Hamilton, *The Root Causes of Sudan's Civil Wars*, Bloomington: Indiana University Press, 2003.

Khalid, Mansour, *The Government They Deserve, the Role of the Elite in Sudan's Political Evolution*, London: Kegan Paul International, 1990.

Lagu, Joseph, *Sudan: Odyssey Through a State: From Ruin to Hope*, Omdurman : MOB Center for Sudanese Studies, Omdurman Ahlia University 2006.

Lynch, Edward A., "The Retreat of Liberation Theology." This appeared in the February 1994 issue of The Homiletic & Pastoral Review.

Lundstrom, Karl-Johan, *The Lotuho and the Verona Fathers: A Case Study of Communication in Development*, Uppsala: EFS Fo¨rlaget, 1990.

Machiavelli, Niccolo, *The Prince*, Penguin Books, Translated with Notes by George Bull & Introduction by Anthony Grafton

Mahòju¯b, Muhòammad Ahòmad, *Democracy on Trial: Reflections on Arab and African Politics*, London: Deutsch, 1974.

Malwal, Bona, *People and Power in Sudan,* London: Ithaca Press, 1981.

McHugh, J.A., *The Catholic Encyclopedia,* Volume X., New York: Robert Appleton Company. Transcribed by Douglas J. Potter [online] http://www.newadvent.org/cathen/10662a.htm

Mirak-Weissbach, Muriel, "Why The British Hate Sudan: The Mahdia's War Against London" Printed in The American Almanac, September 4, 1995.

Morrison, Dan, "Sudan has Bigger Crisis than Darfur: '05 Peace Pact Falling Apart" San Francisco Chronicle, Sunday, August 12, 2007.

New Vision, "Uganda: The Making of Idi Amin," August 6, 2007.

Oduho, Joseph & William Deng, *The Problem of Southern Sudan,* London: Oxford University Press, 1963.

Ohrwalder, Ather Joseph, *Ten Years Captivity in the Mahdi's Camp—1882-1892.* London: Meinerann and Kalestier, 1893.

Paterno, Steve, "Dilemma of Sudan's CPA to the Question of Identity" Sudan Tribune, July 16, 2007 [online] http://sudantribune.com/spip.php?article22863

From Qur'an 9:5 cited on BBC "Religion & Ethics: Islam"[online] http://www.bbc.co.uk/religion/religions/islam/history/earlyrise_1.shtml

_____From Qur'an 9:29 on BBC "Religion & Ethics: Islam"[online] http://www.bbc.co.uk/religion/religions/islam/history/earlyrise_1.shtml

Ratzinger, Cardinal Joseph, "Instruction on Certain Aspects of Theology of Liberation:" Sacred Congregation for the Doctrine of the Faith, August 6, 1984.

_____Ratzinger, Joseph Cardinal, *Milestones; Memoirs 1927-1977*, San Francisco: Ignatius Press, 1998.

Robertson, James, *Transition in Africa: From Direct Rule to Independence: A Memoir*, New York: Barnes & Noble Books, 1974.

Ruay, Deng D., *The Politics of Two Sudans: The South and the North*, Uppsala: Nordiska Afrikainstitutet, 1994.

Simonse, Simon, *Kings of Disaster: Dualism, Centralism and the Scapegoat "King" in Southern Sudan*, Leiden: E.J. Brill, 1992.

Slatin, Rudolf C., *Fire and Sword in the Sudan: A Personal Narrative of Fighting and Serving Dervishes*, London: Edward Arnold, 1903.

Sorenson, John, *Disaster and Development in the Horn of Africa*, New York: St. Martin's Press, 1995.

Sowell, Thomas, *Black Rednecks and White Liberals*, San Francisco: Encounter Books, 2005.

Steiner, Rolf, *The Last Adventurer*, Boston: Little, Brown, 1978.

Time in partnership with CNN, "The Armed Missionary" Nov. 22, 1971.

Tvedt, Terje, *The River Nile in the Age of British: Political Ecology and the Quest for Economic Power*, London: I B Tauris & Co Ltd, 2004.

Tzu, Sun, *The Art of War*, edited & forwarded by James Clavell

The Vigilant, "Fr Saturnino is Dead but His Soul Liveth," February 7th, 1967.

Wadhams, Nick, "Massive Animal Herds Flourishing Despite Sudan War, Survey Reveals" National Geographic News, June 12, 2007. This is accompanied by a video titled "Massive Antelope Herds Seen From the Air in Sudan."

Wai, Dunstan M, *The African-Arab Conflict in the Sudan,* New York: Africana Publishing Company, 1981.

Warburg, Gabriel R., "Sudan: 1898-1989, The Unstable State. (Book reviews)" Middle Eastern Studies, January 4th, 1993.

_____Warburg, Gabriel, *The Sudan Under Wingate: Administration in the Anglo-Egyptian Sudan (1899-1916),* London: Routledge, 1971.

Wheeler, Skye, "International companies to begin exploration for gold and uranium" Gurtong, August 10, 2007.

Wingate, Francis R., *Mahdism and the Egyptian Sudan,* London: Macmillan & Co., 1891.